Pioneers and Newcomers

A Latino History in the United States

First Edition

Edited by **Milagros Denis-Rosario and Luis Álvarez-López**

Hunter College, of the City University of New York

cognella®
SAN DIEGO

Bassim Hamadeh, CEO and Publisher
John Remington, Executive Editor
Gem Rabanera, Project Editor
Casey Hands, Associate Production Editor
David Rajec, Editorial Assistant
Jess Estrella, Senior Graphic Designer
Trey Soto, Licensing Coordinator
Natalie Piccotti, Director of Marketing
Kassie Graves, Vice President of Editorial
Jamie Giganti, Director of Academic Publishing

Cover image: Copyright © 2012 iStockphoto LP/Windzepher.

Printed in the United States of America.

cognella® | ACADEMIC PUBLISHING

3970 Sorrento Valley Blvd., Ste. 500, San Diego, CA 92121

Pioneers and Newcomers

A Latino History in the United States

Contents

Part VII Culture and Identity in the Latino Community

Introduction to Pioneers and Newcomers

A Latino History in the United States

Milagros Denis-Rosario and Luis Álvarez-López

PIONEERS AND NEWCOMERS WAS DEVELOPED TO provide an alternative textbook for introductory courses at the college level. The book title *Pioneers and Newcomers: A Latino History in the United States* ascribes to Latinos a leading role in the making and development of the United States as a nation. The evolution of early pioneers is not static, but dynamic. The process is influenced by many factors that consider early historical presence, US expansionism, imperialism, foreign policies, industrialization, and capitalist development. The second part of the title "*A Latino History in the United States*" originates in the fact that both co-editors are trained in the field of Latin American/Caribbean history fields, and they combined their voices and perspectives to provide their stories about Latinos. Throughout an array of articles and narratives, the book provides an interdisciplinary approach to the understanding of the historical presence, community formation, cultural manifestations, and contemporary issues affecting Latinos in the United States. In the report titled, *The Hispanic Population of the US Census 2010*[1] **Latinos/Hispanics are defined as "the heritage, nationality, lineage, or country of birth of the person or the person's parents or ancestors before arriving in the United States. People who identify as Hispanic, Latino, or Spanish may be any race."** There are approximately fifty-eight million people who self-identify as Latino or Hispanic. Latino or Hispanic as a cultural label gained broad application during the Republican-Nixon administration and did not take into consideration the different experiences or background of what is established as the largest minority group in the United States. Latinos are not a homogenous group. This text provides a set of front-line articles that introduce past and present experiences of Latino individuals and/or national groups.

This first edition is published in a current period of increasing attack of immigration of certain nationalities whose provenances are negatively associated with third-world status (e.g., Africa, Asia, the Hispanophone Caribbean and Latin America). In the provocative piece titled *Who are We? The Challenges to American's National Identity* (New York: Simon & Schuster, 2004), political scientist Samuel Huntington led the unenthusiastic rhetoric portraying people from these nations as a negative influence in the American society. The criticism against Latinos and immigrants, in general, has been followed by a series of legislative initiatives, such as California's Proposition 187, which banned access to public services and non-emergency health benefits to "illegal" aliens residing in the country. Although the measure was defeated in the courts, it demonstrates the direction taken in the society. Similarly is Arizona Senate Bill 1070, enacted in August of 2010. Senate Bill 1070 authorizes the state police to detain any person suspected of being an "illegal alien" or for not carrying or producing immigration documents. This state law generated nation-wide controversy and faced legal challenges to its constitutionality, civil rights violations, and encouragement of racial profiling. The case went to the Supreme Court in 2012, generating a legal opinion 5–3 that helped to deter other states from establishing and enforcing its own immigration policies. However, other provisions were kept in place, including allowing the Arizona State Police to detain individuals for more than twenty-four hours if they do not have documentation to demonstrate their legal status. Despite the atmosphere of denunciation, the readings in this textbook prove that Latino communities grew stronger and managed to carve their own identities within the US framework.

Organization of the Textbook

Pioneers and Newcomers is an academic tool organized into seven sections. Each section addresses themes and issues that facilitate an overall understanding of the evolution and challenges impacting Latinos and their communities, from class, race, gender, activist, and cultural perspectives. Among the topics examined in the book are the theory of migration, Latinos' second generation, the debate about the enclaves, cash remittances, and the integration of Latinos into the labor market, among others. As Latinos, Latinas, and Latinx become more prominent in US society, they confront discrimination in the workplace, housing, politically, and education. All these topics are sampled in the articles presented in this volume.

Furthermore, for students from inner cities, it is essential to deconstruct negative stereotypes and contextualize Latinos historically. The book also takes into consideration the chronology of national groups such as Mexicans that have been living in the US since before it was a nation. Part of the community-building process is the subsequent arrival of Latin American nationals since the late nineteenth and early twentieth centuries. In Part I of the textbook, titled "Historicizing and Theorizing about Latinos," cultural geographer David D. Arreola provides an overview of the antecedents that led to continuous migration of Latin Americans to the United States. Successfully,

Arreola enriches the understanding of migratory patterns with concepts, statistics, and timelines. In the second article, sociologists Carlos Siordia and Ruben Antonio Frias examine two different points of view concerning the profiling of Latinos in American society: the Huntington theory that Mexicans are a danger for the American identity and the Blalock point of view portraying the increasing Latino population in the context of minority group relations.

Part II of the book, "Looking for Work, Building Communities," focuses on the migration and community building of Mexicans and Puerto Ricans. Historian David Badillo documents how supplying the labor for agricultural production in the Midwest led to the development of an immigrant labor force that transformed itself into a stable community. As it is shown in the article, historical events such as the Mexican-American war of 1848 and the Mexican Revolution of 1910, as well as US foreign policy toward Latin America are critical political factors for the Mexican presence and Mexican migration.

Historian Carmen Teresa Whalen focuses on the Puerto Rican colonial experience and the massive migration of US citizens to the mainland United States. Similar to Mexico, foreign policy and political and economic expansions led to the island's "non-incorporated status" and bestowed American citizenship to Puerto Ricans in 1917. The increasing demand for labor during World War II triggered the increase in Puerto Rican migration and a community-building effort on the east coast. Simultaneously, a significant number of Latinos played an essential role in the US military forces in the fight against Nazi Germany.

Part III, "New Immigrants, New Communities," focuses on the new migrations of Latin Americans during the 1960s. The cases of Cubans and Dominicans are examined by John R. Logan and Wenquan Zhang. According to the sociologists, both migrations are linked to the American foreign policy of counter-insurgency and containments following the Cuban revolution of 1959 and 1961 and the assassination of Rafael Leonidas Trujillo in the Dominican Republic.

The US government promoted the migration of both national groups to the mainland as a political strategy to neutralize the political developments in both Caribbean societies. The final result was the migrations and settlements of Cubans and Dominicans in Miami-Dade County and New York City. Both areas became centers for labor rights and political activism.

Maria E. Verdaguer's article about Salvadorian and Peruvian migration to the United States illustrates the timing of increasing international conflict and contested ideology in the region. According to the sociologist, both groups were considered "newcomers" and developed significant communities in New York, New Jersey, and the greater Washington area. Similar to other Latino groups, Salvadorians more than Peruvians followed the socio-economic patterns of other Latinos that became an underclass concentrated in the low-wage service sector of the urban and suburban economy.

Part IV, "Asserting Their Rights: Latinos and Their Quest for Inclusion," focuses on the political activism and organizing efforts of Mexicans and Puerto Ricans. Immigration and law professor Steven Bender centers on the development of the Chicano movement as a "class-based struggle."

The article delves into the multiple struggles of this social movement and students' efforts to achieve political representation.

Latinos and African Americans share histories of oppression and discrimination. Professor Madeleine López explores how the Puerto Rican community organized grassroots coalitions that included parents, students, and government agency officials to break down segregation in the public educational system. The issue for the Puerto Rican community was not only integration in the classroom but quality bilingual education to end exclusion and discrimination against Puerto Rican children and other Latinos. The article sheds a light on the legacy of these interethnic coalitions and the implementation of the bilingual education (today ESL).

Educator and activist Iris Morales's piece is the introduction to an anthology of Latina activism in the twenty-first century that we wanted to include in this volume. The singularity of Morales' essay rests on the clarity and accuracy of the evolution of Latina political activism in the United States. The article emphasizes how gender, class, and racial discrimination obstruct the advancement of women of color in US society. As well-documented in the article, despite the obstacles, Latinas have attained numerous accomplishments in education, politics, academia, and the economy. All are the result of Latina activism and coalitions.

Part V, "Migration and Transnationalism: Opportunities and Challenges," focuses on issues related to the socio-economic profile of the immigrant communities as part of the transnational labor force that characterizes New York City. Political scientist Immanuel Ness analyses how the restructuring of the New York economy based in high tech, financial and service industry impact the immigrant labor force. The article analyzes the decline of manufacturing and the weakening of unionism and their negative impact on the Latino labor force. Unions had often provided an avenue for upward mobility for immigrant workers.

Anthropologist Michelle J. Moran-Taylor tackles the issue of migration and the development of transnational community among Guatemalans and their home country. The article highlights the far-reaching impacts of cash remittances and the role in helping the family, boosting the economy, and promoting better education and healthcare in Guatemalans, creating a globalized culture that operates locally. The intersections of gender and class are explored in the article of civil rights attorney and labor activist, Monica Ramírez. Statistics show that Latina workers are paid an average of fifty-four cents less per dollars than non-Hispanic white male workers, Ramírez outlines how Latinas face disadvantages with the "gender wage gap." She also explains the impact of low incomes on Latinas and their families. At the end, the fight to bridge the gender pay gap is not only an issue about Latinas. As Ramírez put it, it "is a family, a children's women's rights labors' and workers' right issue." It affects the entire community (203).

"*Ni Blancos Ni Negros*: Latinos and the Politics of Race and Identity" is the title of Part VI of the volume. Race and ethnicity are fundamental issues for the Latino community. Contrary to American society where the black or white racial binary is the standard, Latinos navigate different shades of the color spectrum. Furthermore, in some Latin American societies, they do not deal openly with race at all. According to sociologists Fergus et al., for Latinos nationality comes first, then race. The article contains samples from the 2000 and 2010 censuses and analyses how some groups have been forced to take sides regarding their racial identity. The discussion expands the differences from national group to national group, and it takes into consideration geographical provenance (e.g., Caribbean, Europe, Africa, Asia, etc.). The article analyses the response of the census and the emergence of groups that challenge Latino racial paradigms, such as the Afro-Latinos and Latinx.

Latinas do not limit their preoccupations to low salary wages; they also care about racial discrimination. In response to those challenges, Latinas organize a powerful women's resistance movement, challenging the status quo in the Black Lives Matters and #MeToo movements and solidarity with DACA and other efforts to enhance the well-being of migrants' families. In the struggle to gain a more prominent role in their communities Latinas embrace the black feminist movement. A valid argument for this adoption is Black Feminist approaches and views on intersectionality, which provides a better understanding on how male privileges were embedded in all sectors of the capitalist society. According to Kimberly Crenshaw black women are oppressed for multiples variables, such as gender, race, prejudice, and discrimination are embedded in the society and operate a system of oppression against women. This conceptualization applies to Latinas.

In Part VII of the book, titled "Culture and Identity in the Latino Community," cultural anthropologist Deborah Pacini Hernandez traces the fascinating history of Latino music in the United States. She notes that at the beginning, Latino music was labeled as ethnic music and marginalized to the new working-class immigrants from Mexico, Latin America, and the Caribbean. According to the article, in the post-World War II period, Latin music became part of mainstream American music because of famous artists such as the legendary Tito Puente, Carlos Santana, and Fania Records. The development of salsa music placed Latinos in New York in a different category. Latino music record-producing centers in Los Angeles, Texas, and Miami during 1980 became the hub for the creation and fusion of this new American musical genre. The spectacular development of the Latin population expanded the Latino market and opened the door for new generations of Latino musicians and performers in the music genres of Latin Jazz, Merengue, Bachata, Hip Hop, Cumbia, Dembow, and Regetton.

The volume concludes with two classic poems: "I am Joaquín" and "AmeRícan." In "I am Joaquín," Chicano activist Rodolfo González manifests the dualities of sharing Mexican ancestry in the United States. The poem is rich in adjectives, denunciations, criticisms, and historical shout-outs to Mexican heritage, which is typical of the Chicano movement. On the other hand, Tato Laviera plays with Spanglish stanzas to construct a similar dilemma to González but from a Puerto Rican perspective. In "AmeRícan," Laviera refers to his Spanish-speaking Caribbean heritage and, despite the struggle he sees, he finally accepts the United States as his second land without totally assimilating to it. These two poems serve to appreciate from a literary prism the dilemmas of assimilation.

The task of consolidating in one book the dynamics of several Latino groups in different time-lines and from different geographical backgrounds in thematic format requires identifying current and traditional scholarship that does not perpetuate the negative stereotypes and victimization of Latinos in the United States. Combining the scholarship from both the social sciences and the humanities became a very stimulating intellectual and disciplinary exercise. We aim to stimulate a positive learning experience for the reader.

Luis Alvarez-López, Ph.D.
Milagros Denis-Rosario, Ph. D.
Hunter College, the City University of New York

Endnote

1. https://www.census.gov/content/dam/Census/library/publications/2011/dec/c2010br-04.pdf

Part I

Historicizing and Theorizing About Latinos

Hispanic American Legacy, Latino American Diaspora

Daniel D. Arreola

THE ANCESTORS OF HISPANIC/LATINO AMERICANS WERE present in the territory of the United States before it was a nation-state. That legacy extends from the sixteenth century in parts of present-day New Mexico and Florida and from the seventeenth and eighteenth centuries in parts of Arizona, Texas, and California. Yet, we read in our popular media about the explosion of Hispanic/Latino populations across the United States, and we are thus tempted to conclude that this ethnic dispersion is a recent diaspora.

In truth, Hispanic/Latino Americans are one of the oldest and one of the newest groups of American immigrants. They are also enormously diverse, consisting of not one group, but many subgroups. In 1948, writer Carey McWilliams made this prescient observation in his then path-breaking work, *North from Mexico* (McWilliams 1968: 7): "There can be no doubt that the Spanish-speaking constitute a clearly delineated ethnic group. But one must also recognize that there is no more heterogeneous ethnic group in the United States than the Spanish-speaking." Further, as Ilan Stavans cautions (2001: 19), "To begin, it is utterly impossible to examine Latinos without regard to the geography they come from."

In this chapter I introduce the general framework of Hispanic/Latino cultural geography based chiefly on U.S. Census information, and with references to selected writings about these peoples and their places. The chapter pivots on three questions: Who are Hispanic/Latino Americans? How many Hispanic/Latino Americans are there? Where are Hispanic/Latino Americans located? In conclusion, I review some of the debates about the present political and geographical significance of this ethnic population.

Who Are Hispanic/Latino Americans?

About a decade ago, a headline in the *New York Times* proclaimed the following: "What's the Problem with 'Hispanic'? Just Ask a 'Latino'" (González 1992). More recently, in his book *Hispanic Nation*, Geoffrey Fox (1997: 179) notes that, aside from their Spanish-language heritage, the only other thing held in common by these people is the fact that they are "lumped" together as Hispanics. Issues of nomenclature and acceptability have long shrouded what we call people of Hispanic or Latino ancestry. Distinctions are further complicated by official designations versus popular sentiment.

Sociologist Suzanne Oboler (1997) suggests that the definition and uses of the term "Hispanic" in the United States are not to be found in its Spanish colonial heritage or even in the Latin American context. Rather, "Hispanic" as a label is rooted in the political and daily life of this nation, in its past ideological self-image as an immigrant place, and in its present ethnic mosaic. To wit, the U.S. Census has used a number of labels to designate people of Hispanic heritage at different times over the past seven decades. While the 2000 Census uses both "Hispanic" and "Latino" as general referents, people of Spanish/Hispanic/Latino origin could identify specifically as Mexican, Puerto Rican, Cuban, or Other Spanish/Hispanic/Latino. Respondents who marked the last category (Other) in 2000 could further indicate a specific subgroup, such as Salvadoran or Dominican. "Latino" was first used in 2000, because in 1990 and 1980, respondents were designated as only of "Spanish/Hispanic origin or descent" and allowed to select among Mexican, Puerto Rican, Cuban, or Other Spanish/Hispanic. In 1970, respondent options were "origin or descendent Mexican, Puerto Rican, Cuban, Central or South American," or "Other Spanish." During the 1960 and 1950 Censuses, these data were collected for "persons of Spanish surname," but only in five southwestern states (Arizona, California, Colorado, New Mexico, and Texas). The 1940 Census identified those who reported Spanish as their "mother tongue," whereas "Mexican" was included as an optional race response in 1930 (Bean and Tienda 1987; Guzmán 2001).

Nevertheless, there is still considerable discussion about the use of labels like "Hispanic" and "Latino." The *New York Times* reported in 1992 that the King of Spain was asked what name he used for those people in the United States who were related to him by language. "Hispanic," he said with regal certainty. Ricardo Gutiérrez, a salesman from East Los Angeles, responded, with equal certainty, "Latino" when asked the same question (Shorris 1992a).

An independent survey that measured the frequency of use of the terms "Hispanic" and "Latino" corroborated this variability (Skop 1997). Emily Skop compiled data from newspaper indices for the following dailies: the *Los Angeles Times*, the *New York Times*, the *Washington Post*, the *Chicago Tribune*, the *Boston Globe*, the *Houston Post*, the *Denver Post*, the *San Francisco Chronicle*, and the *Atlanta Constitution*. Between 1989 and 1990, "Hispanic" was used 1,606 times in these newspapers, with the greatest frequency in the *Los Angeles Times* (341), the *Denver Post* (221), and the *New York Times* (217); combined, these papers accounted for nearly half of the references. The word

"Latino," by comparison, occurred 357 times from 1989 to 1990 in the same sources, and 261 of those references were in the _Los Angeles Times,_ accounting for some 73 percent of all references for "Latino." Overall, these data suggest newspapers' overwhelming preference at the time for "Hispanic," while "Latino" was clearly an emerging term of preference in Southern California almost exclusively. Richard Rodríguez (2002: 110), who frequently appears in the pages of the _Los Angeles Times,_ notes that "the newspaper's computer becomes sensitive, not to say jumpy, as regards correct political usage. Every Hispanic the computer busts is digitally repatriated to Latino."

In 1999, however, the cover story of the July 12 issue of _Newsweek_ was titled "Latino America" (Larmer 1999). Further, in December 2000 the specialty magazine _Hispanic_ published the results of a poll conducted by Hispanic Trends, Inc., about preferences for use of "Hispanic" and "Latino" (Granados 2000). Some twelve hundred Hispanic/Latino registered voters were polled; 65 percent preferred "Hispanic," and 30 percent chose to identify themselves as "Latino." The poll had a margin of error of plus or minus 3 percent. The results showed that 67 percent of those surveyed in Texas preferred "Hispanic," as did 52 percent of respondents in California and New York.

What most of us know and what the results from the 1992 Latino National Political Survey demonstrate is a preference for place of origin or national identity in what we call ourselves. Face-to-face interviews of 2,817 people were conducted in 1989 and 1990. Some 57 percent to 86 percent of Mexicans and Puerto Ricans—whether born in Mexico or born in the United States, whether born on the island or on the mainland—preferred to call themselves Mexican or Puerto Rican rather than panethnic names like Hispanic and Latino. Only Cubans showed a marked difference in response to the same question. Where 83 percent of those born in Cuba preferred to call themselves "Cuban," the percentage among those born in the United States who favored "Cuban" versus those who favored "American" was almost equal (41 percent and 39 percent, respectively) (de la Garza et al. 1992; González 1992).

Notwithstanding these differences in self-identification, Hispanic/Latino Americans are not one people, but many. When sixteenth-century Europeans from Spain came to politically dominate the Latin American realm, Euro–Native American blending created a mestizo race that includes most, but not all, Latin Americans today. A common Hispanic heritage, roots in varied homelands of Latin America and the Caribbean, differences in historical experience in the United States, and distinctive strains of subgroup identity combine to make Hispanics/Latinos a plural population diverse in several important cultural ways.

Language, for example, is sometimes argued as the glue that holds Hispanic/Latino populations together and that gives them a common bond and unifies them as an ethnic people. Putting aside for the moment that not all Hispanic/Latino Americans speak Spanish and that ability and or desire can vary among subgroups and by generations, the fact remains that varieties of spoken Spanish are now recognized by sociolinguists (Silva-Corvalán 1994; Zentella 2002). These varieties are derived from language drift, evolution in varied environments, and distinctiveness resulting from specific cultural settings. Caribbean Spanish, for example, is known for the practice of swallowing final consonants, thereby creating the impression of a faster spoken Spanish. Puerto Rican Spanish pronounces the trilled *rr* like the English *h*, so that a name like Ramón sounds like *jamón* (ham). It also pronounces some *r's* like an *l*, so that *trabajar* (to work) becomes "*trabajal*" or *carta* (letter) becomes "*calta*." Yet another speech variant is the doubling of consonants, so that *algo* (something) can be said as "*aggo*" or *puerta* (door) can become "*puetta*." Further, Caribbean Spanish vocabularies can be quite different from those of Mexican or Central American Spanish. Some examples include *guagua* rather than *autobús* (bus), *goma* instead of *llanta* (tire), or *ají* as opposed to *chile* (hot pepper). Beans known as *frijoles* in Mexico and Central America are *habichuelas* in the Caribbean, oranges are *chinas* rather than *naranjas*, and bananas are *plátanos* or *guineos* (Lipski 1993).

Beyond the growth of spoken Spanish-language usage, there is considerable variability by generation and income level among Hispanics and Latinos who consume Spanish media. While Spanish radio programming is the fastest growth sector in the American ethnic media, it chiefly attracts lower-income and older Hispanics and Latinos (Carlson 1997). Marketers are sensitive to language segments, and they have created a scale based on usage and proficiency: Spanish Dominant, Spanish Preferred, True Bilinguals, English Preferred, and English Dominant (Valdés and Seoane 1997). A geographical study of Spanish-language newspapers in the United States reveals that the places where Spanish newspapers were published between 1900 and 1929 varied significantly from where such newspapers were published between 1960 and 1992 (Kent and Huntz 1996). Early in the twentieth century, the greatest number of Spanish-language newspapers were published in San Antonio, Santa Fe, Los Angeles, and El Paso, because these places were major centers for the Mexican immigrants who were drawn to the greater Southwest. Between 1960 and 1992, however, the cities that counted the greatest numbers of Spanish-language newspapers were Los Angeles, Chicago, New York, and Miami, municipalities pulsing with large numbers of recent Hispanic/Latino immigrants (Fig. 1.1.1).

Finally, Hispanic/Latino Americans are a relatively youthful population compared with all Americans. In 2000, 35 percent of Hispanics/Latinos were younger than eighteen, whereas only 26 percent of all Americans were under eighteen. The median age of Hispanics/Latinos was twenty-six, while that for all Americans was thirty-five. Although Hispanics/Latinos are clearly a younger population than the entire population of the United States, there is considerable variability in age profiles within subgroups. In 2000, Mexican median age was twenty-four years; Puerto Rican, twenty-seven; Central American, twenty-nine; Dominican, twenty-nine; South American, thirty-three; Spaniard, thirty-six; and Cuban, forty-one (Guzmán 2001). This variation is evident as well when subgroup populations are totaled and compared.

FIGURE 1.1.1 The number of Hispanic/Latino nationalities in Miami is captured by the variety of Spanish-language newspapers from Latin America. *Source: Photograph by D. Arreola, 1985.*

How Many Hispanic/Latino Americans Are There?

Hispanic/Latino Americans are one of the fastest-growing population groups in the United States. In 1960, they totaled 6.9 million, just 3.9 percent of the U.S. population. By 1970, Hispanics counted 9.1 million, some 4.5 percent of all Americans. In 1980, Hispanics had grown to 14.6 million, then 6.4 percent of the total population of the United States (Bean and Tienda 1987: Table 1.1). Hispanic/Latino Americans numbered 22.3 million in 1990, 9.0 percent of all Americans, and in 2000, the number had grown to 35.3 million, 12.5 percent of the U.S. population (Fig. 1.1.2). In 2003, the U.S. Bureau of the Census declared Hispanics/Latinos the largest minority group, estimating their numbers at 38.8 million ("Hispanics Now Largest Minority Group" 2003). By 2010, Hispanic/Latino Americans may well be counted the largest minority in the United States.

Yet, as suggested earlier, Hispanic/Latino Americans are many, not one. A number of subgroups characterize this population, mirroring the varied and historical experiences and interactions of Latin America with North, or Anglo, America. In 2000, the Mexican subgroup included almost six of every ten Hispanic/Latino Americans. No other single subgroup comes close to this number among Hispanic/Latino Americans. The Puerto Rican and Central and South American subgroups are the second and third largest, respectively, at circa four million and three million each. Cubans and Dominicans each account for fewer than two million (Fig. 1.1.2).

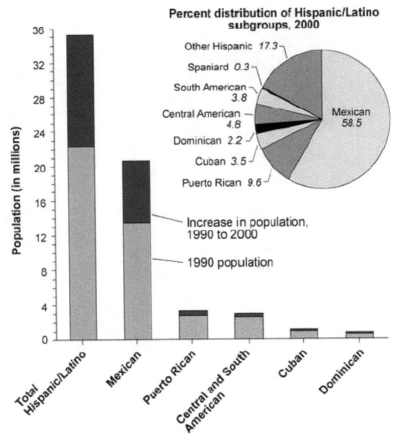

Percent distribution of Hispanic/Latino subgroups, 2000

Other Hispanic 17.3
Spaniard 0.3
South American 3.8
Central American 4.8
Dominican 2.2
Cuban 3.5
Puerto Rican 9.6
Mexican 58.5

Increase in population, 1990 to 2000

1990 population

Population (in millions)

Total Hispanic/Latino · Mexican · Puerto Rican · Central and South American · Cuban · Dominican

FIGURE 1.1.2 Distribution of Hispanic/Latino subgroups, 1990–2000, and percentage distribution, 2000. *Source: U.S. Bureau of the Census 1990, 2000.*

Mexico, ancestral home to the largest subgroup of Hispanic/Latino Americans, is the only Latin American country that borders the United States. Much of the western United States before 1848 was part of the Republic of Mexico. Proximity, a two thousand-mile-long boundary, and demand, especially for labor that could easily migrate from Mexico to the United States, created bonds and cycles of interaction between the nations. This has produced a large resident subgroup of Mexicans in the United States (Mexican Americans and Chicanos/Chicanas), as well as nearly continuous shuttling of thousands of migrants (Mexican nationals) from across Mexico who seek economic opportunity in the United States (Arreola 2000).

Puerto Ricans are unique among Hispanic/Latino Americans because they are the only major subgroup in the population who are American citizens on the mainland United States as well as on their island homeland of Puerto Rico. Puerto Ricans thus have freedom to move back and forth between the island and the mainland without immigration restriction (Fitzpatrick 1987). Unlike most Hispanic/Latino populations rooted in mainland Latin America, but like other

Hispanic/Latino migrants from the Caribbean, Puerto Ricans are of significantly mixed black and white racial ancestry (Boswell and Cruz-Báez 2000).

Cubans, compared with Mexicans and Puerto Ricans, are a more recent Hispanic/Latino subgroup in the United States, having come in large numbers only since 1958, and chiefly as political refugees from Castro's Cuba (Boswell and Curtis 1984). Cubans are distinguishable in several ways from other Hispanics/Latinos. They are an older subgroup, in part resulting from selective migration and low fertility rates. Cubans have also been more successful in occupational achievement, employment levels, and income than most other Hispanic/Latino subgroups (Boswell 2000).

Dominicans are the newest Caribbean Hispanic/Latino subgroup in the United States (Hendricks 1974). The numbers of this subgroup were small before 1990, but they have exploded as a regional population since the 1980s (Grasmuck and Pessar 1991). Dominicans will likely surpass the Cuban subgroup in 2010. Dominicans are a transnational community because they maintain strong connections to their island homeland, returning often from the United States, chiefly New York (Dwyer 1991; Georges 1990; Hernández and Torres-Saillant 1996). Most recently, members of this subgroup have been called "los Dominicanyorks" and are now said to be a "binational society" (Guarnizo 1997). Perhaps Dominican visibility has been greatest as the result of their success in America's national pastime. In the early 1990s, Dominicans represented the largest group of Latin Americans in professional baseball (Oleksak and Oleksak 1991). The 1997 World Champion Florida Marlins included more than a dozen Hispanic/Latino Americans, and more than half of these players were Dominican. In 2002, Dominicans were 8 percent of all professional baseball players ("Strike Would Hit Dominican Economy Hard" 2002).

Hispanics from Central and South America have become some of America's most recent Latino immigrants. In 1990, there were 2.6 million Hispanics/Latinos in the United States from these regions of Latin America; in 2000, there were three million (Fig. 1.1.2). Table 1.1.1 reveals that this large grouping, in fact, comprises Hispanics/Latinos from many nations. Salvadorans and Guatemalans are the largest Central American subgroups, while Colombians and Ecuadorians are the largest subgroups from South America. Salvadorans and Guatemalans have immigrated principally since the 1980s, fleeing civil conflict in their homelands and seeking economic opportunity in the United States. Most are foreign born, from humble origins, with little education, chiefly employed in low-wage service and manufacturing jobs, and largely undocumented (Bachelis 1990; Hart 1997; López, Popkin, and Telles 1996). In fact, the undocumented status of so many Salvadorans and Guatemalans may suggest that the census totals for 2000 were a significant undercount (" 'Other Spanish' Led to Census Missteps" 2002). Colombians and Ecuadorians, like their Central American brethren, are largely foreign born, have chiefly immigrated in large numbers since the 1980s, include undocumented immigrants, and, in the case of Colombians, have sought refuge from political violence in their homeland. Unlike Salvadorans and Guatemalans, however, many Colombians and some Ecuadorians are often middle class and well educated and possess greater employment skills. However, some professionals in these subgroups have experienced downward

TABLE 1.1.1   Central and South American Subgroup Populations, 2000

Subgroup	Population	% Of U.S. Hispanic/Latino Population
Central American	1,686,937	4.8
Salvadoran	655,165	1.9
Guatemalan	372,487	1.1
Honduran	217,569	0.6
Nicaraguan	177,684	0.5
Panamanian	91,723	0.3
Costa Rican	68,588	0.2
Other	103,721	0.3
South American	1,353,562	3.8
Colombian	470,684	1.3
Ecuadorian	260,559	0.7
Peruvian	233,926	0.7
Argentinean	100,864	0.3
Venezuelan	91,507	0.2
Chilean	68,849	0.2
Bolivian	42,068	0.1
Uruguayan	18,804	0.1
Paraguayan	8,769	0.1
Other	57,532	0.2

Source: U.S. Bureau of the Census 2000.

economic and social mobility as a result of migration to the United States (Cullison 1991; Haslip-Viera and Baver 1996; "Coming from the Americas" 2002).

Beyond Mexican, Puerto Rican, Cuban, Dominican, Central American, and South American, there are small numbers of Spaniards in the United States, and a very large undistinguishable grouping labeled "Other Hispanic," some 17 percent of all Hispanic/Latino Americans, and who numbered 6.1 million in 2000 (Fig. 1.1.2). The "Other Hispanic" grouping has baffled census investigators and demographers, because most respondents in this category in the census have simply checked or written in "Hispanic" without further designation of nationality or Hispanic ancestry (Guzmán 2001: Table 1). Some researchers believe that the large numbers of "Other Hispanic" counted in 2000 mirror changes in the way questions were asked on census forms (Suro 2002). In 1990 and again in 2000, "Other Hispanic" respondents were counted mostly in states that had large Hispanic/Latino populations, such as California, Texas, New York, Florida, and New Jersey.

Other researchers believe that those marking "Other Hispanic" in these states represent members of Hispanic/Latino subgroups (Mexican, Puerto Rican, etc.) who choose to designate themselves "Hispanic" because they prefer a panethnic identity rather than a subgroup identity.

In New Mexico, however, some 428,000 respondents to the 2000 Census marked "Other Hispanic." That number represents more than half of all Hispanic/Latino Americans counted in the state in 2000, more even than those who declared themselves "Mexican" (Guzmán 2001: Table 2). This fact supports the assertion by some that the so-called Spanish Americans, also known as Hispanos, are a distinctive subgroup of Hispanic/Latino Americans whose cultural ancestry derives from the earliest Spanish colonial settlement of New Mexico (Carlson 1990; Nostrand 1992). Hispanos do not consider themselves Mexican and thus mark "Other Hispanic" because no census category exists for Spanish American.

The Hispanic/Latino population is growing much faster than the rest of the U.S. population. Assuming moderate levels of fertility and immigration, it is estimated that by 2020, Hispanics/Latinos will number fifty-two million, representing 24 percent of the U.S. population (del Pinal and Singer 1997). By 2050, Hispanic/Latino Americans could total ninety-seven million, a veritable Hispanic nation within a nation (Fox 1997). Yet, Hispanic/Latino American geography is diverse, a spatial mosaic exhibiting high and low population concentrations and composed of regional strongholds and city-state-like nodes, of settlement archipelagos and extensive urban social areas, of compact inner-city and even diffuse suburban barrios.

Where Are Hispanic/Latino Americans Located?

Seven states—California, Texas, New York, Florida, Illinois, Arizona, and New Jersey—contained one million or more Hispanic/Latino Americans in 2000. These states counted some 27 million of the 35 million members of this population group in the United States, 77 percent of all Hispanic/Latino Americans (Guzmán 2001: Table 1.2). Half of all Hispanic/Latino Americans live in two states: California (10.9 million) and Texas (6.6 million).

In nineteen states, Hispanic/Latino Americans were the largest minority group in the state in 2000 (Fig. 1.1.3). Most of these states were in the western United States, but four were New England states. New Mexico was the most Hispanic/Latino in 2000: 42.0 percent of the state's population was from this ethnic group. Both California and Texas had greater than 30.0 percent Hispanic/Latino population, and Arizona had more than 25.0 percent. Five additional states—Florida, Colorado, Nevada, New York, and New Jersey—counted greater than the national percentage of 12.5 percent Hispanic/Latino, but less than 25 percent.

Six states in the South—North Carolina, South Carolina, Georgia, Alabama, Tennessee, and Arkansas—experienced Hispanic/Latino population gains of 200 percent or more in the 1990s (Fig. 1.1.3). Excluding the peripheral southern states of Florida and Virginia, the number of Hispanics/Latinos in the South more than tripled, from 402,000 to 1.3 million, between 1990 and 2000.

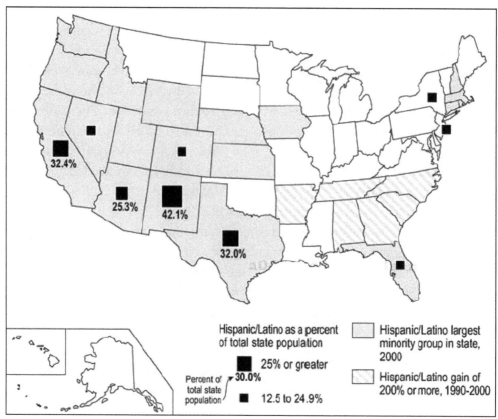

FIGURE 1.1.3 Hispanic/Latino percentage of total state population, 2000. *Source:* Brewer and Suchan 2001: 17, 86, 87.

Shifting scale from states to counties illuminates another geography of Hispanic/Latino Americans. While some states, like New York and Illinois, have large absolute numbers of the ethnic group, Hispanic/Latino Americans in those states are a small percentage of individual county populations. Figure 1.1.4 shows, for example, that Hispanic/Latino Americans in New York and Illinois did not anywhere exceed 50 percent of a county's population. Along the East Coast, only Dade County (greater Miami), in southern Florida, counted more than 50 percent Hispanics/Latinos. Moving west on the national map, not until one reaches the northeastern edge of South Texas are there counties that are predominantly Hispanic/Latino. This emphasizes the substantial vacuum of Hispanic/Latino concentration at the county level across the middle of America. In fact, only Nebraska, South Dakota, North Dakota, and Montana had counties in 1990 without a single Hispanic/Latino resident (Roseman 2002: Map 1.3).

Hispanic/Latino population concentration is most pronounced along the southwestern borderland, where the Mexican subgroup is dominant. A rimland of counties in South and West Texas that are overwhelmingly Mexican is the most intensive and extensive Hispanic/Latino

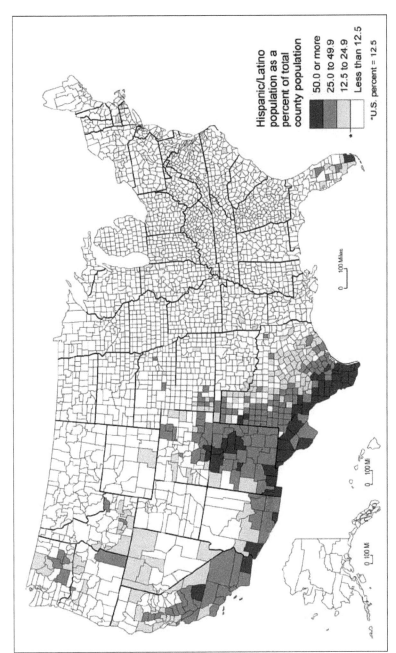

FIGURE 1.1.4 Percentage Hispanic/Latino population, by county, 2000. *Source: Guzmán 2001: Fig. 3.*

zone (Arreola 1995). Outlier clusters of counties that also have high (greater than 50 percent) concentrations of the ethnic group are notable in southwestern New Mexico, southwestern Arizona and southeastern California, the western Panhandle of Texas, and single counties in South-Central Arizona and California (Fig. 1.1.4). The large cluster of counties in North-Central New Mexico and southern Colorado is chiefly the remnant of the once-extensive highland Hispano homeland (Nostrand 2001).

In borderland states, there is a substantial domain of counties more than 25 percent but less than 50 percent Hispanic/Latino. These extend from coastal, Trans-Pecos, and Panhandle Texas across parts of western Oklahoma and Kansas, touching parts of southern Colorado, most of New Mexico, scattered counties of southern Arizona, most of Southern California, and pieces of central and coastal California, especially the San Joaquin Valley (Fig. 1.1.4). This area was early identified as the Hispanic-American borderland, "a culture region because of the intensity of a distinctive subculture, the longtime existence of Hispanic settlements, a rich Hispanic legacy, and the presence of Anglo-Americans who have been 'Hispanicized' (Nostrand 1970: 638)."

Pieces of central Washington, eastern Oregon, Idaho, and Colorado, too, have scattered counties where Hispanics/Latinos make up a significant, if relatively smaller, concentration (Fig. 1.1.4). On the margins of these areas, there are other and greater numbers of counties where Hispanic/Latino Americans are recent arrivals, especially in the Yakima River, Columbia River, and Snake River stretches of Washington and Oregon, the South Platte River area of Colorado, and northern Nevada. These concentrations have been documented as "new" communities where recent Hispanic/Latino immigrants have settled among Anglos in small towns that are still tied to rural economies (Haverluk 1998; McGlade 2002).

A breakdown of Hispanic/Latino Americans by major subgroup populations creates yet another picture of this ethnic mosaic. Figure 1.1.5 emphasizes how Mexicans are not only the most numerous of Hispanic/Latino Americans, but also the most geographically distributed. In each of thirty-five states, there are at least twenty-five thousand Mexicans, and four of those states have at least one million. The borderland focus is explained by the legacy of Spanish and Mexican entrenchment there, but the range of the distribution is attributable in part to the long history of Mexican migrant labor, both inside of and, especially, outside of borderland states (Cardoso 1980; Grebler, Moore, Guzmán 1970; Reisler 1976). Mexicans were drawn to mining districts, railroad centers, farming regions, and industrial nodes. Today, immigrant labor continues to be a major component of urban service economies, and Mexicans labor in many sectors of regional economies across the country. A comparison of the distribution shown in Figure 1.1.5 with Mexican population distributions from 1980 and 1990 shows that Mexicans are now extended to parts of the South, the Middle Atlantic, and New England where they were not concentrated earlier (Allen and Turner 1988: Mexican Origin map: 154; Arreola and Haverluk 1996: Maps 1 and 2).

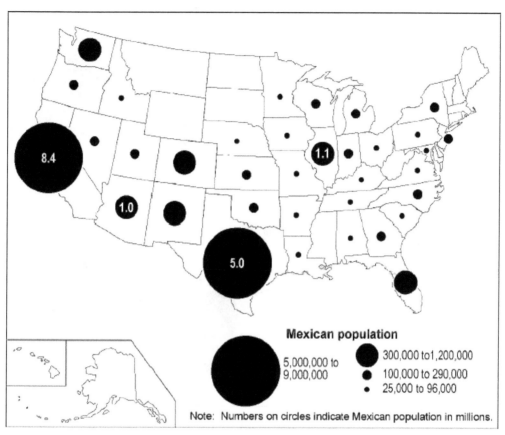

FIGURE 1.1.5   Mexican population greater than 25,000, by state, 2000. *Source: Guzmán 2001: Table 2.*

Puerto Ricans and Cubans are unevenly distributed compared with Mexicans. Figure 1.1.6 illustrates the pronounced geographic skew to the East Coast and upper Midwest for Puerto Ricans. New York and neighboring New Jersey combined account for almost half the population of the subgroup, and Florida alone is a significant concentration. Secondary distributions are found in Massachusetts, Connecticut, Pennsylvania, and Illinois. Only California in the West maintains a large number of Puerto Ricans, who are otherwise a minor population in the middle of the country. The geography for this subgroup has not changed significantly from that mapped in 1980 and 1990 (Allen and Turner 1988: Puerto Rican Origin map: 154; Boswell and Cruz-Báez 2000: Fig. 1.5). Further, secondary migration appears to account for the greater part of the Puerto Rican relocation from New York to other regions (Allen and Turner 1988: U.S.-born Puerto Rican Origin Population map: 158).

Cubans are even more geographically concentrated than are Puerto Ricans. Figure 1.1.6a shows that more than two-thirds of all Cubans in the United States reside in Florida. New Jersey, California, and New York are secondary centers of this subgroup population, and only five other

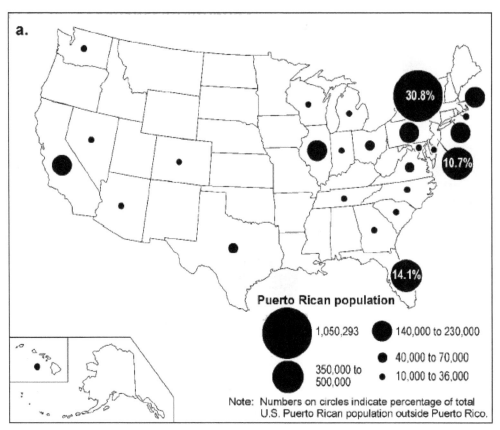

FIGURE 1.1.6a Puerto Rican population as percentage of total, by states with more than 10,000 population, 2000.

states have concentrations greater than ten thousand. Cuban ethnic geography has been equated to an "archipelago" consisting of small islands, because the distribution of population is diffuse beyond Florida, the "big island" (McHugh, Miyares, Skop 1997: Fig. 1.1). Further, the 2000 national map for Cubans did not change fundamentally from distributions plotted in 1980 and 1990 (Allen and Turner 1988: Cuban Origin map: 162; McHugh, Miyares, Skop 1997: Fig. 1.2).

Salvadorans and Guatemalans are the leading Central American subgroups in the United States (see Table 1.1.1). Although Salvadorans are almost two times as numerous as Guatemalans, their respective geographies are amazingly similar (Figs. 1.1.7a, 1.1.7b). California ranks first as the destination of choice for each subgroup, with approximately 40 percent of both Salvadorans and Guatemalans resident in the Golden State. A West Coast proximity of origin and destination may contribute to this skewed distribution, but one cannot discount the perceived economic opportunities of California, one of the world's major regional economies, as well as any preexisting channels for overland migration through Mexico (Jones 1989; Menjívar 2000). Texas and New York are secondary centers of Salvadoran immigrants, whereas New York and Florida serve as secondary destinations for Guatemalans. While the Lone Star State is linked to conduits of

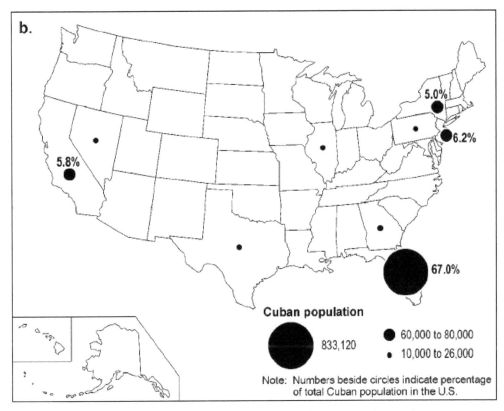

FIGURE 1.1.6b Puerto Rican population as percentage of total, by states with more than 10,000 population, 2000.

overland migration via Mexico, Houston and Miami are each closer by air to both El Salvador and Guatemala than the Central American countries are to California. Massachusetts, New Jersey (Bailey et al. 2002), and Virginia are tertiary destinations for both subgroups, while Maryland and the District of Columbia are separate, significant locations of Salvadorans. Other Central American subgroups like Nicaraguans and Hondurans are concentrated, albeit in small numbers, in Florida (Miami) and Louisiana (New Orleans), respectively (Hamilton and Chinchilla 1991; Portes and Stepick 1993).

Colombians and Ecuadorians are the major South American subgroups in the United States, although Peruvians rank a very close third (see Table 1.1.1). More than half of all Colombians in the United States are concentrated in Florida and New York. These concentrations appear to represent Colombians from different parts of the homeland. The oldest migrant channel is chiefly from Bogotá and first came to New York after World War I. However, the largest migrations have occurred since 1960, especially since 1970, and the population of this subgroup has nearly doubled every decade since 1960 (Haslip-Viera and Baver 1996: Table 3). Colombians who migrated to New York City found residence in the Jackson Heights area of Queens and began to call their neighborhood "Chaperino" after a middle-class suburb of Bogotá. The migrant stream that

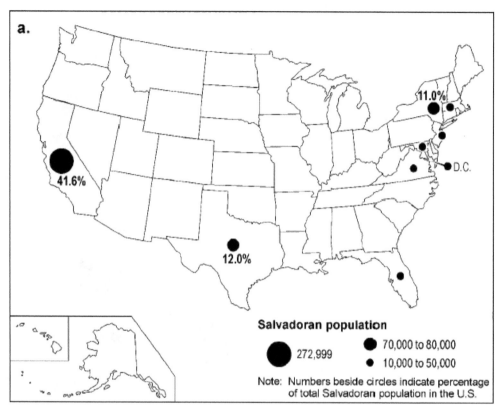

FIGURE 1.1.7a Salvadoran population as percentage of total, by states with more than 10,000 population, 2000.

settled Florida, however, is said to be mostly *costeños*, from the coastal regions of Colombia and chiefly of mixed African, Native American, and Spanish ancestry (Gann and Duignan 1986: 121–122) (Fig. 1.1.8a).

Ecuadorian emigration is a relatively recent phenomenon, stimulated in part by changes in agrarian structure in the homeland. Most emigrants come from the provinces of Cañar and Azuay in South-Central Ecuador, and their primary destination has been New York City, via stopovers in Central America and overland through Mexico (Jokisch 1997; Jokisch and Pribilsky 2002). Because Ecuadorians are chiefly illegal immigrants, the total given in the 2000 census (Table 1.1.1 may be a serious undercount and populations may be several rimes higher, possibly making Ecuadorians the largest South American subgroup, exceeding even Colombians. Like Colombians, however, Ecuadorians in the United States are highly concentrated, with approximately two-thirds in New York—especially Queens—and New Jersey, and smaller numbers in Florida, Illinois, and California (Fig. 1.1.8b).

Notwithstanding the geographical dispersion of Hispanic/Latino Americans, the ethnic group is more urban than the national population as a whole. In 2000, nine of every ten members of the

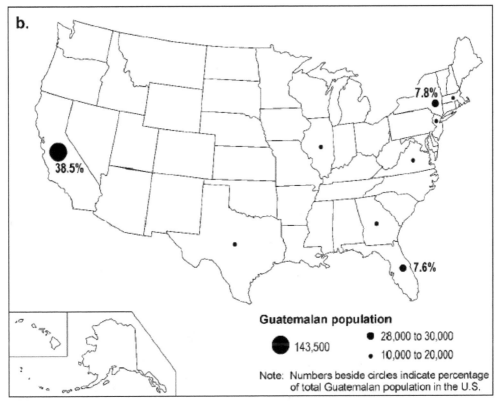

FIGURE 1.1.7b Guatemalan population as percentage of total, by states with more than 10,000 population, 2000. *Source:* U.S. Bureau of the Census 2000.

group lived in metropolitan areas, whereas only seven of every ten non-Hispanic whites lived in metropolitan regions. Further, nearly half of all Hispanic/Latino Americans lived in the central city of a metropolitan area, whereas the percentage in similar areas for non-Hispanic whites was about 20 (Therrien and Ramírez 2001). Nevertheless, Hispanic/Latino Americans are now predominantly a suburban population in the one hundred largest metropolitan areas, having grown 71 percent in these districts in the 1990s (Suro and Singer 2002).

Figure 1.1.9 illustrates cities with more than one million population, more than two hundred thousand Hispanic/Latino residents, and more than 25 percent Hispanic/Latino in 2000. New York and Los Angeles have the greatest numbers of the ethnic group, but only Miami and San Antonio are places that are predominantly Hispanic/Latino. Los Angeles (see Allen and Turner 1997: Figs. 4.2–4.9; Allen and Turner 2002: Figs. 5.2–5.4) is nearly half Hispanic/Latino, and cities like Houston, Dallas, and Phoenix are now more than one-third Hispanic/Latino. In seven of these nine cities, Mexicans are the leading Hispanic/Latino subgroup, and only in Miami is another subgroup, Cuban, a plurality. Even New York City, which contains the greatest number of Hispanics/Latinos, is now a mixed population where "Other Hispanic" is the leading category, exceeding

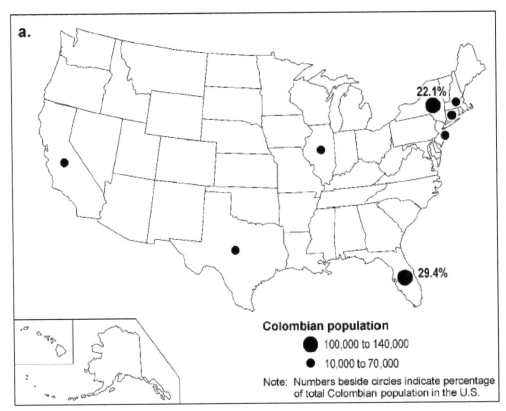

FIGURE 1.1.8a Colombian population as percentage of total, by states with more than 10,000 population, 2.000.

even Puerto Ricans. In fact, in all remaining cities, with the exception of New York and Chicago, "Other Hispanic" is the second-ranking category. Central and South Americans in Los Angeles, New York, Miami, Houston, and Washington, and Dominicans in New York and Miami are now part of the ethnic mix in major cities with Hispanic/Latino populations (Arreola 1997; Boswell and Skop 1995; Davis 2000; Hamilton and Chinchilla 2001; Haslip-Viera and Baver 1996; Miyares and Gowen 1998; Moore and Pinderhughes 1993; Padilla 1987; Portes and Stepick 1993; Waldinger and Bozorgmehr 1996).

Is This a Nation?

In the introduction to his considerable tome, *Latinos: A Biography of the People*, Earl Shorris (1992b: 12) writes, "Although the name of this book is *Latinos*, the theory of it is that there are no Latinos, only diverse peoples struggling to remain who they are while becoming someone else." In his own struggles with the word "Hispanic," Richard Rodríguez (2002: 117) writes, "You won't find Hispanics in Latin America ... not in the quickening cities, not in the emasculated villages. You need to come to the United States to meet Hispanics ... What Hispanic immigrants learn within

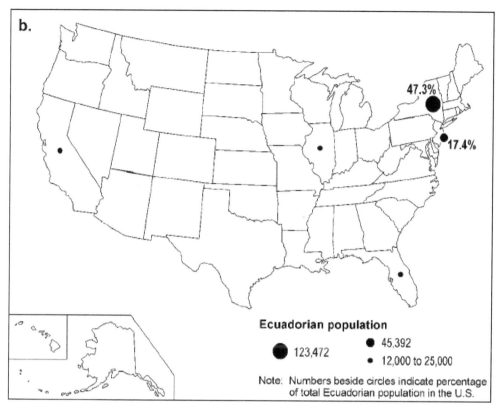

FIGURE 1.1.8b Ecuadorian population as percentage of total, by states with more than 10,000 population, 2000. *Source:* U.S. Bureau of the Census 2000.

the United States is to view themselves in a new way, as belonging to Latin America entire—precisely at the moment they no longer do."

These antipodes of inclusion and exclusion—are Hispanic/Latino Americans Latin Americans, or some new nation within the United States—are stimulating volatile debates in scholarly as well as popular literature. To a large extent, these debates center on the idea of cultural confrontation and identity. Cultural critic Ilan Stavans (2001) explores this notion in the context of his stimulating book *The Hispanic Condition*, where he also asks questions about the ways in which cultures behave among themselves and toward others.

Among Hispanic/Latino Americans, perhaps the most intense exploration of the issue of exclusion has been trained on Mexican Americans. Historians especially have deliberated on Anglo attitudes toward Mexicans in Texas (De León 1983), in California (Monroy 1990), and in Los Angeles (Acuña 1996). In his 1999 book, *¡Pobre Raza!*, Arturo Rosales explores how elite Mexican immigrants in the early twentieth century formed a "México Lindo" (beautiful Mexico) nationalism to confront discrimination and violence against Mexicans in the United States.

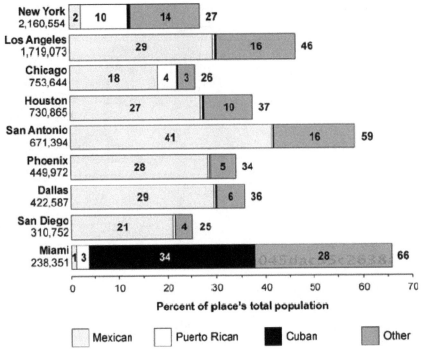

FIGURE 1.1.9 Cities with more than one million population, at least 200,000 Hispanic/
Latino residents, and more than 25 percent Hispanic/Latino population, 2000. *Source:* U.S.
Bureau of the Census 2000.

Borrowing anthropologist Renato Rosaldo's term "cultural citizenship," some social scientists have refashioned his concept to mean "a range of social practices which, taken together, claim and establish a distinct social space for Latinos in this country" (Flores and Benmayor 1997:1). Arguably, the most advanced discussion about the idea of a Hispanic/Latino consciousness is sociologist Geoffrey Fox's *Hispanic Nation.* Fox (1997: 4) starts with anthropologist Benedict Anderson's concept of nation as "an imagined political community" where members have very little in common beyond language and a few traditions, yet where they may feel affiliated with one another and with some larger collective entity. The media have largely carried the nationalist banner for Hispanics/Latinos. Fox examines how and why this component of society, especially, has worked to forge a national agenda. Improvements in communications technologies are spreading notions of imagined community. Nationally broadcast Spanish-language television, for example, creates a united Hispanic/Latino audience, where the same events in the same homogenized Spanish accent get communicated. A large part of these media, not surprisingly, is tied to marketing geared toward Hispanic/Latino Americans. Other segments of society, like political organizations, are much more fragmented by alliances that hold tightly to subgroup identity.

And, geographically, most Hispanic/Latino Americans do not lay claim to a united Territory. "It may therefore be objected," says Fox (1997: 7) "that Hispanics cannot become a 'nation' because they have neither a flag nor a land to fly it over. And if they did, where would it be? A secessionist chunk of the American Southwest? East Harlem? Miami?"

If there is a geographical Hispanic/Latino nation, it is a largely fragmented confederation of regional zones and nodes, not a unified area in any real sense. And it is precisely because Hispanic/Latino Americans are diverse and diffuse that we can best understand and appreciate their geographical identities through the lens of regional inspection, across settlement scales, and through time.

Finally, what might a future Hispanic/Latino American geography look like? I would contend that the fundamental geographical anatomy of this ethnic population is already in place. Although Hispanic/Latino Americans will no doubt increase as a percentage of all Americans, and while subgroup concentrations may increase or erode, it seems unlikely that the ratios of subgroup populations will change too greatly, because the homeland populations for many subgroups are small. Puerto Ricans who currently reside on the mainland are nearly equivalent to the total number of Puerto Ricans on the island, and Guatemala, Ecuador, Cuba, Dominican Republic, and El Salvador each have fewer than 15 million people today. Only Mexico, which counted some 104 million people in 2002, is a large country that also contributes significantly to the total number of Latin American emigrants. In 2000, Mexico accounted for more than half of the foreign born in the United States from Latin America ("Coming from the Americas" 2002).

California and Texas, the most Hispanic/Latino American states, and chiefly Mexican, are also states with the greatest number of Hispanic/ Latino elected officials (National Directory of Latino Elected Officials [NALEO] 2000). If political influence on a regional scale is to develop, it will likely emerge first in these areas.

It is not inconceivable, then, that Mexico, homeland to the largest share of Hispanic/Latino Americans, will continue to be the source of the greatest number of new Hispanic/Latino Americans. And this, in all likelihood, means that Mexicans (Mexican Americans and Chicanas/Chicanos) will, in the near future, continue to represent the vast majority of Americans of Hispanic/Latino ancestry.

In *Crossing Over: A Mexican Family on the Migrant Trail,* Rubén Martínez (2001: 136) relates his discussions with Purépecha migrants from the town of Cherán in Michoacán. The residents of this village, like villagers in so many other mountain valleys of these highlands, have been migrating to *el norte* (the north, i.e., the United States) for generations. One migrant who has journeyed to the San Joaquin Valley in California, then to Los Angeles, and finally to Arkansas remarked with optimism, "Within a decade … Hispanics will be the largest minority in the United States." That statistic, says Martínez, which is today cited with regularity in our media, has been a truth among Mexican migrants for years. A Latino American diaspora has been transforming this country for many generations, and as surely as a Hispanic American legacy has shaped the

American Southwest, so, too, will it spread across and spice up the far corners of these United States. As the contributions to this volume attest, it is already happening.

Reading 1.1

Define the following concepts/phrases:

cultural geography

nation (according to Benedict Anderson)

transnational community

the antipode of inclusion and exclusion

Latin American diaspora

majority–minority population

Answer the following questions:

1. Why are Latinos one of the oldest and newest groups of American immigrants at the same time?
2. Why do some Hispanics identify themselves as Latinos? Explain the reasons for the different labels.
3. Why are Hispanics/Latinos "a plural population and diverse in several important ways"?
4. Identify the reasons for the increase and projection of the Latino population from 1960 until 2000?
5. Where did Latinos settle in the United States?
6. Discuss how the settlement process changed geographically and by historical period.
7. Who are the "other" Latinos?
8. Describe a listing of the books quoted in this essay about Hispanics or Latinos.

A Multilevel Analysis of Latinos' Economic Inequality

A Test of the Minority Group Threat Theory

Carlos Siordia and Ruben Antonio Farias

I N SEPTEMBER 2010 THE NEWS MEDIA alerted the public that: the "ranks of the working-age poor climbed to the highest level since the 1960s ... leaving one in seven Americans in poverty" (CBS News, 2010). Four months later, in January 2011, the media raised the alarm further by reporting that the "number of poor people in the United States is millions higher than previously known, with one in six Americans" struggling in poverty (CBS News, 2011). Finally, the *New York Times* ran a story on the United States' "lost decade," showing that the recent increase in the depth and severity of poverty underscored the overall economic challenges facing a substantial portion of Americans. As the author reports, "[national poverty data] brought into sharp relief the toll the past decade—including the painful declines of the financial crisis and recession—had taken on Americans at the middle and lower parts of the income ladder (Tavernise, 2011). Overall, the mass media's message is clear: *many U.S. residents are experiencing financial troubles*.

Which individuals and groups have been adversely affected by the economic downturn of the last decade? A closer look at poverty data reveals that: *financial trouble has affected some racial/ethnic groups more severely than others*. Notably, Latinos and Blacks have been the two most distressed racial groups with 26% of Latinos and 27% of African Americans living in poverty (Tavernise, 2011). In contrast, the poverty rate among non-Hispanic Whites stands at 9.9%. Due to the volume's focus on Latinos,[1] this chapter concentrates on Latino poverty in the United States [...].

Studying Latino poverty—especially in relation to non-Hispanic Whites—is important. Such information contributes to the ongoing national discussions (as exemplified in the media, politics, and academic circles) on how, if at all, the increase in the Latino population will "change the face" of the United States. Some commentators argue that Latinos' growing group size (and hence influence) will weaken and disunite the nation-state (for an interesting discussion see the 2004 study by R. Yzaguirre and his colleagues). Leo Chavez (2008) has called such rhetoric the

Carlos Siordia and Ruben Antonio Farias, "A Multilevel Analysis of Latinos' Economic Inequality: A Test of the Minority Group Threat Theory," *The Economic Status of the Hispanic Population: Selected Essays*, ed. Marie T. Mora and Alberto Dávila, pp. 65-79. Copyright © 2013 by Information Age Publishing. Reprinted with permission.

"Latino Threat Narrative," which is a pervasive national narrative that portrays Latinos in general, and people of Mexican origin in particular, as a "danger" to the basic sovereignty of the United States nation-state. In contrast, many observers conjecture that in the near future (around the time when Latinos are projected to become largest racial-ethnic group in the United States) the nation will become a more multicultural and racially egalitarian nation.

Poverty in the United States

Notwithstanding numerous governmental and private initiatives, poverty levels in the United States were roughly the same in 1980 as in 2009. As reported by the Annual Social and Economic Supplement (ASEC) from the Current Population Survey, in 1980, about 13% of the U.S. population lived at or below the poverty line, compared to 14% in 2009. The one percentage-point difference between these two times hides the fact that in 2009 there was a bigger population base—which means there are more people living in poverty now than thirty years ago.

Recent U.S. Census Bureau reports indicate that poverty has, in fact, increased in the last couple of years. For instance, there was a statistically significant increase in the poverty rate from 2008 (13.2%) to 2009 (14.3%) (DeNavas-Walt, Bernadette, & Smith, 2010). In absolute numbers, the number of people living in poverty increased from 39.8 million in 2008 to 43.6 million in 2009. The 2009 poverty rate was the highest since 1994, but lower than the first official poverty rate estimate (of 22.4%) in 1959.

What are some notable characteristics of contemporary poverty? The recent increase in poverty is characterized by geographic and demographic concentration. In terms of geography, previous publications indicate that 13 states contain almost two thirds of the individuals living in poverty (see Bishaw & Macartney, 2010, Figure 1). Poverty is not only geographically clustered along southern states (Holt, 2007); it is also concentrated along detectable racial/ethnic groups. For example, of the 43 million people living in poverty during the 2009 survey period, non-Hispanic Whites only had 9.4% (or about 1 in every 10) of their population living in poverty while more than one in every four Latinos (or 25.3%) were in poverty (DeNavas-Walt, Bernadette, & Smith, 2010). In sum, two trends are clear from the poverty data:

1. Economic recessions and booms have come and gone while poverty has persistently retained its firm place in American society.
2. The absolute number of people categorized as poor in 2009 is the largest since poverty estimates were first published.

The history of poverty in the United States is admittedly complex. Nevertheless, people continue to enter, exit, and remain in poverty during their lifetime. The very real consequences of poverty are important points to remember. As we next discuss, the minority group threat theory high-lights such consequences on the lives of racial-ethnic minorities.

Group Threat Theory

Forty years ago, it was eloquently stated that when "a person thinks, more than one generation's passions and images think in him" (Novak, 1972, p. 32). In this section we investigate *how* the per-cent of Latinos in an area of residence is associated with the likelihood of experiencing poverty. Prior research demonstrates that there are significant statistical associations between poverty, racial-ethnic status, and place level measures (e.g., Siordia, 2011). Before exploring these associa-tions, a review of the chapter's main theory is in order. In particular, the review underscores how the percent of Latinos in the area of residence influences an individual's chances for experienc-ing poverty—*over and above the influence of the individual characteristics*. In short, the occurrence of poverty is significantly influenced by geographic and place-level attributes.

Huber M. Blalock Jr. (1970) formulated empirically testable propositions on minority-group relations.[2] He outlined a theory with two primary components:

1. Groups of individuals who are aligned by some detectable characteristic (e.g., race-ethnicity) seek out ways to either obtain or retain a "dominant group" status.
2. When the dominant group (i.e., the one with the largest control over political, economic, and social power) perceives that a competing group is acquiring power, they fear them and seek ways to hinder or prohibit the subordinate group from advancing.[3]

In other words, when inter-group competition for tangible (e.g., money) and intangible (e.g., lan-guage) resources increases, perceptions of out-groups as threats increase within the dominant group. Dominant group members then respond with "exclusionary anti-outgroup attitudes" which serve to protect their individual and group interests (Schlueter & Scheepers, 2010).

The most pertinent component of Blalock's minority group threat theory is that "exposure to large numbers of minority members" threatens "*individual* members of the dominant group" (Blalock, 1970, p. 28 italics by original author). Rephrased to fit our case, when non-Hispanic White group members perceive a growth in the Latino population and interpret it as a threat, non-Hispanic White *individual* members will act in such a way so as to reduce their level of fear.

Under what specific conditions will the dominant group act, via discrimination, to maintain group control? A discriminatory response occurs when non-Hispanic Whites:

1. Perceive an increase in the Latino population
2. Interpret the increase as posing a threat.

In the words of Gary Becker (1971, p. 123), "tastes for discrimination against non-whites vary directly with their proportion in a community." Blalock's theory directly links a minority group's population size with perceived fear in the dominant group. The higher the population size of a minority group, the more the group can be seen as posing a threat to the dominant one.

It is important to consider how "threats combine with personality variables to produce motivation to discriminate" (Blalock, 1970, p. 28), because "different kinds of persons will not be similarly motivated by the minority percentage variable" (Blalock, 1970, p. 31). The main component of the group threat theory—that an increase in a minority group's population leads to perceived fear and discriminatory actions—underscores another important proposition of the theory: the main motivation compelling dominant group discrimination is the desire to keep group control. Ultimately, in response to the perceived threat (fear) of the minority group, the dominant group works to maintain their privileged status.

How does Blalock's theory apply to the case of Latinos? We expect that as the percent of Latinos in an area of residence increases, fears of them by non-Hispanic Whites will increase, such that they would respond to increase their ability to retain political and economic control. Specifically, the rise in fear among non-Hispanic Whites can result in discriminatory practices against Latinos—which can lead to economic marginalization. By arguing that Latino poverty is in part a product of discrimination,[4] we contribute to the literature describing the process by which oppressed groups become the recipients of their disadvantages.

What is the result of long term discrimination of the dominant group (non-Hispanic Whites) against the minority group (Latinos)? When discriminatory behaviors by non-Hispanic White individuals are sustained over time, they form structural elements (e.g., laws, financial agencies, school funding policies) that systematically inhibit Latinos from obtaining social and human capital resources. According to Herbert Blumer (1958), when historically advantaged group members (in our case non-Hispanic Whites) perceive minority-group members (in our case Latinos) as threatening their entitlements, non-Hispanic Whites manifest their prejudice towards the challenging minority group. The positive association between discrimination and minority presence occurs because similarly motivated non-Hispanic Whites "interact with each other in such a way as to bring about concerted action leading to actual discrimination" (Blalock, 1970, p. 28). This is how individual-level behaviors combine over time to create durable and unjust discriminatory distributive processes (Massey, 2007). If non-Hispanic White group members discriminate similarly and consistently against Latinos, then their behaviors will contribute towards instituting systemic discriminatory practices that collectively constrain Latinos.

Some have convincingly argued that Latinos are seen by some as a threat to the "American way of life" (Sáenz, Cready, & Morales, 2007). When thinking of how individual-level behaviors combine to form macro-level social structures, we can frame our discussion on racial-ethnic discrimination as follows. The more non-Hispanic Whites are threatened by Latinos, the more they cooperate, and the more likely discrimination against Latino occurs. Consequently, as the Latino population proliferation continues, it could represent a threat that fuels the prevailing stratification system by allowing non-Hispanic Whites the ability to erect "formidable structural obstacles" (Sáenz, 1997, p. 207)

Prior research has given support to Blalock's relative group size-inequality theory in the case of Latinos. For example, Rogelio Sáenz (1997) found a positive relationship between the relative size of the Chicano population and the group's poverty rate. Additionally, related work has shown that Latinos residing in communities with heavy co-ethnic concentrations have a labor market penalty (e.g., Bean & Tienda, 1987; Cort, 2011; Kaplan & Douzet, 2011; Wang, 2010). Recent arguments have advanced "that the animosity toward Latinos by both the majority white *and* minority Black populations may be more intense than those shaping contemporary White-Black relations" (Markert, 2010). Support for Blalock's power-threat theory has been given elsewhere (Kane, 2003), and some have pointed out that in highly segregated areas "the relative size of the Latino population is a predictor of fear of crime among White residents" (Eitle & Taylor, 2008, p. 1102).

A great amount of space is dedicated elsewhere (Siordia, 2011) towards delineating the assumptions of how "individual goals, motives, and needs are major causal agents in social systems" (Blalock, 1970, p. 28). For now, there is one theoretical premise (as adapted from Blalock) that will suffice in advancing our understanding of the ethno-racial discrimination-poverty link. We outline and adapt it to our Latino versus non-Hispanic White comparison. As may be clear by now, we perceive non-Hispanic Whites to be the dominant racial-ethnic group in the United States. We make this the case because non-Hispanic Whites have historically controlled most of the governmental, economic, and social structures in the United States; they "have more balanced distribution of labor and capital" (Becker, 1971, p. 32) than Latinos. Thus, when we mention the dominant group in the context of our chapter, we are referring to non-Hispanic Whites.

In passing, we would like the reader to be aware of an extensive literature on how inter-group contact works (see Allport, 1954). It is beyond the scope of this chapter to address how this topic plays a role in our investigation. In the most general sense we should keep in mind that "since people discriminate little against those with whom they have only indirect [contact] in the market place, some direct contact must be necessary for the development of a desire to discriminate" (Becker, 1971, p. 154). On the one hand, inter-ethnic contact can result in the reduction of racial-ethnic discrimination under the right circumstances (Burton-Chelley, Ross-Gillespie, & West, 2010). On the other hand, the increased presence of Latinos may escalate the potential for non-Hispanic Whites to be in contact with them, which may in turn provide the social-psychological material necessary for fearing Latinos and subsequently desiring to discriminate against them. We bring up the "contact hypothesis" to simply point out that our chapter only focuses on the "negative aspects" arriving from inter-ethnic contact.

By following our delineated theoretical views, we utilize an empirical model to measure how Latinos' co-ethnic concentration relates their likelihood of being in poverty when compared to non-Hispanic Whites. Our quantitative investigation focuses on individuals as units of analysis while using macro-level variables as indicators of racial-ethnic exposure to Latinos. In particular, our analysis estimates how the percentage of Latinos in the area of residence affects a Latino's likelihood of being in poverty after accounting for several other individual-level and context-level factors. The latter factors (also referred to as macro-level factors) pertain to the characteristics of the geographic area in which the individual resides.

The investigation in effect tests how "contextual effects" (Blalock, 1970, p. 26) affect the Latino status with respect to the likelihood of being in poverty. Even though our model allows for comparisons between non-His-panic-Blacks to non-Hispanic Whites, such a discussion deserves detailed attention, which is not possible in this chapter.

Data and Methodology

Our analysis of Latino poverty is conducted using a Public Use Microdata Sample (PUMS) from the American Community Survey (ACS), specifically the ACS 2005–2007 three-year PUMS files. The Data Appendix chapter provides more information on the ACS. For the United States government to release microdata files, they must employ various techniques to ensure the confidentiality of survey participants, including limiting the ability of public users to geographically locate respondents. The U.S. Census Bureau protects the identity of survey participants by introducing small demographic alterations to the sample and by only allowing public data users the ability to physically locate respondents to geographical areas with at least 100,000 people, called Public Use Microdata Areas (PUMAs). PUMAs are the smallest identifiable geographic unit. As such, our measure of Latino concentration is the percentage of Latinos in the PUMA.

Our sample of interest only includes individuals ages 20–64 who directly participated in the survey, and who resided in one of the mainland contiguous states (and D.C.).[5] Our primary individual-level variable of interest is an individual's racial-ethnic identity. We use ethnicity along with race because previous research has found that "people with specific ethnic self-conceptions" use different self-images in the course of interaction with others (Sáenz & Aguirre, 1991, p. 17). Given this chapter's focus, the sample only includes Latinos/as, single-race non-Hispanic-Blacks, and single-race non-Hispanic-Whites (referred to here as non-Hispanic Whites).

It is important to note that "ethnicity" is an inherently qualitative and complicated concept first instrumentalized at a large scale by the United States government to capture a broad group of peoples. The U.S. Census Bureau collects race and Hispanic-origin information following the guidance of the United States Office of Management and Budget—which defines "Hispanic" as a person of Cuban, Mexican, Puerto Rican, South or Central American, or other Spanish culture or origin regardless of race. As a consequence of this grouping scheme, and since the umbrella term includes a very identity-fluid group of individuals, Hispanics/Latinos are a heterogeneous ethnic group.

We now describe our empirical model for our analysis. Our empirical model predicts the likelihood of being in poverty when controlling for observable individual-level and geographic-level characteristics.[6] Since our interpretation focuses on contrasting how Latinos differ in their odds of being in poverty with non-Hispanic Whites, the latter group represents the reference category. Studies [...] have shown that racial-ethnic minorities are more likely than non-Hispanic Whites to be in poverty—this is not our primary interest (although the models confirm it). The primary question under investigation is on how the Latino concentration at the PUMA-level influences the Latino status as it predicts the likelihood of being in poverty.

A driving motivation behind this investigation is that many poverty-related studies have been lacking in one respect: the recognition and modeling of multilevel data. If racial-ethnic context matters, then accounting for it is not only important but *necessary*. More generally, our basic argument "... is that through its opportunity structure, the place of residence affects the ability of households to raise their economic status and avoid falling into poverty, above and beyond the human resources and work behavior of its residents" (Lewin, Stier, & Caspi-Dror, 2006, p. 178). In short, place matters.

Sample Characteristics and Empirical Findings

As seen in Table 1.2.1, the average age of individuals in our analytic sample was 45, about 57% of them were male, 14% had some form of disability, 58% were married, about 15% had served in the military at some point in their lifetime, and approximately 90% had a high school degree and beyond. From this table, Latinos (of all races) made up 11% of the sample, and that non-Hispanic Whites comprise the majority (79%). Nearly four out of five individuals in our sample were U.S.-born, while immigrants were, on average, 21 years of age at time of arrival.

About one in every ten persons in our sample resided below the poverty line in 2005–07. In terms of the association of poverty with race and ethnicity, 17% of Latinos, and 20% of non-Hispanic Blacks were impoverished, compared to only 7% of non-Hispanic Whites. When it comes to language, 10% were bilingual (speak another language other than English at home and speak English "very well" or "well") and 3% were monolingual in a non-English language (i.e., they speak English "not well" or "not at all"). Unfortunately, the bilingual variable offers little insight on the details of bilingualism; since it measures language spoken at home, it fails to capture those who may be bilingual but lived in a monolingual English household. Consequently, as the bilingual variable is constructed here, it only informs us that the individual spoke English and another language at home.

From the geographic-level characteristics in Table 1.2.1, PUMAs in 2005–07 averaged a 14-percent Latino population concentration, followed by an average 13% non-Hispanic Black population concentration. When it comes to formal educational attainment, on average, the PUMAs had populations in which 19% have a bachelor's degree and beyond.

TABLE 1.2.1   Characteristics of Latinos, Non-Hispanic Blacks, and Non-Hispanic Whites: 2005–2007

Characteristic	All	Latinos	Non-Hispanic Blacks	Non-Hispanic Whites
Panel A: Individual-level characteristics				
In poverty	10%	17%	20%	7%
Latinos	11%	100%	—	—
Non-Hispanic Blacks	10%	—	100%	—
Non-Hispanic Whites	79%	—	—	100%
U.S.-born	90%	46%	90%	96%
Age at immigration (range: 20-64 years)	21	22	24	20
Bilingual	10%	55%	6%	4%
Monolingual non-English household	3%	25%	1%	0.4%
Age (range: 20-64 years)	45	41	44	46
Male	57%	58%	40%	60%
Disabled	14%	13%	20%	14%
Married	58%	59%	36%	61%
Served in Military	15%	7%	13%	16%
At least a high school education	90%	68%	85%	93%
Panel B: Area-level variables				
Percent Latinos	14%	—	—	—
Percent Non-Hispanic Blacks	13%	—	—	—
Percent with a bachelors degree and beyond	19%	—	—	—

Source: Authors' estimates using 2005–2007 ACS data in the IPUMS. The sample only contains the reference persons ages 20–64 who filled out the questionnaire; see the text for more information.

We now turn to the findings from our empirical model, which predicts a persons' likelihood of being in poverty when controlling for other characteristics. Table 1.2.2 only consists of "percent change" values, which are the odds ratio minus one times 100. The "direct effect" column reflects the micro-level association between the variable and the outcome (i.e., likelihood of being in poverty). The "Area's % Latino" column shows the cross-level interaction between the area's Latino concentration and the variable in the row. Readers may contact the authors for a more detailed set of results.

We focus on the findings for the two primary coefficients of interest: how being Latino influences the chances of being in poverty, other things the same, as well as how the geographic Latino concentration relates to these chances. At the individual-level, our results indicate that in 2005–07, Latinos had a 25% *greater* likelihood of being in poverty than otherwise similar

TABLE 1.2.2   Individual-Level and Geographic-Level Determinants of the Likelihood of Residing below the Poverty Line: 2005–2007

Characteristic	Direct Effect (I)	Area's % Latino (II)	Area's % Non-Hispan- ic-Black (III)	Area's % College Graduates (IV)
Intercept	46%*	–66%*	–48%*	–97%*
Racial-ethnic group				
Latino	26%*	20%*	72%*	–15%
Non-Hispanic Black	74%*	9%	15%	42%*
Demographic covariates				
U.S.-born	–25%*	–17%*	33%*	15%
Age at immigration	1%*	–1%*	–2%*	1%
Bilingual	20%*	–17%*	–15%*	13%
Non-English monolingual household	26%*	26%*	–13%	363%
Age	–4%*	1%*	0.20%	–1%
Male	–55%*	28%*	15%*	195%*
Disabled	279%*	–41%*	–20%*	91%*
Married	–74%*	146%*	67%*	–49%*
Served	–11%*	–17%*	–16%*	47%*
At least a high school edu- cation	–65%*	49%*	–2%	–21%*

*Statistically significant at conventional levels.

Source: Authors' estimates using 2005–2007 ACS data in the IPUMS for the reference persons ages 20–64.

Notes: Column I shows the percent change in odds ratio for the individual-level relationship between the characteristics and the probability of being impoverished. The remaining columns show the percent changes in the odds ratio for the cross-level interactions with the (1) percentage of Latinos in the PUMA (Column II), percentage of non-Hispanic Blacks in the PUMA (Column III), and (3) the percentage of individuals with a bachelors degree or higher in the PUMA (Column IV).

non-Hispanic-Whites. This confirms other reports that Latinos are more likely to experience poverty than non-Hispanic Whites. Our results indicate that when it comes to predicting the likelihood of poverty, being a Latino is a disadvantage, even when controlling for other observable characteristics (such as age, English-language fluency, etc.) related to the odds of being in poverty.

It is worth mentioning that all the other individual-level characteristics played a role in the likelihood of being poor. Being female, disabled, having less than a high school education, and not residing in a monolingual-English household, for example, all increased this likelihood. Since these conditions are prevalent among Latinos, they compound the risk of impoverishment within this population.

Just as Blalock's group threat hypothesis predicted, moreover, Table 1.2.2 suggests that as the concentration of Latinos increases, a Latino's chances of being in poverty increase further as well—a social context influence that is above and beyond their individual-level characteristics. When investigating the indirect effects of the share of Latinos on the association between Latinos and the odds of being in poverty, we find that the "Latino disadvantage" increases with the concentration of Latinos in the PUMA of residence. Although not shown here, the raw estimated coefficient for this cross-level interaction is 0.22, which in technical terms means that for every increase of 0.01 in a community's percent Latino, the micro-level association between "Latino and poverty" status on the log odds of being in poverty increase by 0.0022%.[7]

In short, our hypothesis is supported because we find that as the geographic presence of Latinos increases, the odds of being in poverty rise for Latinos. Our investigation is important because Blalock's proposition—a minority-group's proliferation increases discrimination against them— is supported in our findings in the context of Latinos.

The fundamental argument underlying this investigation suggests that economic inequality occurs on an unequal basis, as a function of ascribed and attained characteristics in a socially stratified society. We do not appear to be born into a level-playing field. The existence of poverty has material consequences with the potential to alter our society, for better or worse. Since Latinos are, and will continue to be, a force in the formation of North America, their observed disadvantage can affect all U.S. residents. If fear continues to rise and produce discriminatory behaviors that victimize the economic condition of Latinos, then Latinos might eventually learn to abstain from participating in the U.S. democracy experiment.

Conclusion

The chapter began by arguing and providing evidence for how social disequilibrium asymmetrically affects Latinos. Seeking the cause of economic inequality is primarily driven by the desire to blame somebody. Because the subtle but prevalent belief is that if the source of a problem is found, a solution is possible. Finding the source(s) of Latino inequality is the first step towards developing a response that may negate the initial formation of inequality—because Latino poverty is a national issue, not just a Latino issue.

Both "structure" and "agency" factors affect a Latino's life chances. Our chapter offers evidence for how structural factors affect Latinos. As with all academic investigations, there are some limitations with the present study. For example, the measure of poverty is bounded in how the U.S. federal government measures it. Also, we frame poverty as the product of discrimination and thus interpret its presence as evidence that discriminatory practices have negatively affected Latinos. Beyond these measurement assumptions and limitations, and because we are using cross-sectional data, we are unable to determine how "lifetime factors" (e.g., childhood economic status) play a role in a Latino's adult poverty status. On a more theoretical aspect, our study is limited in that it assumes individual-level prejudices by non-Hispanic Whites coalesce to influence the formation of unjust and systematic discriminatory systems against Latinos, without regard to how agency plays a role.[8]

Notwithstanding these limitations, our investigation is valuable because it lends support to the minority-group threat theory by showing that a Latino's co-ethnic concentration influences his/her chances of being in poverty. Future research should investigate the theoretical essence driving multilevel modeling. First, researchers should seek to better measure how people feel they belong to a community. Then, they should determine if the geographical boundaries of said community can be drawn in such a way so as to apply to most people's perception of a "neighborhood." We suspect standardizing community geographical boundarization will prove challenging since people may vary greatly in their perceptions of where their community starts and ends. Lastly, more standardized measures on the social characteristics of environment should be created. These efforts will allow for a more scientific measure of how minority population growth is perceived by non-Hispanic Whites.

Blalock's predictions have not been falsified here. If Blalock's theories are correct and Latino's proliferation in the United States continues, then fear, conflict, and discrimination may continue to rise. One of the major contributions of this chapter lies in the empirical modeling of minority-group status related variables in the prediction of poverty. We are unable to falsify the main argument that Latinos are at a disadvantage when compared to non-Hispanic Whites, and that their co-ethnic concentration further aggravates their individual-level economic-penalty.

Endnotes

1. Please note that because the "Hispanic" label is a contested category within some academic circles, we opted to use Latino (Aguirre & Turner, 2011). In truth, some investigations have found that Latinos/as prefer to ethnically identify with a "national origin" label and that such preference can even vary by geographical settings (e.g., Kiang, Perreira, & Fuligni, 2011). We use the term Latino since in our models we include all sub-ethnic groups subsume under the ethnic label (e.g., Mexicans, Dominicans, Puerto Ricans, etc.). It is more appropriate to use Latinos/as, but we have chosen to use masculine-singular "Latino(s)" in order to keep chapter more readable. We use the term racial-ethnic status in reference to "racial and ethnic" groupings outlined in greater detail in the methods section of the chapter.

2. We reference Blalock's 1970 paper because it more clearly delineates all his previous and subsequent work. It should be noted that the "group threat" idea was first introduced to academic literature more than 60 years ago by a Texan (Key, 1949) and was subsequently brought into the academic main stage by Blalock and others.

3. A full discussion, explaining the five general ways in which fear towards minorities occurs is given elsewhere, as are the details underlying the theoretical assumptions in this area of research (Siordia, 2011).

4. It is important to note here that socioeconomic inequality is a resultant of discriminatory behavior *and* "of other factors as well" (Blalock, 1970, p. 17). A full discussion on the "other factors" is important but beyond the scope of this study. We do however acknowledge that there are components (e.g., agency, biology, etc.) beyond social structures that can influence life chances. Some of these other factors were discussed in the previous chapter.

5. More technically, we only include "reference" persons in ACS data (i.e., those who filled out the questionnaire) because *self-identification* on both the race and ethnic variable matters deeply. Age selection is done to increase our chances of only evaluating working-age adults. Also, we only selected states in the mainland because we are unsure if spatial auto-correlation may be playing a role in the diffusion of Latino population.

6. The federal government determines "poverty thresholds" by family types to determine if individuals are in poverty (for more details see http://aspe.hhs.gov/poverty/11poverty.shtml). Their poverty thresholds do not vary geographically, and as such, do not account for the relative cost of living. The thresholds are however annually updated for inflation using the Consumer Price Index.

7. The reason why the value is moved two decimal places to the rights is that the *percent Latino* variable is measured as a proportion that ranges from 0.00 to 0.98. This means that a one unit change in the percent *Latino variable* would result in a change in the log-odds of 0.21. But a change of 0.01 in the same variable results in a change in the log-odds of 0.0021.

8. Hobbes (1839) first introduced the term "agency" to social science over 170 years ago. However, the agency versus structure debate remains unresolved (e.g., see Fuchs, 2001, p. 24). "Systemic discrimination" involves a pattern where differential treatment has deep and broad impacts on people (e.g., see Feagin, 2006).

References

Aguirre, A., & Turner, J. H. (2011). *American ethnicity: The dynamics and consequences of discrimination*. New York: McGraw-Hill.

Allport, G. W. (1954). *The nature of prejudice*. Garden City, NY: Doubleday.

Becker, G. S. (1971). *Human capital: A theoretical and empirical analysis, with special reference to education*. Chicago: University of Chicago Press.

Bean, F. D., & Tienda, M. (1987). *The Hispanic population of the United States*. New York: Russell Sage Foundation.

Bishaw, A., & Macartney. S. (2010). U.S. Census Bureau, American Community Survey Briefs, ACSBR/09-1, *Poverty: 2008 and 2009*, U.S. Government Printing Office, Washington, DC.

Blalock, Jr., H. M. (1970). *Toward a theory of minority-group relations*. New York: Capricorn Books.

Blumer, H. (1958). Race prejudice as a sense of group position. *Pacific Sociological Review, 1*, 3–7.

Burton-Chellew, M. N., Ross-Gillespie, A, & West, S. A. (2010). Cooperation in humans: Competition between groups and proximate emotions. *Evolution and Human Behavior, 31*, 104–108.

Cort, D. A. (2011). Reexamining the ethnic hierarchy of locational attainment: Evidence from Los Angeles. *Social Science Research, 40*(6), 1521–1533.

Chavez, L. R. (2008). *The Latino threat: Constructing immigrants, citizens, and the nation*. Palo Alto: Stanford University Press.

DeNavas-Walt, C., Bernadette D. P., & Smith, J. C. (2010). U.S. Census Bureau, Current Population Reports, P60–238, *Income, poverty, and health insurance coverage in the United States: 2009*, U.S. Government Printing Office, Washington, D.C.

Eitle, D., & Taylor, J. (2008). Are Hispanics the new "threat"? Minority group threat and fear of crime in Miami-Dade county. *Social Science Research, 37*, 1102–1115.

Feagin, J. R. (2006). *Systemic racism: A theory of oppression*. New York, NY: Routledge

Holt, J. B. (2007). The topography of poverty in the United States: A spatial analysis using county-level data from the community health status indicators project. *Preventing Chronic Disease, 4*, 4–9.

Kane, R. J. (2003). Social control in the metropolis: A community-level examination of the minority group-threat hypothesis. *Justice Quarterly, 20*, 265–95.

Kaplan, D. H., & Douzet, F. (2011). Research in ethnic segregation III: Segregation outcomes. *Urban Geography, 32*(4), 589–605.

Key, V. O. (1949). *Southern politics in state and nation*. New York: Knopf.

Kiang, L., Perreira, K. M., & Fuligni, A. J. (2011). Ethnic label use in adolescents from traditional and non-traditional immigrant communities. *Journal of Youth Adolescence, 40*, 719–29.

Lewin, A. C., Stier, H., & Caspi-Dror, D. (2006). The place of opportunity: Community and individual determinants of poverty among Jews and Arabs in Israel. *Research in Social Stratification and Mobility, 24*, 177–91.

Markert, J. (2010). The changing face of racial discrimination: Hispanics as the dominant minority in the USA—a new application of power-threat theory. *Critical Sociology, 36*, 307–327.

Massey, D. S. (2007). *Categorically unequal: The American stratification system*. New York: Russell Sage Foundation.

Novak, M. (1972). *The rise of the unmeltable ethnics: Politics and culture in the seventies*. NY: The Macmillan Company.

Sáenz, R. (1997). Ethnic concentration and Chicano poverty: A comparative approach. *Social Science Research, 26*, 205–228.

Sáenz, R., Cready, C. M., & Morales, M. C. (2007). Adios Aztlan: Mexican American outmigration from the Southwest. In L. M. Lobao, G. Hoods, & A. R. Tickamyer (Eds.), *The sociology of spatial inequality* (pp. 189–214). Albany, NY: State University of New York Press.

Schlueter, E., & Scheepers, P. (2010). The relationship between outgroup size and anti-outgroup attitudes: A theoretical synthesis and empirical test of group threat- and intergroup contact theory. *Social Science Research, 36*, 285–295.

Siordia, C. (2011). Sociospatial inequality: A multilevel and geo-spatial analysis of Latino poverty. (Doctoral dissertation). Texas A&M University, College Station, Texas. Available at: http://gateway.proquest.com/openurl%3furl_ver=Z39.88-2004%26res_dat=xri:pqdiss%26rft_val_fmt=info:ofi/fmt:kev:mtx:dissertation%26rft_dat=xri:pqdiss:3500095.

Tavernise, S. (2011, September 13). Soaring poverty casts spotlight on 'Lost Decade' The New York Times. Available at: http://relooney.fatcow.com/0_New_11194.pdf

Wang, Q. (2010). The earnings effect of ethnic labour market concentration under multi-racial metropolitan contexts in the United States. *Tijdschrift voor Economische en Sociale Geografie, 101*(2), 161–176.

Yzaguirre, R., Suro, R., Ajami, F., Daniels, R., Jacoby, T., Buchanan, P., et al., (2004). Huntington and Hispanics. *Foreign Policy, 142*, 4, 6, 8–10, 12–13, 84–91.

■ Reading 1.2

Define the following concepts/phrases:

minority

dominant group

poverty threshold

economic marginalization

"Latino Threat Narrative"

contact hypothesis

Answer the following questions:

1. Discuss Blalock's minority group relations theory.
2. What are the specific theories of social disequilibrium and minority-threat that Siordia and Farias are challenging?
3. Identify some of the sources used by Siordia and Farias in support of the impact of social disequilibrium among Latinos.

Part II

Looking for Work, Building Communities

Tejanos, Mexican Immigrants and Mexican American Communities

David A. Badillo

I N THE EARLY DECADES OF THE twentieth century Mexican Americans in the ranches, towns, and farms of the lower Rio Grande Valley and the Winter Garden area in Texas began expanding as far north as Montana and Minnesota. Large corporations involved in the growing and processing of beet sugar contracted with local growers for the employment of out-of-state seasonal labor, thereby introducing Mexicans into the Michigan economy. The Texas Mexicans, or *tejanos*, Michigan's first Latinos, had lived in Texas for varying periods—sometimes decades, even centuries—because they or their ancestors were born there, because they had crossed the border at some earlier point, or because their arrival predated U.S. annexation of the area in 1845. Their experience as migrant laborers, picking cotton or other crops for low wages, prepared them to work on Michigan farms, at first seasonally and then later permanently. Culturally Mexican and often predominantly Spanish speakers, they readily ventured north to the Great Lakes region and elsewhere in the United States as opportunities developed, and they customarily returned to winter in Texas. Labor recruiters targeted the huge Mexican population residing in San Antonio, the gateway to the Midwest during the 1920s, where railways and highways from El Paso to Brownsville converged. Track work, particularly for the Pennsylvania Railroad Company, also drew many *tejanos* as well as immigrants directly from Mexico to Michigan, where they took jobs in agriculture, increasingly remaining in *el Norte* to work until the following spring, or settling into opportunities in industry.

Tejanos arrived in the Michigan's eastern "thumb" area around 1915 to work in sugar beets, at which time a vacuum had been created in the rural Michigan workforce by the flight of Hungarian and Russian laborers to the cities. Thereafter, the Saginaw-based Michigan Sugar Beet Company brought up thousands of migrants from Texas to replace European-origin immigrants who had "settled out" from the beet fields, often after having accumulated small properties.

David A. Badillo, "Tejanos, Mexican Immigrants, and Mexican American Communities," *Latinos in Michigan*, pp. 3-14, 61-62.

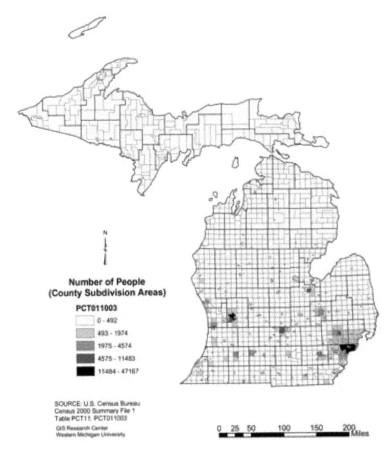

**Number of People
(County Subdivision Areas)**

PCT011003

	0 - 492
	493 - 1974
	1975 - 4574
	4575 - 11483
	11484 - 47167

SOURCE: U.S. Census Bureau
Census 2000 Summary File 1
Table PCT11, PCT011003

GIS Research Center
Western Michigan University

0 25 50   100   150   200
Miles

FIGURE 2.1.1 Distribution of Michigan's Population claiming Hispanic Ancestry (1990).

By the 1920 growing season, almost five thousand Mexicans had arrived in the different parts of southern Michigan, and they soon came to dominate this agricultural sector. These workers, who called themselves *betabeleros*, most of whom had been farmers, sharecroppers, or ranch hands prior to heading north, spearheaded the permanent settlement of Mexican Americans in Michigan. At first they came alone (often having been smuggled into the state aboard covered trucks), but later they arrived with their families, as children and all able-bodied adults effectively served as additional hands to tend the acreage.[1]

Growers and local residents believed that utilizing the family as the basic work unit helped ensure the "reliability" of the seasonal migrants. *Betabeleros* faced many forms of discrimination and exploitation by growers, who treated them as transients, to be unceremoniously returned home after each season—at company expense, if necessary. It was especially feared that they would break their contracts and wander off from the low-paying beet work in isolated communities into cities and towns, competing economically and mixing socially at the end of the season.

By the mid-1920s, Michigan's sugar beet work had created what one historian calls an "agricultural proletariat" of almost seven thousand primarily Mexican and *tejano* workers, clearly distinguished by ethnic background, language, and mode of entry from the established residents of rural and urban midwestern communities.[2]

Given the seasonal nature of their migration and the presence of interethnic hostility, the *betabeleros* realized that few opportunities existed for the acquisition of even small farms. For them, therefore, survival often meant stability, and they seized whatever opportunities existed to pursue year-round industrial work. Many remained in beet work for a season and then instead of heading South went to the booming urban centers of southeastern Michigan. As production in Michigan's fruit belt expanded sharply in the 1940s, migrants expanded into the picking of asparagus, cherry, blueberry, and apple crops in western Michigan; they also moved to nearby cities and formed new *colonias*. Undocumented *betabeleros* joined their ranks, in spite of greater immigration restrictions and more tenacious, although always selective (due to the power of the growers' lobby) enforcement.

After 1910 the disruption, violence, and dislocation of society caused by the Mexican Revolution accelerated the movement of Mexicans to the Southwest. It also spurred emigration from the interior states of the *mesa central* (central plateau), primarily Michoacán, Jalisco, and Guanajuato, to the Midwest. Railroads linked central Mexico with the Texas border cities of Laredo and El Paso and then connected with Kansas City, allowing for further direct passage. Track

FIGURE 2.1.2 Mexican sisters visiting a Mexican migrant worker family in the Archdiocese (Archives of the Archdiocese of Detroit).

maintenance workers, in particular, obtained easy access to points farther north, and they sometimes established the first *colonias*, or *barrios* (urban settlements), in midwestern cities. At first, labor agents called *enganchistas* recruited workers, but soon family networks precipitated a chain migration and formed a migrant stream coordinating the needs of farmers and the Mexican workers. This second group of Latinos in Michigan entering directly from Mexico had more diverse occupational backgrounds, with some even skilled as tradesmen and industrial workers, although most were agricultural workers in their home country.

Mexico's church-state crisis, the Cristero Revolt of the mid-1920s, and its attendant disorders, strongly stimulated emigration from Mexico's central plateau to the Great Lakes states, including Michigan. The dynamic factor in the outward flow of population was a peonage system in place on the haciendas that hindered economic development for the populace. Revolutionary violence and economic destabilization, meanwhile, undermined individual security, and the promise of high wages and better opportunities launched many migrants on northward adventures. Most Mexicans expected at first to work in agriculture or for the railroads. Many immigrants arrived in Detroit and other cities only after making preliminary stops in Texas or elsewhere in the Southwest.

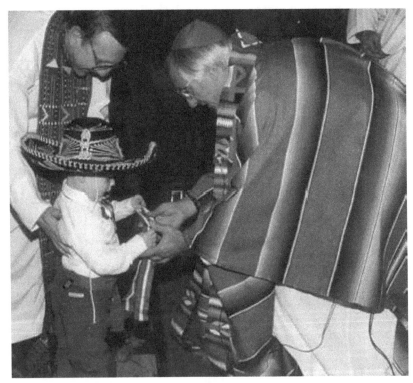

FIGURE 2.1.3 Auxiliary Bishop Thomas Gumbleton (right) participating in a Cinco de Mayo celebration (Archives of the Archdiocese of Detroit).

By the end of World War I, with the mass production of the automobile and the labor shortages of the period, the number of Mexican immigrant laborers swelled. Mexicans and a few *tejanos* began filtering in to Saginaw, Flint, Pontiac, and Detroit. Immigrants also found jobs with firms that subcontracted for the major automobile producers, such as Fisher Body, which employed several hundred Mexicans in its southeastern Michigan plants. The first Mexicans came to Flint around 1923, after having been recruited in San Antonio by company agents. Many migrants subsequently took work in industrial jobs developing at General Motors. By the late 1920s, Flint Mexicans had formed a mutual aid society that had a branch for women, as well as a Catholic parish. Detroit soon became the foremost employer of Mexican labor; however, its "Little Mexico," while not as concentrated as the ethnic enclaves of Italians and Poles, was nonetheless a considerably larger and denser *colonia* than that which existed, for example, in Flint, the budding General Motors "company town." Lansing did not develop a solid settlement until the mid-1930s. Saginaw County, in the sugar beet heartland, had attracted Mexican migrants before 1920, but its permanent *colonia* emerged slightly later.[3]

The Mexican colony in Detroit first arose around 1917, when several hundred Mexicans came to the city. This number included over two hundred young men from Mexican engineering and technical schools specifically chosen to work as apprentices on cars, trucks, and tractors in the Highland Park and Fordson plants. After their training they became technicians for fledgling plants and dealerships in Mexico and elsewhere in Latin America. Many remained in Detroit instead, however, where they ascended to higher-income positions. Soon, laborers poured in to replace workmen who had been sent off to fight in World War I. By late 1920, the colony was estimated at eight thousand members, but, facing recession, the colony months later had dwindled to twenty-five hundred persons. As economic conditions improved, Michigan beet companies again called for workers. Ford soon became the largest midwestern employer of Mexicans, with some one thousand workers at the River Rouge plant alone, and other plants and businesses connected with the auto industry soon began to offer good wages and attract Mexican immigrants.[4]

The Motor City, as the nucleus of the nation's fastest-growing metropolitan area, attracted European immigrants and thousands of migrants from the South on its way to becoming the nation's fourth-largest city. Large numbers of African American migrants came to Detroit around 1916 and then again after 1924, when the full effects of restrictive immigration policies had opened the local market to unskilled laborers. Within this urban mosaic some three thousand Mexicans had entered by 1920; this number had increased to fifteen thousand by the late 1920s, according to some unofficial estimates. During these early years Detroit's Mexican population ratio greatly favored males over females, reflecting the prominence of *solos*, or unaccompanied males, coming to work in the assembly lines, foundries, and related areas. High manufacturing wages allowed for the continual sending of remittances back home to help families survive.[5]

Detroit's barrio developed near downtown, close to the factory districts. Characterized by poor housing and restrictive renting practices, it also served to focus cultural life, with a handful of grocery stores, along with pool halls and barbershops (both of which served as social centers) catering to the tastes of Mexicans. Here several distinct waves of migration with differing cultural patterns existed—one involving the offshoots from the agricultural migrant stream (usually *tejanos*) and others consisting of those workers either recruited by labor agents along the border or proceeding directly from the interior. Not all Detroit Mexicans lived within the barrio, which initially lacked well-defined boundaries.

As their numbers increased, a more distinct settlement formed, where, in 1926 several hundred men, mostly transients, lived in boardinghouses, or *casas de asistencia*, which proved to be more economical than renting an apartment or house. These rooming houses usually possessed names of homeland provinces or cities, and they tended to serve persons from the same regions in Mexico. Women helped run the houses, cooking and cleaning, providing a familiar cuisine, and packing lunches for workers as they left in the morning to take the streetcar to the factory. Some individual families also took in relatives and *paisanos* (fellow countrymen) in need of inexpensive dwellings. By the close of the 1920s Mexican women began to expand their workplaces throughout the urban landscape, taking jobs in downtown businesses as packers, cutters, and even machine operators. Second-generation Mexican American women, especially clerks and office workers, also found work outside of heavy industry. The family, nonetheless, always remained an important institution, as it had in agricultural settings.

The attachment of Detroit Mexicans to their homeland and culture necessitated periodic return travel, causing immigrants to view immigration (albeit often mistakenly) as a temporary phenomenon. Mexican nationals overwhelmingly preferred to retain their citizenship, shunning naturalization out of a sense of nationalism and also for practical reasons, since ties with the consul's office often provided assistance and intervention in times of individual or group crisis, and such services would largely be forfeited with U.S. citizenship. The Mexican government appointed representatives, or consuls general, to help support the sprouting *colonias* in U.S. cities, including one in Detroit. In 1926 this office promoted "cultural retention" as well as allegiance to the homeland through the establishment of La Comisión Honorífica Mexicana, the Mexican Honorary Commission. It supervised and assisted in the observance of *fiestas patrias*, religious and patriotic celebrations, such as the 12 December Feast of Our Lady of Guadalupe and the commemoration of Mexican Independence Day on 16 September. These occasions strengthened the sense of community among immigrants far from home. Movie houses with Latin American films and Spanish-language newspapers reporting both international and local news served a similar purpose.[6]

The collapse of auto manufacturing and the subsequent shutdowns in the early years of the Great Depression triggered mass layoffs in southeastern Michigan, causing thousands of Mexican

FIGURE 2.1.4 Our Lady of Guadalupe Procession (Archives of the Archdiocese of Detroit).

nationals to lose their jobs. The Civil Works Administration provided employment for a large segment of the Mexican population of Detroit in the winter of 1933 and the spring of 1934. As factory employers began restricting employment to citizens, Mexicans realized that their alien status made them vulnerable to further discrimination. Workers on Detroit track and sewer construction projects similarly found themselves permanently unemployed after municipal authorities required all foreign-born workers to be naturalized. Some turned to railroad track work, while others went on relief, but until the Depression ended relatively few Mexicans took out citizenship papers. Yet, when compared with Los Angeles or El Paso, Detroit enjoyed higher, though still meager, naturalization rates, which stood at about 10 percent during the 1930s.[7]

In the early 1930s Mexicans throughout the state experienced massive repatriation, both voluntarily and coerced, from rural and urban areas. In 1932 more than five thousand Detroit Mexicans returned across the border, including thirteen hundred offered "free transportation" on rail lines to the border and then to points in the Mexican interior. Various governmental officials opted for this solution, since it was cheaper to return individuals, at about fifteen dollars per person, than to sustain them in Michigan with the dwindling relief funds. This drastic measure ignored the rights of the repatriated workers, many of whom had U.S.-born children. The Welfare Department paid their fares to the Mexican border, and the Mexican government did the rest. Even the families of naturalized citizens were urged to repatriate, and the rights of American-born children to citizenship in their native land were explicitly denied or not taken into account. By the end of 1932, fifteen hundred Mexicans had been sent from Michigan, with lesser numbers returning from other nearby states. Repatriates were disappointed with the mode of travel provided and with the facilities offered for adjustment when they arrived in Mexico; land and tools had been promised, but no adequate provisions were made. In any event, this "reverse immigration" throttled the development of small *colonias* throughout Michigan, including those in Port Huron, Saginaw, and Grand Rapids.[8]

Industry, unfortunately, revived very slowly, and by 1936 the number of Mexicans in Detroit had dwindled to twelve hundred, less than 10 percent of the predepression figure; few former employees were sent for before 1939. By then, after the passing of the most violent phases of the Mexican Revolution and its social and economic repercussions, the points of origin of emigrants from Mexico had shifted from the central plateau northward. Thereafter, *norteños*—immigrants from Mexico's northern states, within easy reach of Texas cities—made up the largest group of Mexican nationals traveling to Michigan. Like those from the interior, they were unaccustomed to small town life in the United States, and they sought to work and live in the Detroit metropolis and other large cities. *Tejanos*, also having resumed the cycle of seasonal migration with the revival of economic opportunities, adapted to the isolated, rural areas of Michigan. They often faced discrimination in restaurants, hotels, churches, and other public places, but their greater familiarity with English eased their adjustment into cities after 1940, as it had previously in the fields.[9]

In the late 1930s, Mexican Americans once more sought work in Michigan sugar beet fields, again replacing European workers (who had left the cities in search of agricultural work early in the Depression). The Beet Growers Employers Committee streamlined the process of recruitment, using Mexican American workers to depress wages and undermine future organizing attempts (they reportedly worked for $2 an hour under the union rate), sparking a renewed wave of migration from Texas. The imposition of a higher tariff for imported sugar in 1937 also boosted the domestic industry, until mechanization of the harvest phase of the beets decades later conclusively reduced the need for hand labor. Seasonal migrations north of several thousand *betabeleros* in jalopies, trains, or trucks (generally the same ones used during the season to haul sugar beets to the refinery) became the norm. Although workers remained in Michigan in fulfillment of their contracts for as long as seven or eight months, they actually worked in sugar beets for only seventy-five or eighty days. Therefore, during slack periods, or after the season ended, they often looked for fieldwork in pickles, tomatoes, and onions, as well as in the fruit orchards.[10]

With the defense boom of the 1940s a new influx of Mexicans occurred. By 1943 some four to six thousand Mexican immigrants and their children had been crowded into commercial and factory areas west of Detroit's central business district. In 1942, facing a national labor shortage with the military draft in effect, the United States and Mexico negotiated contract labor agreements under the Bracero Program (which was repeatedly extended until 1964), allowing for the temporary or seasonal use of imported Mexican labor in various sectors of the economy. The War Manpower Commission began the recruitment of railroad hands directly from Mexico for maintenance work on the Michigan Central Line. Many of these midwestern braceros lived in boxcars on railroad property; others worked in agriculture, bunking in abandoned shacks and sheds. [11]

Wartime employment helped bring better jobs to all segments of the population and allowed some mobility for those workers fortunate enough to find work in defense plants. The Mexican *colonia* in Ecorse, outside of Detroit, developed as the Great Lakes Steel Company procured Mexican employees by obtaining certification; a similar process occurred in Pontiac. *Tejanos*, moreover, began moving from agriculture to work in industrial towns, benefiting from the higher wages of unskilled factory jobs and from improved housing in federal projects such as that constructed in Adrian, which constituted a marked improvement over nearby Blissfield's congested migrant camps and substandard facilities. Detroit's relatively real wages, as well as the requirements of many defense factories that first papers be taken out before workers were hired, increased naturalization rates. In general, the more economically successful the immigrant family had become and the more rooted it was in American culture, the greater became the likelihood of naturalization.[12]

Mexico's predominantly rural culture and habitat aided in the preservation of folk culture. The roles of boys and girls in the Mexican immigrant family were considerably altered in Detroit as compared with those in Mexico. Mexican American children, for example, often served as translators for their parents, giving these children greater freedom and responsibility. Similarly, the necessities of industrial employment resulted in lesser parental control over children as they entered factories and engaged in social activities. Intermarriage with Anglo-Americans, moreover, blurred the formation of the kind of fixed caste lines that characterized discrimination against the Mexicans in Texas. Discrimination undeniably occurred at various points, but the immigrant context of the midwestern mosaic more readily muffled ethnic conflicts. These persistent cultural differences, as well as very real socioeconomic fissures, arguably pale, however, before the historic segregation patterns experienced by Michigan's African Americans.

Endnotes

1. Francisco A. Rosales, "Mexican Immigration to the Urban Midwest during the 1920s" (Ph.D. diss., Indiana University, 1978), 92, 99, 107.

2. Dennis N. Valdes, "Betabeleros: The Formation of an Agricultural Proletariat in the Midwest, 1897–1930," *Labor History* 30 (fall 1989): 556–58, 562.

3. Eduard A. Skendzel, *Detroit's Pioneer Mexicans: A Study of the Mexican Colony in Detroit* (Grand Rapids, Mich.: Littleshield Press, 1980), 7, 27–30.

4. Zaragosa Vargas, *Proletarians of the North: A History of Mexican Industrial Workers in Detroit and the Midwest, 1917–1933* (Berkeley: University of California Press, 1993), 20.

5. Zaragosa Vargas, "Life and Community in the 'Wonderful City of the Magic Motor': Mexican Immigrants in 1920s Detroit," *Michigan Historical Review* 15 (spring 1989): 49; John R. Weeks and Joseph Spielberg Benitez, "The Cultural Demography of Midwestern Chicano Communities," in T*he Chicano Experience*, Stanley A. West and June Macklin, eds. (Boulder, Colo.: Westview Press, 1979), 231.

6. Louis C. Murillo, "The Detroit Michigan 'Colonia' from 1920 to 1932: Implications for Social and Educational Policy" (Ph.D. diss., Michigan State University, 1981), 33, 34.

7. Norman D. Humphrey, "Employment Patterns of Mexicans in Detroit," *Monthly Labor Review* 61 (November 1945): 914, 921.

8. Norman D. Humphrey, "Mexican Repatriation from Michigan: Public Assistance in Historical Perspective," *Social Service Review* 15 (September 1941): 501–3, 512; Vargas, "Life and Community," 65, 67. For an account of repatriates in Mexico, see Paul S. Taylor, *A Spanish-Mexican Peasant Community: Arandas in Jalisco, Mexico* (Berkeley: University of California Press, 1933).

9. Rosales, "Mexican Immigration," 107–10.

10. Kay D. Willson, "The Historical Development of Migrant Labor in Michigan Agriculture" (Master's thesis, Michigan State University, 1978), 22–25, 39–43; Carey McWilliams, "Mexicans to Michigan," in *A Documentary History of the Mexican Americans*, ed. Wayne Moquin (1941; reprint, New York: Praeger, 1971), 311–14. See also Carey McWilliams, *Ill Fares the Land: Migrants and Migratory Labor in the United States* (Boston: Little Brown and Company, 1942).

11. Valdes, "Betabeleros," 59–61.

12. Reymundo Cardenas, "The Mexican in Adrian," *Michigan History* 42 (September 1958): 346–49.

Image Credits

Define the following concepts/phrases:

seasonal migrations	remittances
agricultural proletariat	massive repatriation
interethnic hostilities	reverse immigration
Mexican Revolution-1910	Cristero Revolt
family networks	bracero program

Answer the following questions:

1. Identify the places of Mexican migration in Michigan.
2. Which American industry recruits Mexican workers?
3. Why does the author characterize this migration as a "seasonal migration"?
4. Why were the boardinghouses (Casas de Asistencia) so important in the process of settlement and community building of Mexican immigrants?
5. How did the Mexican government strengthen Mexican culture in the Mexican immigrant communities?
6. When did female immigrants became incorporated into the labor markets in Detroit?
7. Why were Mexicans repatriated during the 1930s?
8. Why did Mexican migration increase during the decade of 1940 to 1950?
9. Why was the bracero program eliminated by the United States government?

Colonialism, Citizenship, and Community Building in the Puerto Rican Diaspora

A Conclusion

Carmen Teresa Whalen

P UERTO RICANS' COMMUNITY-BUILDING EFFORTS HAVE BEEN shaped by both the continuing colonial ties between the United States and Puerto Rico, and the resultant ambiguous U.S. citizenship. Colonial status framed U.S. policymakers and residents' perceptions and treatment of Puerto Ricans in the States. Puerto Ricans' U.S. citizenship facilitated migration, but has not always eased settlement and incorporation. While U.S. citizenship made it easy for employers and policymakers to recruit Puerto Ricans as a source of cheap labor, citizenship sometimes provided leverage, making Puerto Ricans less vulnerable than noncitizen workers. Puerto Ricans have used their U.S. citizenship to claim their rights, in the realms of employment, housing, education, and electoral politics, as well as to claim access to public spaces and public services. At times invoking citizenship rights, Puerto Ricans have also directly contested second-class citizenship, demanding respect, equality, and social justice in terms that extend beyond formal legal rights.

Colonialism and citizenship have also meant continued migration and the formation of transnational communities, created at the intersections between Puerto Rico and the States. These ongoing links between Puerto Ricans in the States and Puerto Rico, as well as the social movements of the late 1960s and 1970s, fostered approaches to adaptation that promoted bilingualism and biculturalism. Instead of assimilating to white, Anglo-Saxon Protestant dominance, many Puerto Ricans sought to retain Spanish language and Puerto Rican culture, while learning English and adapting to life in the States. Colonialism has proved a persistent political issue for Puerto Ricans in the States, as well.[1] Early political exiles fought for an end to Spanish colonial rule in Puerto Rico and Cuba, and since 1898, some Puerto Ricans have advocated Puerto Rico's independence from the United States. In recent decades, others have promoted statehood for Puerto

Rico, mobilizing around a plebiscite on what Puerto Rico's permanent status should be. Still others have sought to influence U.S. policies in Puerto Rico in a variety of ways, including economic and social welfare policies, as well as most recently and visibly in efforts to get the U.S. military removed from the offshore island of Vieques. The chapters in this book examine a range of historical periods and various Puerto Rican communities, providing an opportunity to explore historical trends and comparative dimensions of community building in the Puerto Rican diaspora.

U.S. Perceptions and Receptions

In 1898, as the United States set about establishing colonial rule in Puerto Rico, the beliefs embodied in manifest destiny justified U.S. expansion and shaped U.S. perceptions of the people living under U.S. rule. U.S. policymakers viewed Puerto Ricans as incapable of self-government and as a pliable labor force. These U.S. perceptions followed Puerto Ricans, who were recruited to the then U.S. territory of Hawai'i in 1900, as well as those who migrated to the States. As Iris López demonstrates, Puerto Ricans in Hawai'i were racialized as "temperamental knife wielders." Plantation growers cultivated racial and ethnic divisions among their diverse workforce as an intentional strategy to control their workers, keeping wages low and profits high. Although the U.S. Congress declared all Puerto Ricans U.S. citizens in 1917, U.S. citizenship did not guarantee Puerto Ricans full citizenship rights or equality. Puerto Ricans in Hawai'i were initially denied the right to vote. As the Puerto Rican community in New York City grew dramatically, Linda Delgado reveals, Puerto Ricans confronted a racial binary that defined people only as white or black, leaving little room for Puerto Ricans, a multiracial group with significant degrees of racial mixing. Puerto Ricans, like Jesús Colón, experienced the full intensity of racism, as discrimination prevented him from getting a better job and negatively affected his daily interactions. Puerto Ricans confronted racism and discrimination alongside economic exploitation.

This racial binary continued to define Puerto Ricans and shape their experiences, as migration and dispersion increased in the post–World War II era. Confusion abounded with the arrival of a group that did not fit neatly into a white or black category. Even siblings could be treated differently depending on their skin color. In 1958 Hartford, Connecticut, a fair-skinned sister could get her hair cut without incident, while her darker-skinned sister was sent to the back of the shop so that black women could cut her hair, and she was not permitted to interact with white shop patrons, presumably even her own sister. As labor contracts brought Puerto Rican workers to Lorain, Ohio, in 1948, one reporter tried to ascertain, "Are Puerto Ricans predominantly Spanish, predominantly Negro, or what?" Alluding to indigenous, European, and African ancestry, this reporter assured readers that Puerto Ricans were not "Negro." Another newspaper ran a series of photographs to show "What They Look Like." African ancestry was censored out, and as Eugenio Rivera reveals, initially Puerto Ricans were portrayed as "civilized," and as likely to become "good citizens" instead of a "troublesome minority." Indeed, labor recruiter Samuel

Friedman and some reporters emphasized Puerto Ricans' U.S. citizenship and how "American" they were to make them more palatable to Lorain's residents. This approach would soon change, and Puerto Ricans would increasingly be portrayed as more akin to a "troublesome minority."

The chapters in this book suggest that wherever they settled, Puerto Ricans confronted discrimination in several realms, including employment, police relations, education, politics, religious institutions, access to public spaces, and the provision of social services. The most striking, for several authors, was the discrimination that Puerto Ricans encountered in their efforts to find a decent place to live. As Olga Jiménez de Wagenheim argues, Puerto Ricans faced obstacles in renting apartments and in purchasing homes in Dover, New Jersey. Puerto Ricans were confined to renting in the "Spanish barrio," the poorest section of town where they were overcharged for tiny, inadequate rooms or apartments. With few houses available in the "Spanish barrio" trying to buy a house created its own challenges. The hostility and the obstacles were every bit as jarring in Lorain, Ohio. Given that most Puerto Ricans worked in factory jobs covered by union contracts, had decent wages, and could have afforded better housing, Rivera concludes, "The primary factor contributing to their poor and unhealthy living conditions was discrimination". Nor were urban areas necessarily more welcoming, as housing discrimination plagued Puerto Ricans who settled in Chicago as well. Puerto Ricans recalled having doors closed in their faces, being told, "We don't rent to Puerto Ricans," and being charged higher rents.

Racial tensions often increased as Puerto Ricans settled, becoming permanent residents instead of temporary workers. In Lorain, the press, policymakers, and employers all deemed the recruitment of Puerto Rican workers a "success." However, as Puerto Rican men began to move out of the company barracks and send for their families, they were transformed from a "success story" to "the Puerto Rican problem". Indeed, in the postwar era, policymakers, social scientists, and the press increasingly spoke of Puerto Ricans in the language of "social problems." Instead of speaking of them as recruited workers who confronted discrimination, Puerto Ricans were portrayed as people with "social problems," who created even more "problems" for the communities where they settled.[2] This was, as Delgado suggests, the era of the "culture of poverty" discourse and "blaming the victim" studies.

Puerto Ricans also confronted racial hostility from the police and their new neighbors, as depicted by Jiménez de Wagenheim. Yet policymakers often interpreted the resultant incidents through their own "culture of poverty" perspectives. In 1953 Philadelphia, white neighbors responded to Puerto Rican settlement in the Spring Garden neighborhood with street fighting. In Chicago, when a white police officer shot a young Puerto Rican man in 1966, the Division Street riots erupted. In both cases, city politicians and policymakers became more aware of Puerto Rican residents. They responded, however, in ways that pinned the blame on Puerto Ricans and on their assumed "social problems." In Philadelphia, the violence was transformed from a racially motivated attack against Puerto Ricans into an indication of Puerto Ricans' "problems of adjustment." The city conducted their first major study on Puerto Rican residents and their neighbors' attitudes.[3] In Chicago, Puerto Ricans were transformed from hardworking people and a representation of a modern Horatio Alger—comparable to Lorain's "success story"—into a "dangerous, decaying community, ruled by gangs and filled with drug dealers and poor people on welfare".[4]

By the late 1970s, policymakers, social scientists, and others invoked the label of "Hispanic" and applied it to all groups who traced their origins to Spanish-speaking Latin America and the Caribbean. Suzanne Oboler argues that the Hispanic label served to squelch Puerto Ricans and Chicanas/os' demands for recognition.[5] This label also sought to encompass the rapid increase of Latinas/os in the United States, following the passage of the Immigration Act of 1965. Yet this umbrella term grouped together diverse peoples, with diverse histories. The term encompassed Chicanas/os, whose U.S. citizenship dated to the end of the War with Mexico in 1848 when the United States conquered half of Mexico's territory, the border moved, and an estimated 80,000 Mexicans found themselves in the United States. The term also encompassed the most recent arrivals.

Numerous issues arose from the term Hispanic. One was that negative, entrenched stereotypes, which had emerged from years of racism toward Puerto Ricans and Chicanas/os, were now applied to all Hispanics. Hence, despite Puerto Ricans' U.S. citizenship, there are important parallels in how other Latinas/os are labeled and treated in the States. Another issue was that the propensity to stereotype all Latinas/os as people "who got off the boat yesterday" was intensified by the erasure of histories that came with the term. Migration histories were obliterated, as were Puerto Ricans and Chicanas/os' long histories of struggle to improve the conditions of their lives in the States. Indeed, as Víctor Vázquez-Hernández argues, "The 'new' phenomenon of a growing Latino population is not so new—a diverse Latino population in Philadelphia was evident as early as the 1890s". Puerto Ricans settled in diverse areas and sought to re-create supportive communities that would counter hostile environments.

Resistance and Community Building

Persistent challenges wrought equally persistent resistance, community building, and social movements on the part of Puerto Ricans. Yet changing contexts, both historically and geographically, shaped Puerto Ricans' efforts to improve their lives and their communities. As Jiménez de Wagenheim suggests, Puerto Ricans' community building was about "overcoming challenges" and "creating alternatives". Puerto Rican migrants did not start from scratch; rather, as Rivera notes, they confronted hostile environments with organizing skills they brought with them from Puerto Rico. There was, as several authors suggest, a certain evolution from informal networks responding to immediate needs to more organized community responses. This evolutionary approach reveals important dynamics in several communities. However, this approach should not obscure the remarkable degree of community organization in the periods before World War II, nor the extent to which community life at any moment reveals diverse and multilayered dimensions. Hence, the chapters in this book highlight the diversity, as well as historical trends, in Puerto Ricans' community building.

Migration itself can be seen as a form of resistance, to both economic exploitation and racial hostilities. Puerto Ricans, who had migrated from Puerto Rico to improve their lives, proved willing to migrate again, if they deemed it necessary. Workers recruited to Hawai'i's sugar plantations resisted horrendous conditions on the journey by escaping in San Francisco and resisted poor conditions on the plantations by moving from one plantation to another in search of better circumstances, or sometimes to San Francisco. In the post–World War II era, employers' complaints that Puerto Ricans broke their labor con-tracts reflected Puerto Ricans' efforts to find better jobs and living conditions than those offered by seasonal farm work. Or as Ruth Glasser puts it, "Many Puerto Rican farmworkers decided to improve their conditions by 'voting with their feet'". The growth of Puerto Rican communities in Philadelphia, Dover, Lorain, Connecticut's cities, and Boston were shaped, in part, by farmworkers seeking better work and perhaps more hospitable environments.

The migration process also sparked informal networks of family and friends. These networks, through which people helped each other migrate and settle, became the building blocks for communities. Cigar makers' networks, as Vázquez-Hernández suggests, facilitated migration to Philadelphia and elsewhere, as they were accustomed to traveling in search of work. Cigar maker Jesús Colón arrived in New York City with visible manifestations of his networks—letters of introduction as a member of a tobacco workers' union and of the Socialist Party. The impact of these networks continued in the communities where they settled. As Vázquez-Hernández argues, "Cigar makers, many of whom were political activists, were well known for their keen sense of organization." They established mutual aid societies, and contributed to the late nineteenth-century labor movements, in part through a Spanish-speaking local of the Cigar Makers International Union in Philadelphia in 1877. In Philadelphia and New York City, cigar makers continued their political activism in new contexts.

Networks, often based on hometowns, sparked community organizations. Communities evolved with significant numbers of people coming from the same hometowns in Puerto Rico. In Connecticut, Hartford's Puerto Rican community hailed from the Comerío/Cayey/Caguas region; Meriden's from Aguada; Waterbury's from Ponce, Guánica, and Peñuelas; and New London's from Añasco. Hometown clubs proliferated, and hometown connections played a role in electoral politics in Hartford, as well as in Meriden, which elected the first Puerto Rican official in the state in 1959. Boston's Puerto Rican neighborhoods, Cambridge, and nearby Waltham, all reflected town-specific migrations. Chicago's organizations included home-town clubs, El Vegabajeño and El Club de Lares. In Dover, most migrants came from Aguada. When turned away from Dover's

Catholic Church, Aguadans formed a purchasing committee and bought their own church in 1962. Problems with the police fostered the founding of the Aguada Social Club, named in honor of their hometown. The club provided space for weddings and other celebrations, while addressing continuing problems with the police. As hometown clubs provided mutual support and social activities for their members, these same networks could provide the foundation for broader community-based organizations.

Networks played a critical role in meeting migrants' immediate needs for housing and for countering the discrimination they confronted in renting and purchasing homes. In Dover and Boston, Puerto Rican-run boarding houses met immediate housing needs, while providing much needed income to those who ran them. In Chicago, migrants moved in with relatives. The "crowded apartment with lots of family members" could either provide "a sense of continuity, security, and community" or create "difficulties adjusting to living with other relatives". As they moved out of company-owned housing, boarding houses, and their relatives' homes, Puerto Ricans confronted discrimination. To ease its impact, Puerto Ricans in Dover and Chicago established credit unions. In 1970, the Spanish-American Federal Credit Union opened in Dover, to address the challenges Puerto Ricans and other Latinos confronted in getting credit and loans. The credit union succeeded in increasing home ownership and fostering the growth of small businesses. In Lorain, Puerto Ricans left the company barracks and crafted their solution to the housing crisis by buying old houses above market value, renovating them with the help of fellow workers, and creating a Puerto Rican neighborhood along Vine Avenue. Perhaps a more unique solution was purchasing unincorporated, wooded land near a railroad yard. Unshaken by the lack of municipal services and roads or by their lack of building permits, they built their own homes and "christened 'El Campito'".

The same networks that helped men and women find jobs helped working-class Puerto Rican women balance the demands of paid employment and caring for their families. Networks provided a means to arrange childcare, as women cared for each other's children in their homes.[6] Again, informal networks and immediate needs shaped community building, as Maura Toro-Morn argues, "Given the demands of work and family life, Puerto Rican working-class women focused their energies in community activities that complemented their roles as working mothers." As "working-class Puerto Ricans cared a great deal about the education of their children," Puerto Rican mothers struggled to make the public school system responsive to their needs. Puerto Rican women played important roles in Connecticut and Massachusetts' community organizations, as well.

Recruited as a source of low-wage labor, Puerto Ricans responded by struggling to improve conditions for workers. Many cigar makers, as Delgado explores, sought improved working and living conditions for workers through Socialism. Jesús Colón's condemnation of exploitative working conditions and false promises of "easy job, good money," came with his lifelong activism in search of solutions. In addition to his extensive writings, he founded twenty-five organizations, "all inspired by his leadership and energy". In the post–World War II era, Puerto Ricans continued efforts to improve working conditions through union activities. They participated, for example, in Lorain's strike by the Congress of Industrial Organizations. Well-paid, steady union jobs, as Rivera points out, then strengthened Puerto Ricans' community-building efforts, as well as improved their quality of life. In Connecticut, farmworkers' "anger over their treatment was often intense," and as Glasser demonstrates, that anger gave way to organizing. In 1972, Puerto Rican workers created the Asociación de Trabajadores Agrícolas (Agricultural Workers Association or ATA). The ATA and other supportive organizations sought to improve living conditions and health care; increase wages, sick and overtime pay; and gain unrestricted access to the camps for outsiders, many of whom were activists striving to improve conditions. The ATA won some victories. The increased attention to the plight of farmworkers, as well as the government of Puerto Rico's role in the contract labor program, fostered a drastic reduction from 12,760 to 5,639 contract farmworkers between 1974 and 1975.

While struggles to improve working conditions continued, by the 1960s Puerto Ricans faced another challenge. Deindustrialization brought the loss of manufacturing jobs and unemployment for many Puerto Ricans living in urban areas, as well as deteriorating wages and working conditions in those jobs that remained. Puerto Ricans crafted new responses. To meet basic human needs, Puerto Ricans demanded that existing institutions respond, and that federal antipoverty programs address the pressing needs of Puerto Rican communities. Puerto Ricans also established their own social service agencies. At times, Puerto Ricans and African Americans worked well together in federally funded social service and community action agencies, while at other times there was competition for positions and federal dollars. According to Glasser, "From this struggle for antipoverty positions and culturally specific services were born many Latino-oriented organizations that still exist today." In Bridgeport, the Spanish American Development Agency was born, and in Danbury, the Spanish Learning Center grew from a split in an earlier agency in 1971. Similarly, in Boston, as Félix V. Matos Rodríguez argues, "During the late 1960s and early 1970s, many of the most important community service organizations were created." Leadership positions in these social service agencies became stepping-stones for political positions, and "an intense struggle for the leadership of Puerto Rican and Latino social service agencies" reigned during the 1970s. In 1977, the Morris County Organization for Hispanic Affairs was established in Dover, providing social and educational services. Although this agency closed, federal monies were channeled through the Dover Office of Hispanic Affairs, which continued providing social services during the 1980s.

As Puerto Ricans created their own community-based organizations and social service agencies, they contested the role that the government of Puerto Rico's Migration Division had claimed as the representative of Puerto Rican communities in the States. The Migration Division fostered migration and oversaw the farm labor program. Yet as historian Michael Lapp argues, given the centrality of U.S. investment and tourism in Puerto Rico's economic development program, Puerto Rico's policymakers worried about hostility toward Puerto Rican migrants. Along with encouraging more dispersed settlement in the States, the Migration Division sought to reduce the hostilities Puerto Ricans encountered, especially in New York City, by serving as a liaison to the city administration and social services and by working with Puerto Rican organizations.[7]

Scholars have debated whether the Migration Division ultimately fostered or hindered Puerto Ricans' community-building efforts. According to Roberto Rodríguez-Morazzani, the Migration Division office's "island-born leadership was viewed as elitist and racist, reflecting a class bias in their interactions with stateside Puerto Ricans" and was viewed as "accountable not to the Puerto Rican community, but to the colonial government of Puerto Rico and, by extension, that of the United States." For Rodríguez-Morazzani, the stateside Puerto Rican founders of community organizations and social service agencies "were able to effectively challenge the old elite for leadership and within a few years establish themselves as the recognized representatives of the community."[8] While this debate continues, still less is known about the impact of the Migration Division in other communities where it opened offices, such as Chicago, Camden, New Jersey, Philadelphia, and Boston, where the Migration Division's successor, the Puerto Rican Federal Affairs Administration, seemed most interested in shaping attitudes toward Puerto Rico's status in the late 1990s.[9] Nevertheless, the Migration Division's role reveals the continuing ties between Puerto Rico and the United States, as well as the government of Puerto Rico's awareness that Puerto Ricans' U.S. citizenship did not assure a warm welcome or an easy adjustment to life in the States.

Along with deindustrialization, Puerto Ricans confronted urban renewal, which threatened the communities they had struggled to build. In city centers, so called "urban renewal" programs actually demolished low-rent housing and the small businesses that had sprung up to serve their residents. Urban centers became the hubs for office buildings, hospitals, retail and entertainment establishments, and for the gentrified housing that accompanied economic restructuring. Puerto Ricans in Hartford, Connecticut, were among those forced to relocate. In 1965, the Boston Redevelopment Authority planned to convert Parcel 19, the part of the South End where most Puerto Ricans lived, into shopping malls, schools, and other facilities. Puerto Ricans organized to "save the 'parcela,'" forming the Emergency Tenants Council. After a five-year struggle, Villa Victoria was born—a housing complex with commercial and public spaces. Villa Victoria, home to 3,000 residents, "remains the symbolic center of Boston's Puerto Rican and Latino community". More recently, Puerto Ricans in Chicago confronted gentrification by constructing two steel Puerto Rican flags, measuring fifty-nine feet high and fifty-nine feet across, at the ends of Division Street. In a symbolic gesture, the flags remember the community's history of migration and settlement, and the sculpture "physically marks a space as 'the Puerto Rican community'".

The destruction wrought by economic restructuring, urban renewal, and poverty also sparked a militant, political response from second-generation Puerto Ricans in several communities. Puerto Rican youth were tired of second-class citizenship, racism, and poverty, as well as with the United States' continuing colonial domination of Puerto Rico. Puerto Rican radicalism of the late 1960s and early 1970s occurred during an era of global activism marked by anticolonial struggles throughout the Third World and by student movements. In the United States, civil rights, black power, student, antiwar, Chicano, Native American, Asian American, as well as women and gay liberation movements, challenged the United States to live up to its professed ideals and become an inclusive society.[10]

Puerto Rican youth's militant politics and grassroots organizing reflected the ideals and tactics of the era, sometimes conflicting with the more established leadership in Puerto Rican communities. In Chicago, a gang became the Young Lords, as politicized youth resisted gentrification. Other branches of the Young Lords started in New York City, Philadelphia, Haywood, California, Newark, New Jersey, and several Connecticut cities. The Young Lords advocated independence for Puerto Rico, and Socialism, while providing grassroots, community-based services in their barrios, thereby "bridging homeland and barrio politics."[11] In Bridgeport, Connecticut, Young Lords protested the local gas company's discriminatory consumer and employment practices, and police brutality, while organizing lead poisoning testing, free breakfast programs, and rent strikes. Like the Young Lords, the Puerto Rican Socialist Party (PSP) played an important role in several communities, advocating independence for Puerto Rico and addressing issues affecting Puerto Ricans in the States. In Boston, the PSP chapter, created in 1972, addressed police brutality and was active in labor organizing, housing, and educational issues, such as bilingual education and busing.

Despite political, generational, and other differences, Puerto Ricans joined forces and increasingly claimed victories in electoral politics. Glasser found that it was "the informal community leaders—the shopkeepers, factory foremen, and church activists—who became the first explicitly political leaders." They provided patronage links between Puerto Ricans and the Democratic Party, and Democratic clubs proliferated. Some, however, felt taken for granted and joined up with Republicans. Such was the case in Meriden, when Emilio Varona was elected to the Board of Aldermen, becoming the first elected Puerto Rican in the state in 1959. Other firsts followed. In 1971, Marina Rivera became Norwalk's first Puerto Rican city councilwoman and the first Puerto Rican woman elected in the United States. And in 2001, community activist and first-time political candidate Eddie Pérez was elected mayor of Hartford, Connecticut's capital city. In Boston, as Matos Rodríguez notes, "it took almost three decades for the Puerto Rican community to elect one of its own into local or state politics." But in 1988, Nelson Merced became a state representative and the first Puerto Rican or Latino elected to statewide office in Massachusetts. Like many other Puerto Rican elected officials, heading a multiservice Latino service agency was an important step on the road in electoral politics. Other communities had electoral victories, too.

Puerto Rican politics in the diaspora had come full circle in some ways. For New York City through the 1930s, as Delgado suggests, "leadership in this community came mostly from the radical sectors." The International Workers' Organization, the Socialist Party, and progressive unions played central roles. The political repression of the 1950s took its toll on the Socialist, working-class culture to which Puerto Ricans contributed, and not just in New York City. As Rivera indicates, the anti-Communism hysteria of the postwar era affected Puerto Rican organizations in Lorain, as those accused of Communist leanings merged in efforts to diffuse the accusations, and others prohibited Communist members in their by-laws. Yet by the late 1960s and early 1970s, new Left politics influenced the activism of another generation. Puerto Rican political activism, nevertheless, has been continuous, even as it has ranged within and beyond electoral politics, including Socialist groups and more mainstream antipoverty social service agencies, as well as campaigning for Congressman Vito Marcantonio and for Puerto Rican candidates. In other words, sweeping trends should not mask the political diversity among Puerto Ricans. One of the most contentious issues has remained Puerto Rico's unresolved political status. During the late 1960s and 1970s, advocacy for Puerto Rico's independence reinforced transnational links between Puerto Rico and Puerto Ricans in the States, provided a foundation for racial and ethnic pride, and unified segments of Puerto Rican communities in the States. Yet political perspectives on the proper political status for their homeland remains as potentially divisive for Puerto Ricans in the States as it is for those residing in Puerto Rico. Even with this diversity of views, however, there has been widespread agreement on the importance of sustaining Puerto Rican identities and pride.

Constructing Identities

Puerto Ricans arrived in the States as a colonial people in the metropolis, as U.S. citizens, and as a racially diverse group in a biracial system of classification that deemed people as either white or black, despite the far greater racial complexity that has always existed in the United States. In the earliest era, some Puerto Ricans built their lives among African Americans and sometimes identified primarily as black, like Arturo Schomburg who came to New York City in 1891.[12] Yet as Puerto Rican migration increased after 1898, and even more so after World War I, Puerto Ricans also settled in communities with diverse Latino populations that were predominantly working class. Such was the case with the New York City that Jesús Colón encountered in 1917, and with Philadelphia. In 1900, the few Puerto Ricans in Connecticut were found scattered geographically and living among Spaniards, Cubans, and other Latinos. By the early 1940s, most Puerto Ricans "mingled with a variety of European immigrants and their descendents." Glasser suggests that the pre–World War II generation often intermarried and raised their children as English speakers; however, the "massive post–World War II migration allowed ensuing settlers to form strong ethnic enclaves and preserve their language and culture".

Indeed, Puerto Ricans have settled in diverse communities with striking regional variations. In the earliest large-scale migration to Hawai'i in 1900, Puerto Ricans encountered a "uniquely multicultural society." As López notes, a "complex multiethnic local culture" had evolved "as a product of the daily contact and consequent alliances between Puerto Ricans, Japanese, Chinese, Portuguese, Hawai'ians, and Filipinos who all worked side by side in the sugar plantations in the early part of the twentieth century". On the East Coast, Puerto Ricans settled in diverse Latino communities in places like New York City, Philadelphia, and Florida's cigar-manufacturing centers. In the aftermath of World War I and World War II, Puerto Ricans shared many of their destinations with African American migrants, including New York City, Philadelphia, and Chicago.[13] Puerto Ricans settled in predominantly Mexican American regions in their early settlement in California, stemming from the 1900 migration to Hawai'i, and in their post–World War II migrations to the Midwest.[14] More recently, Puerto Ricans have headed to Texas, predominantly Mexican American, and Florida, predominantly Cuban. Perhaps, as Vázquez-Hernández hints, it is the post–World War II era, when Puerto Rican migration peaked and many communities became overwhelmingly Puerto Rican, that is something of an aberration. During the 1970s and continuing to the present, areas of Puerto Rican settlement, both old and new, have become home to increasingly diverse Latino populations, as the authors here reveal.

Although much research remains to be done on how Puerto Ricans interacted with their neighbors and how these interactions shaped identities, the chapters in this book suggest that wherever they settled, Puerto Ricans sought to retain a sense of identity and pride. Colonialism and continuing migration facilitated transnational ties, which in turn facilitated adaptation that promoted bilingualism and biculturalism. In addition to continuous migration and two-way migrations, Puerto Ricans kept connected to Puerto Rico in a variety of ways. Political activism forged connections, whether it was protesting the Ponce Massacre in New York City in 1937, promoting independence in the late 1960s and 1970s), or election campaigning by Puerto Rico's politicians in the States. So did activities such as fundraising relief efforts following hurricanes, and sports events [...]. In Hawai'i, Centennial Celebrations resulted in cultural exchanges between the 100-year-old Puerto Rican community there and Puerto Rico. Working-class Puerto Rican women, ac-cording to Toro-Morn, "played an important role in the transmission of cultural traditions in Chicago and transnationally," maintaining the connections in extended families and between Chicago and Puerto Rico.

Throughout the diaspora, Puerto Ricans' persistent educational activism focused on promoting bilingual and bicultural education, as well as on mitigating discriminatory treatment. In Dover, Puerto Ricans established a "pre-kinder" program, so that children could learn English before starting school and not be separated or at a disadvantage. In Chicago, Puerto Rican women were particularly active in demanding changes in the school system. One result was the Roberto Clemente High School, which grew out of the struggles of the 1960s and 1970s, and another was a teacher exchange program with Puerto Rico to meet their demands for more bilingual teachers). In Boston, two programs prepared children for elementary school, with an explicit agenda, "The Escuelita provided bilingual education and used Puerto Rican heritage and culture as a pedagogical strategy to teach the children." Puerto Ricans and other Latinos played a key role in the passage of legislation for state-mandated bilingual education in 1970. Just four years later, court-ordered busing to desegregate the city's schools threatened bilingual education, and Puerto Rican parents responded to protect these programs. In the late 1960s and 1970s, Puerto Rican students demanded Puerto Rican Studies departments and programs in colleges and universities. With their newly asserted racial and ethnic pride, students sought an inclusive curriculum, courses that reflected their histories and cultures, as well as programs to recruit and retain Puerto Rican students and faculty. In 1973, the Centro de Estudios Puertorrique ños was established at Hunter College, City University of New York to promote the research, study, and dissemination of knowledge of Puerto Ricans in the States. While the Centro celebrates its thirtieth anniversary as this book goes to press, the pressure on colleges and universities to be inclusive has also continued to this day.

Community organizations aimed not only at meeting pressing human needs, but also at fostering identity and pride. In Boston, Inquilinos Boricuas en Acción (IBA) had a "philosophy centered on promoting a deep sense of identity and pride among Puerto Rican residents of the South End, as a way to mobilize and empower that community." IBA sponsored festivals and cultural activities, in addition to its educational programs for children. Parades, festivals, and cultural centers became communal focal points throughout the Puerto Rican diaspora. Chicago's community opened La Casita de Don Pedro, and held an annual Fiesta Boricua, while the Puerto Rican Cultural Center encouraged "a critical appraisal of U.S. policies toward Puerto Rico ... and offers barrio youth an educational alternative through the development of the Pedro Albizu Campos High School (PACHS), an independent high school founded on nationalist ideology". In Hawai'i, Puerto Ricans, along with other locals, "have been directly involved in shaping" the Plantation Village Museum, set up as a series of houses, with each house representing one of the early twentieth-century immigrant groups. Puerto Ricans' house, La Casita, provides a link to their past and a space for special cultural activities. As for the long-term outcomes for Puerto Rican culture and identity, perhaps the multiethnic context of Hawai'i provides a model. López predicts, "Local Puerto Ricans will expand the meaning of what it means to be Puerto Rican by becoming more multiethnic while continuing to preserve certain parts of their Puerto Rican heritage".

During the 1960s and 1970s, radical social movements boldly asserted racial and ethnic pride, and the Puerto Rican movement was no exception. Composed primarily of second-generation

Puerto Rican youth, groups like the Young Lords demanded "a true education of our Afro-Indio culture and Spanish language."[15] This activism shaped identities not only of youth but of the previous generation as well. In June of 1971, a Philadelphia newspaper reported, "A new wave of ethnic pride has been sweeping the Puerto Rican community here recently." Businessman Domingo Martínez emphasized the shift, "Before, people who made it didn't want to be called Puerto Rican, now they are proud of it. One of the things we won't sell at any price is our culture."[16] In asserting racial and ethnic pride, the Puerto Rican movement challenged the dominant assimilation paradigm that insisted that Puerto Ricans and others should lose their culture and shed their native language in order to become full participants in U.S. society. In calling attention to persisting racism, discrimination, and second-class citizenship, the Puerto Rican movement questioned the notion that if they assimilated, the doors to full participation were open to them. Throughout the communities of the Puerto Rican diaspora, alternatives emerged in the form of racial and ethnic pride, celebrations of bilingualism and biculturalism, and demands for full inclusion. The exception appears to have been Hawai'i, where radical movements may have had less impact in a society that was already more accepting of its multiracial dimensions and where the "second" generation had matured long before the 1960s and 1970s.

The chapters in this book raise important questions for Puerto Rican identities and communities in the long run. One concerns subsequent generations' notions of identity and their involvement in community building. Given that migration occurred to different communities in different eras and that migration to most destinations has continued, there is no clear-cut delineation of migrant generations. Still, one can ask what roles second, third, and subsequent generations will play in reshaping Puerto Rican identities and communities. While some authors point to continued engagement, others suggest a lapse. In contrast to the biracial system of classification that confronted earlier migrants, these subsequent generations come of age in a context that includes their designation as "Hispanic." Other important questions center on the increasing diversity within Puerto Rican communities. In addition to migrant generations, this diversity includes class differences. There are indications that more recent migrants have brought higher socioeconomic backgrounds to predominantly working-class communities. At the same time, even limited social mobility has contributed to an increasingly bipolar economic status among Puerto Ricans, with a few at higher socioeconomic levels, and most at lower socioeconomic levels. Finally, many Puerto Ricans find themselves as one part of increasingly diverse larger communities, as the 1965 immigration reforms increased immigration from Latin America, the Caribbean, and Asia. Whereas one could say that Puerto Ricans in Hawai'i landed in a multiracial society, that Puerto Ricans in California settled in a predominantly Chicano area, that Puerto Ricans in New York City and Philadelphia settled in pan-Latino areas, that Puerto Ricans in the Midwest settled in predominantly African American and Chicano areas, that Puerto Ricans in New England settled in predominantly African American areas, and that Puerto Ricans in Florida settled in predominantly

Cuban areas, the racial composition of these areas has continued to change. Scholars and others will grapple with, and most likely debate, whether Puerto Rican identities and communities are waning or whether we are witnessing the creation of something new and different. Culture and identity, after all, have never been static constructs, not even in Puerto Rico.[17]

Meanwhile, challenges and issues remain. The most blatant forms of stereotypes resurface, as the 1999 *Boston Herald* column depicted Puerto Ricans as "un-assimilable, welfare-driven, crime-prone aliens". This insult encapsulated the 1900s portrayal of Puerto Ricans in Hawai'i as knife-wielding criminals; the post–World War II portrayal of Puerto Ricans as lazy, unwilling to work, mired in a "culture of poverty," and hence welfare dependent; and the "Hispanic" notion of recently arrived, "un-assimilable ... aliens." Yet, as Matos Rodríguez suggests, Puerto Rican history reveals that "Boston's Puerto Rican community has been engaged in a struggle to 'save their parcela,'" and that the parcela has been defined and redefined, "At times it has been concrete neighborhoods, at others, political clout, cultural recognition, or full citizenship". This holds true for Puerto Rican communities throughout the diaspora. As Puerto Ricans have struggled against invisibility and demeaning stereotypes, the effort has been to de-fine visibility, belonging, and meaningful citizenship on their own terms. Revisiting the histories of migration, settlement, community building, and activism is another dimension of that task.

Endnotes

1. For an earlier overview of community building, see Carmen Teresa Whalen, "Puerto Ricans," *A Nation of Peoples: A Sourcebook on America's Multicultural Heritage*, ed. Elliott R. Barkan (Westport, CT: Greenwood Press, 1999), 446–63.

2. Carmen Teresa Whalen, *From Puerto Rico to Philadelphia: Puerto Rican Workers and Postwar Economies* (Philadelphia: Temple University Press, 2001), especially Chapter 6.

3. Ibid.

4. See also Gina M. Pérez, "An Upbeat West Side Story: Puerto Ricans and Postwar Racial Politics in Chicago," *Centro: Journal of the Center for Puerto Rican Studies* 14:2 (Fall 2001): 46–71.

5. Suzanne Oboler, *Ethnic Labels, Latino Lives: Identity and the Politics of (Re)presentation in the United States* (Minneapolis: University of Minnesota Press, 1995).

6. See also Virginia Sánchez Korrol, *From Colonia to Community: The History of Puerto Ricans in New York City, 1917–1948* (Westport, CT: Greenwood Press, 1983).

7. Michael Lapp, "The Migration Division of Puerto Rico and Puerto Ricans in New York City, 1948–1969," *Immigration to New York*, ed. William Pencak, Selma Berrol, and Randall M. Miller (Philadelphia: Balch Institute Press, 1991), 200, 204–5.

8. Roberto Rodríguez-Morazzani, "Puerto Rican Political Generations in New York: Pioneros, Young Turks and Radicals," *Centro de Estudios Puertorriquenos* 4 (Winter 1991–1992): 102.

9. On Philadelphia, see John H. Stinson Fernández, "Hacia una antropología de la emigración planificada: El Negociado de Empleo y Migración y el case de Filadelfia," *Revista de Ciencias Sociales* 1 (June 1996): 112–55.

10. Andrés Torres and José E. Velázquez, *The Puerto Rican Movement: Voices from the Diaspora* (Philalephia: Temple University Press, 1998).

11. Carmen Teresa Whalen, "Bridging Homeland and Barrio Politics: The Young Lords in Philadelphia," *Puerto Rican Movement*, ed. Torres and Velázquez, 107–23.

12. Winston James, "Afro-Puerto Rican Radicalism in the United States: Reflections of the Political Trajectories of Arturo Schomburg and Jesús Colón," *Centro* 8 (Spring 1996): 92–127.

13. Few works address the interactions or comparative analysis of Puerto Ricans and African Americans; see Carmen Teresa Whalen, "Displaced Labor Migrants or the 'Underclass': African Americans and Puerto Ricans in Philadelphia's Economy," *The Collaborative City: Opportunities and Challenges for Blacks and Latinos in U.S. Cities*, ed. John J. Betancur and Douglas C. Gills (New York: Garland Publishing, 2000), 115–36; and Andrés Torres, *Between Melting Pot and Mosaic: African Americans and Puerto Ricans in the New York Political Economy* (Philadelphia: Temple University Press, 1995).

14. Victor M. Rodríguez, "Boricuas, African Americans, and Chicanos in the 'Far West': Notes on the Puerto Rican Pro-Independence Movement in California, 1960s–1980s," *Latino Social Movements: Historical and Theoretical Perspectives*, ed. Rodolfo D. Torres and George Katsiaficas (New York: Routledge, 1999), 79–110.

15. "Young Lords Party 13 Point Program and Platform," *Palante: Young Lords Party*, ed. Young Lords Party and Michael Abramson (New York: McGraw-Hill Book Company, 1971), 150.

16. "Puerto Ricans Feel New Wave of Pride," *Evening Bulletin*, 13 June 1971. For discussion see Whalen, "Bridging Homeland and Barrio Politics."

17. On cultural interactions in the shaping of Puerto Rican culture, see José González, "Puerto Rico: The Four Storeyed Country," *Puerto Rico: The Four Storeyed Country* (Princeton, NJ: Markus Wiener Publishing, 1993), 1–30; and Ruth Glasser, *My Music Is My Flag: Puerto Rican Musicians and Their New York Communities, 1917–1940* (Berkeley: University of California Press, 1995).

Define the following concepts/phrases:

colonialism

citizenships

transnational community

community building

manifest destiny

Immigration Act of 1965

deindustrialization

ethnic enclaves

social movement

culture of poverty

non-incorporated status

Answer the following questions:

1. What reasons explain the Puerto Rican migration to the United States? Examine several waves and different periods.
2. Are the Puerto Ricans living in the United States a diaspora?
3. What role did the informal networks of family and community organizations play in the settlement process of the Puerto Rican communities?
4. Why doesn't the concept "racial binary" fit within the Puerto Rican community?
5. How did Puerto Rican immigrants organize themselves at the community level? Provide an example.
6. How does the gentrification process affect the Puerto Rican community?
7. Are Puerto Rican communities a transnational community?

Part III

New Immigrants, New Communities

Cubans and Dominicans

Is There a Latino Experience in the United States?

John R. Logan and Wenquan Zhang

W HAT WE CALL THE HISPANIC POPULATION in the United States is actually a mixture of many different groups from around the world whose common link is language. As Hispanics become the nation's largest minority (up from 22.4 million to 35.3 million in the past decade alone), it is increasingly important to understand not only the similarities but also the differences among them. This chapter focuses on Hispanic immigrants from the Caribbean and the two largest of these groups, Cubans and Dominicans. It compares them in broad strokes to other Hispanics and then focuses on their situation in their principal settlement areas of Miami and New York. We emphasize their socioeconomic position and their residential patterns in these metropolitan regions, as revealed in the most recent census data.

Counting Hispanic National Origin Groups

Census 2000 did an excellent job of counting Hispanics but performed poorly in identifying their origin. In previous years, a single "Hispanic question" on the census has served reasonably well to distinguish Hispanics from those of different national origins. In the last two decennial censuses, people who identify as Hispanic were asked to check one of three boxes (Mexican, Puerto Rican, or Cuban) or to write in another Hispanic category. In Census 2000, no examples of other categories were provided to orient respondents. It is likely that this caused an unprecedented number of Hispanics to provide no information or only the broad category of "Hispanic" or "Spanish." As a result, 6.2 million, or 17.6 percent, of all Hispanics were counted in census reports as "Other Hispanics." This represents nearly double the share of the Other Hispanics category in the 1990 census.

John R. Logan and Wenquan Zhang, "Cubans and Dominicans: Is There a Latino Experience in the United States?" *Caribbean Migration to Western Europe and the United States: Essays on Incorporation, Identity, and Citizenship,* ed. *Margarita Cervantes-Rodriguez, Ramon Grosfoguel, and Eric Mielants,* pp. 191-207. Copyright © 2009 by Temple University Press Reprinted with permission.

There is good evidence that the sharp jump in the Other Hispanics category has to do with the change in the wording of the question itself. A census study conducted in 2000 (Martin 2002) compared results from a questionnaire using the old and new wording. Using the new wording, 20.1 percent of Hispanics gave responses that had to be coded "Other Hispanics." Using the old wording, only 7.6 percent gave such responses. The result is a severe underestimate of the numbers of specific Hispanic groups in 2000. National studies that rely solely on the Hispanic origin question of the decennial census find only modest growth for major sources of Hispanic immigration such as El Salvador (up 16 percent) and Colombia (up 24 percent). States and metropolitan areas where Latino immigrants from sources other than Mexico and Puerto Rico are particularly concentrated are dramatically affected by this problem. In the State of California, for example, the census estimated the number of Salvadorans in 1990 as 339,000; ten years later, the estimate is only 273,000. In Miami, the census counted 74,000 Nicaraguans a decade ago, but only 69,000 in 2000. It is implausible that these groups actually decreased in this period of intensified immigration.

This chapter uses improved estimates of the size of every Hispanic group compared with those relying solely on the Hispanic origin question in Census 2000 (these are referred to as the Mumford estimates; see Logan 2001). Our procedure uses the Current Population Survey, which has the advantage of being conducted in person or by telephone, as the basis for determining the percentage of Hispanics who "really" should be classified as Other Hispanics. We then apply this target to Census 2000 data at the level of census tracts. Where the census has an excessive number of Other Hispanics, we allocate them across specific national-origin groups according to a pre-established formula. Details of the procedure for 1990 and 2000 are documented in the appendix. For comparison, Table 3.1.1 also provides the Census Bureau's alternative estimates, prepared in 2003 and taking into account additional information on people's country of birth and

TABLE 3.1.1   Estimates of the Hispanic Population in the United States, 1990 and 2000

	Mumford Estimates			Census Reports		
	1990	2000	Growth	1990	Original 2000	Simulated 2000
Hispanic total	21,900,089	35,305,818	61%	21,900,089	35,305,818	35,305,818
Mexican	13,576,346	23,060,224	70%	13,393,208	20,640,711	22,338,311
Puerto Rican	2,705,979	3,640,460	35%	2,651,815	3,406,178	3,539,988
Cuban	1,067,416	1,315,346	23%	1,053,197	1,241,685	1,312,127
Dominican	537,120	1,121,257	109%	520,151	764,945	999,561
Central American	1,387,331	2,863,063	106%	1,323,830	1,686,937	2,435,731
South American	1,095,329	2,169,669	98%	1,035,602	1,353,562	1,847,811
Other Hispanic	1,530,568	1,135,799	_26%	1,922,286	6,211,800	2,832,289

ancestry (Cresce and Ramirez 2003). These are described by the authors as "simulated" counts, and they have not replaced the bureau's official numbers.

Table 3.1.1 provides a detailed breakdown of the Hispanic population at the national level (not including Puerto Rico) in 1990 and 2000. In absolute numbers, the Mexicans are the group most affected by our reallocation of Other Hispanics, increasing by 2.4 million from the census count. In proportion to their number, however, it is the New Latinos for whom the figures changed the most. Taken together, the Mumford estimates show that New Latinos more than doubled their number, compared with an increase of about a third reported by the Census Bureau. We calculate more than 350,000 additional Dominicans and Salvadorans, 270,000 additional Colombians, and 250,000 additional Guatemalans.

- By all estimates, Mexicans are by far the largest Hispanic group: about two-thirds of the total and still growing rapidly. They number over 23 million, an increase of 70 percent in the past decade.

- Puerto Ricans and Cubans remain the next largest Hispanic groups, but their expansion is now much slower, up 35 percent and 23 percent, respectively, since 1990.

- The largest newer groups are Dominicans and Salvadorans, both of whom have doubled in the past decade and have now reached over 1.1 million. Salvadorans are listed in the table with other Central Americans, who now total nearly 3 million. Guatemalans (over 600,000) and Hondurans (nearly 500,000) are the next largest Central American groups.

- South Americans are also growing quickly, doubling to over 2 million. The largest numbers of these are Colombians (nearly 750,000), and Ecuadorians and Peruvians are quickly approaching the half-million mark.

These numbers place Hispanic immigration from the Caribbean into a wider perspective. On the one hand, they make clear that Mexico continues to be by far the major origin of Hispanic Americans in the United States. On the other hand (and this is why it is so important for the census figures to be corrected), there are more than a million Hispanics from each of several different origins, and these smaller groups are increasingly important—particularly outside the Southwest, where Mexicans are most highly concentrated. Among these groups, Cubans represent an older immigration that has at least temporarily slowed; Dominicans represent a newer and faster-growing Hispanic community.

The Hierarchy of Success

This chapter will first describe the many Hispanic groups in broad strokes. We will examine the extent to which Cubans' current experience matches their usual portrayal as one of the country's most successful immigrant groups. They certainly benefit from their development of an enclave economy based on entrepreneurial activity in the Miami region (Portes and Bach 1985). However, the distinctions between different generations of Cuban immigrants, particularly between early exiles and more recent economic refugees, are also significant (Portes and Stepick 1993), and there is evidence that many self-employed Cuban workers benefit from the enclave primarily because of its opportunities for long working hours (Logan et al. 2003). The more difficult incorporation of Dominicans into U.S. society has been analyzed by numerous scholars, though here also there are distinctions to be made among cohorts of immigrants (Grasmuck and Pessar 1991; Pessar 1995). We also compare these groups' residential patterns, looking for additional indicators of their incorporation into mainstream society. Have Cubans succeeded in part by establishing unusually separate community areas, or is greater residential separation more clearly a reflection of failure of economic mobility?

Our best current information about people in each group is from the Current Population Survey, because this data source allows us to use their parents' birthplace as part of the identification of national origin. To maximize the size of the sample on which they are based, our figures here are pooled estimates from the Current Population Surveys conducted in March 1998 and 2000 (see Table 3.1.2).

TABLE 3.1.2 Social and Economic Characteristics of Hispanics, by National Origin (Pooled Estimates from Current Population Survey, March 1998 and March 2000)

	% Foreign-Born	% Post-1990 Immigrants	Years of Education	Mean Earnings	% Below Poverty Line	% Unemployed	% Public Assistance
All Hispanics	38.5	17.2	10.7	$9,432	25.2	6.8	3.0
Mexican	36.5	18.0	10.2	$8,525	26.3	7.0	2.6
Puerto Rican	1.3	0.3	11.4	$9,893	30.4	8.3	7.3
Cuban	68.0	18.2	11.9	$13,567	18.3	5.8	2.2
Dominican Republic	62.7	28.4	10.8	$7,883	36.0	8.6	8.2
Central America total	71.3	34.3	10.3	$9,865	22.3	6.4	2.4
South America total	73.6	32.7	12.6	$13,911	13.6	4.3	0.8

Nativity and Year of Entry

Puerto Ricans are considered by definition born in the United States. The majority of Cubans are foreign-born (68 percent), though relatively few of those entered the country in the past ten years (27 percent). They mainly represent a pre-1990 immigration stream. In contrast, only about a third of Mexican Americans (36 percent) were born abroad, but nearly half of these (18 percent) arrived in the previous ten years.

The newer groups are like Cubans in having a majority of foreign-born people, ranging from 63 percent for Dominicans to over 70 percent for Central Americans and South Americans. But they are like Mexicans in that they represent the most recent wave of immigration—generally close to half of their foreign-born arrived in the past ten years.

Education

Mexicans are the least educated of the older Hispanic groups, with an average education of only 10.2 years (for those age twenty-five and older). Puerto Ricans average 11.4 years, and Cubans 11.9 years. Central Americans and Dominicans have the least education (fewer than 11 years). But Hispanics from South America are better educated than Cubans, averaging 12.6 years.

Income

Compared with Puerto Ricans and Mexicans, Cubans in the United States have always been regarded as economically successful. The mean earnings of employed Cubans are above $13,500, compared with about $10,000 for Puerto Ricans and $8,500 for Mexicans. Only 18 percent of Cubans fall below the poverty line, compared with 26 percent of Mexicans and 30 percent of Puerto Ricans.

Among the newer groups, Dominicans stand out for their very low income: mean earnings below $8,000 and more than a third in poverty (36 percent). Central Americans are roughly equivalent to Puerto Ricans in average earnings, although they are less likely to fall below the poverty line. Hispanics from South America do considerably better: on average, they earn more and have lower poverty rates than do Cubans.

Unemployment and Public Assistance

Levels of unemployment among Hispanic groups are generally consistent with their average earnings. Dominicans have higher-than-average unemployment, and they are the group most likely to receive public assistance (above 8 percent). In fact, in both of these respects, they are less successful than Puerto Ricans. Those from South America have the lowest levels of unemployment and are even less likely than Cubans to receive public assistance.

Thus, a new and wider range of social and economic characteristics accompanies the growing diversity of national origins among Hispanics in the United States. It is becoming harder to view Hispanics as one group. As their growth and diversity continues, we must recognize that there are many Hispanic situations in America, apparently creating a continuum with Cubans and South Americans at one end and Dominicans at the other.

National Trends in Hispanic Segregation

Another way to assess a group's experience in the United States is to ask where its members live and, especially, to what degree they live in different neighborhoods from the non-Hispanic white majority. Hispanic segregation, as measured by the Index of Dissimilarity (reported in Logan et al. 2004), is intermediate between that of blacks (who have values about 14 points higher) and Asians (about 9 points lower). These figures were calculated by computing levels of segregation in every metropolitan area, then taking a weighted average, giving more weight to areas with more group members. We can use the same procedure for individual Hispanic groups, with one provision. The 1990 Census reported counts for Dominicans, Central Americans, and South Americans only for a one-in-six sample of persons. This means that there is sampling error, especially at the census-tract level. In metropolitan areas with fewer than 25,000 group members, we believe that the 1990 indices for these groups are unreliable. Therefore, we limit our calculations for both 1990 and 2000 to those metropolitan regions with larger numbers of group members. (In the case of Dominicans, this means that only the New York metropolitan area is included.)

Table 3.1.3 shows that there is considerable variation in Hispanic groups' settlement patterns at a national level. Consider first segregation from non-Hispanic whites (the Index of Dissimilarity). The index ranges from 0 to 100, giving the percentage of one group who would have to move to achieve an even residential pattern—one where every tract replicates the group composition of the metropolis. A value of 60 or above is considered very high. Values of 40 to 50 are usually considered moderate levels of segregation, while values of 30 or less are considered low.

The national average for all Hispanics in 2000 is 51.5—meaning that 51.5 percent of either Hispanics or whites would need to move to a different tract for the two groups to become equally distributed. Three groups have substantially higher levels of segregation from whites: Dominicans (the extreme, measured for New York only, at 80.8), Central Americans (64.1), and Puerto Ricans (56.5). South Americans and Cubans, by contrast, have segregation levels below 50.

The national average increased very slightly in the last decade, while segregation declined for every group except Mexicans. This illustrates the importance of the Mexican experience, since two-thirds of Hispanics in the United States are Mexican. It also reflects the fact that the two most segregated groups—Dominicans and Central Americans—grew faster than the others.

Segregation from (non-Hispanic) African Americans is another important feature of the Hispanic experience. Overall, Hispanics are about as segregated from blacks as they are from whites. In fact, although many Dominicans and Cubans classify themselves in the census as non-white,

TABLE 3.1.3 Metropolitan Segregation of Hispanics: National Averages for 1990 and 2000

	Population		Segregation from Whites		Segregation from Blacks	
	1990	2000	1990	2000	1990	2000
Hispanic total	21,900,089	35,305,818	50.6	51.5	54.0	49.2
Mexican total	13,576,346	23,060,224	51.4	53.1	53.4	49.3
Puerto Rican total	2,705,979	3,640,460	61.9	56.5	56.0	50.2
Cuban total	1,067,416	1,315,346	55.4	49.5	76.1	71.5
Dominican total	537,120	1,121,257	82.0	80.8	69.7	64.3
Central American total	1,387,331	2,863,063	67.2	64.1	63.8	56.3
South American total	1,095,329	2,169,669	51.4	47.8	73.0	68.8

	Group Isolation		Exposure to Whites		Exposure to Hispanics	
	1990	2000	1990	2000	1990	2000
Hispanic total			41.8	36.5	42.4	45.5
Mexican total	40.3	38.7	40.2	35.0	46.7	49.5
Puerto Rican total	19.1	14.0	42.1	42.4	33.5	31.6
Cuban total	29.8	26.2	37.6	34.5	51.9	52.8
Dominican total	24.1	19.5	16.3	12.7	56.2	57.4
Central American total	12.0	7.9	27.9	23.6	47.6	50.4
South American total	7.2	7.4	46.8	38.4	34.3	39.6

they are more segregated from African Americans than are Mexicans. Nevertheless, segregation from blacks has declined 5 points for each Hispanic group, so the trajectory is clearly downward.

Table 3.1.3 also shows levels of group isolation (the percentage of same-group members in the census tract where the average group member lives). This is an indicator of the extent to which a group has developed residential enclaves in metropolitan areas. Mexicans, who make up less than 10 percent of the nation's population, live on average in neighborhoods that are almost 40 percent Mexican and nearly 50 percent Hispanic. Cubans, not even 1 percent of the nation's population, live in neighborhoods were more than a quarter of residents are Cuban and more than half are Hispanic. Every group has a similar experience. Of course, the smaller the group, the lower is its isolation. But even the smaller groups, such as Central Americans and South Americans, whose neighborhoods are only 7–8 percent Central American or South American, live in neighborhoods that are half, or nearly half, Hispanic. There is a high degree of residential mixing among these groups: each tends to concentrate in its own specific neighborhoods, but the presence of people from other Hispanic national origins reinforces the Hispanic character of those neighborhoods.

Conversely, exposure to whites (defined as the percentage of non-Hispanic whites in the census tract where the average group member lives) is lower and has fallen over time for every group except Puerto Ricans. Dominicans have the lowest exposure to whites; the average Dominican lives in a neighborhood where only one of eight residents is a non-Hispanic white.

Miami and New York

We now take a closer look at Cubans and Dominicans in the two metropolitan regions where they are found in the largest numbers, Miami and New York. Table 3.1.4 lists several social and economic characteristics of group members and provides a comparison with the total Hispanic population in each metropolis. Cubans represent just above half of Miami's Hispanic residents; Dominicans now are over a quarter of New York's Hispanics, where a majority are Puerto Rican. (These data are from the Census Bureau's Summary File 3 and Summary File 4. Note that the census population estimate for Dominicans, which is the basis for this table, is fewer than half a million.)

Cubans are significantly older than other Hispanics in Miami, with a median age of nearly forty-four years, and they include a smaller share of recent immigrants. In other respects they are very similar to Hispanics from other national origins in the Miami region.

TABLE 3.1.4 Characteristics of Persons and Households in the Miami and New York Metropolitan Regions, 2000

	Miami		New York	
	Cubans	Hispanics	Dominicans	Hispanics
Population (census estimates)	656,751	1,291,681	444,174	2,341,108
Median age	43.8	36.9	29.9	29.3
% English only	5.3	5.6	6.2	13.0
% Foreign-born	79.3	71.4	68.7	41.8
% Post-1990 immigrant	22.8	25.3	28.6	18.7
% College educated	10.5	11.0	6.1	7.0
% Below high school	14.9	13.4	15.2	13.4
% Unemployed	7.8	8.6	14.5	13.2
Median household income	$33,427	$33,536	$26,218	$28,791
% in poverty	15.6	17.5	32.1	29.8
% Households with public assistance	7.9	6.9	18.2	14.5
% Female-headed households	13.4	15.6	37.7	29.1

Compared with other Hispanic New Yorkers, Dominicans stand out most prominently for their high percentage of female-headed households—just under 40 percent. This level is high for New York and more than double the figure for Miami. Dominicans are less likely than other Hispanic New Yorkers to speak only English at home, and they have somewhat lower education and income levels. But in these respects also the greater contrast is between New York and Miami as contexts of reception: Hispanics in New York are much younger and more likely to be recent immigrants than Hispanics in Miami; they are also considerably less educated, less likely to be employed, poorer, and more likely to receive public assistance. This means that when we compare Cubans and Dominicans in the United States overall, we need to be aware that a very large share of them live in parts of the country where the Hispanic community as a whole has a different character.

One would expect that Cubans, given their age, longer average residence in the United States, and greater human capital resources, would be more fully integrated with other groups than are Dominicans at the neighborhood level. This is only partly the case. Table 3.1.5 shows that Cubans in Miami have become less segregated from non-Hispanic whites in the past decade, from a level that most would consider "high" in 1990 (59.8) to a more moderate level in 2000. Yet there are other population dynamics at play. Cubans are unusually highly segregated from Miami's black minority (the value of the Index of Dissimilarity [D] is over 80). Also, because Hispanics are actually a majority of metropolitan residents, they live in neighborhoods with relatively little exposure to non-Hispanic whites (20.4 percent on average), where Cubans are a near-majority and Hispanics are three-quarters of the population. Cuban Miami is very Cuban and even more Hispanic.

Dominicans in New York (as noted earlier) have a different pattern. They are remarkably segregated from non-Hispanic whites (Dover 80), though more intermixed with blacks. The average Dominican lives in a census tract where only one in five residents is Dominican but a majority is Hispanic. Their residential mixing with other Hispanics is especially pronounced in the western portions of the Bronx, formerly dominated by Puerto Ricans, where Dominicans have recently been moving.

TABLE 3.1.5 Segregation of Cubans and Dominicans, 1990 and 2000

	Miami Cubans		New York Dominicans	
	1990	2000	1990	2000
Population	563,979	681,032	351,377	602,714
Segregation from whites	59.8	53.6	82.0	80.8
Segregation from blacks	82.4	81.3	69.7	64.3
Isolation	50.3	46.3	24.1	19.5
Exposure to whites	20.4	16.4	16.3	12.7
Exposure to Hispanics	73.5	76.5	56.2	57.4

These differences are represented in part by maps of Miami and New York that show how each group is distributed across census tracts (Figure 3.1.1). The map of Miami shows that relatively few tracts have fewer than 10 percent Cuban residents (the legend notes that the number of such tracts is 106), and nearly as many tracts (78) have a Cuban majority. Cuban settlements extend from the southwestern corner of the city, where Little Havana is located, across the Miami city line in both a western and northern direction. A large concentration of African Americans is found to the northeast, and whites are settled in the very high-income neighborhoods along the coast to the south of the Cuban area.

The map of New York, in contrast, shows that most of the metropolitan area has very few Dominican residents—indeed, more than 2,000 census tracts are less than 10 percent Dominican, and only 97 tracts have as high as 20 percent Dominican residents. Dominican neighborhoods are highly clustered in upper Manhattan (the area known as Washington Heights) and in adjacent portions of the Bronx. There are smaller but well-known clusters of Dominicans in Corona (Queens) and in northeastern sections of Brooklyn that border on Queens.

A final step that we can take is to describe the social and economic characteristics of these ethnic neighborhoods and assess what living in a distinctively Cuban or Dominican neighborhood means for members of each group. We are guided here by expectations about spatial assimilation of ethnic groups in American cities (Massey 1985). Cities like Miami and New York have both grown mainly by attracting newcomers, whose customs or language often set them apart from the majority population—never more so than in the current period of intensive immigration. Concentrated immigrant settlement areas seem to be a permanent feature of cities, but the predominant view among social scientists is that they are also transitional places. People live in them as long as they need the affordable housing, family ties, familiar culture, and help in finding work that they provide. They search for areas with more amenities as soon as their economic situation improves and they become better able to function without assistance from co-ethnics— that is, they assimilate. An alternative view is that members of some groups seek ways to sustain a strong ethnic identity even as they move to neighborhoods with a better environment and greater community resources. We would expect Dominicans as a newer and less affluent minority to be more likely to manifest the traditional pattern in which group members who live in ethnic neighborhoods are not only less integrated with other racial and ethnic groups, but also are limited to areas with substantially more newcomers and lower socioeconomic standing.

Do Cuban neighborhoods in Miami also resemble such immigrant enclaves? To answer this question, we use new spatial-analysis techniques that have been developed to determine the extent to which an aerial characteristic is spatially clustered (Logan et al. 2002). Geographers have developed several indicators of the extent to which the spatial distribution of place characteristics departs from a random pattern. Luc Anselin (1995) has extended this work to a class of "local indicators of spatial association" (LISA), which offer a measure for each place of the extent

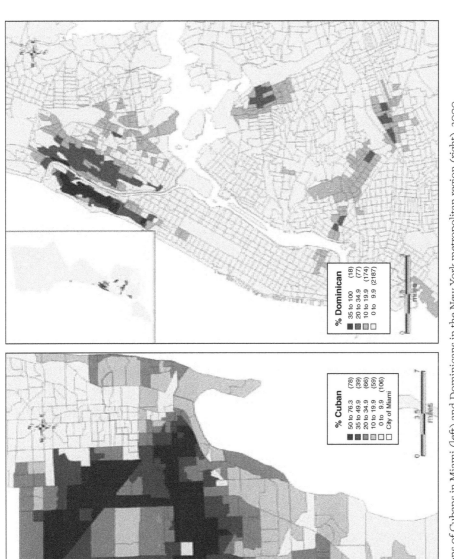

FIGURE 3.1.1 Concentrations of Cubans in Miami (left) and Dominicans in the New York metropolitan region (right), 2000.

% Dominican
- 35 to 100   (18)
- 20 to 34.9   (77)
- 10 to 19.9   (174)
- 0 to 9.9   (2187)

% Cuban
- 50 to 76.3   (78)
- 35 to 49.9   (39)
- 20 to 34.9   (66)
- 10 to 19.9   (59)
- 0 to 9.9   (106)
- City of Miami

TABLE 3.1.6 Characteristics of Cubans' and Dominicans' Neighborhoods

Neighborhood Type:	Miami Cubans		New York Dominicans	
	Cuban	Mainstream	Dominican	Mainstream
Group total (Mumford estimate)	383,427	298,036	351,456	251,297
Race and ethnicity				
% Non-Hispanic white	11.5	23.0	6.1	21.9
% Black	2.0	12.4	22.4	28.3
% Hispanic	86.7	63.0	70.6	39.3
% Group	63.3	28.7	40.0	9.0
Language and nativity				
% English only	10.2	28.3	26.6	47.0
% Foreign-born	69.6	52.2	46.0	34.6
% Post-1990 immigrant	23.2	19.2	20.7	15.3
Socioeconomic status				
% College+ educated	9.6	14.7	7.2	11.9
% Below high school	14.5	10.5	14.8	11.5
% Unemployed	8.5	8.2	16.5	12.5
Median household income	$36,303	$42,545	$25,347	$33,331
% Below poverty line	11.6	12.6	26.6	20.5
% with public assistance	7.7	5.4	17.2	11.0
% Female-headed households	15.7	15.2	32.5	24.8

of *significant spatial clustering* of similar values around it. In brief, LISA indicators identify "hot spots" that take into account not only unusually high or low values in a single place (such as a census tract) but also the values in nearby places. Such spatial clustering provides a method for identifying ethnic neighborhoods. This approach takes advantage of an underlying statistical theory through which only sets of tracts that depart significantly from a random distribution are assigned to clusters.

A majority of Miami Cubans (56 percent) live in the Cuban neighborhoods that we identified in this way, as do 60 percent of Dominicans in New York. But this means that substantial minorities live outside ethnic clusters. Table 3.1.6 summarizes the characteristics of census tracts where group members live (i.e., they are averages that have been weighted by the number of Cubans or Dominicans who live in each tract), classified as Cuban/Dominican or mainstream neighborhoods.

Cuban neighborhoods are defined by the presence of Cubans, so it is not surprising that, on average, 61 percent of residents are Cuban, compared with 27 percent in the mainstream neighborhoods where Cubans also live. Cuban neighborhoods are almost entirely Hispanic (one in eight residents is black or non-Hispanic white). Almost 70 percent of residents are foreign-born and nearly a quarter are recent immigrants, and only 10 percent of residents speak only English at home. Mainstream neighborhoods have a less pronounced ethnic character, but even these are nearly two-thirds Hispanic. Mainstream neighborhoods have a higher share of English-only speakers and a lower percentage of immigrants than do Cuban neighborhoods.

There are systematic differences in socioeconomic standing, and these mostly favor mainstream neighborhoods. For example, the median income of mainstream neighborhoods is nearly 20 percent higher than that of Cuban neighborhoods. This means that moving away from Cuban areas of Miami does represent social mobility as well as increased exposure to other groups. It should be noted, though, that there is a socioeconomic gradient within the heavily Cuban portion of the region, and it is also possible to move to a somewhat more affluent but still Cuban neighborhood beyond the city limits.

Dominican neighborhoods of New York are less intensely ethnic than are these Cuban neighborhoods. Table 3.1.6 shows that they average 29 percent Dominican, well above the 6.5 percent level in mainstream neighborhoods but still definitely a minority of residents. But Dominican neighborhoods are over 70 percent Hispanic, while mainstream areas are only 40 percent Hispanic. Nearly half of residents in mainstream neighborhoods speak only English, which is much more than in Dominican neighborhoods, and they also have a lower share of foreign-born and recent immigrants.

Socioeconomic disparities between ethnic and mainstream neighborhoods are similar and in some respects even more pronounced that what we found in Miami. For example, the median income in Dominican neighborhoods is 30 percent below that of mainstream neighborhoods. In this case, there is also a distinction in household formation, as Dominican neighborhoods also have higher shares of female-headed households. Again we see that moving out of ethnic neighborhoods represents a degree of upward social mobility, as the spatial assimilation model anticipates. More detailed analyses show that there are more affluent sections within Washington Heights, and at a greater distance the Corona neighborhood in Queens is much more middle class, but on average moving up means moving out for Dominicans in New York.

Is There an Average Latino?

The scale of immigration from nontraditional Hispanic sources brings new and less-well-known groups into the United States. Because they are highly concentrated in a few regions, often in a fairly narrow set of neighborhoods, every Hispanic group has local significance. And their growth expands the range of variation in what could be considered the typical Latino experience.

Of the groups studied here, Cubans and South Americans stand out for their high degree of economic success. This success translates into moderate levels of segregation from whites, although members of both groups still tend to live in neighborhoods where non-Hispanic whites are outnumbered by His-panics. They are also the most segregated from African Americans, although this dimension of separation is on the decline. On the other hand, two of the newer and fastest growing groups—Dominicans and Central Americans—lag behind in economic standing. Dominicans are clearly the least successful as well as the most segregated. These differences show up even more clearly when we study these groups in places like Miami and New York where they are most highly concentrated. Looking to the future, it is likely that the Hispanic population will maintain or accentuate the diversity we see today. Our ability to distinguish among the national-origin groups is therefore crucial to understanding Hispanic Americans. There is no "average Hispanic."

Yet we found some commonalities among Cubans, Dominicans, and other Hispanic groups. The differences between Miami and New York for Hispanics of all national origins are so large that they make variations between groups within these metropolitan regions seem minor. Even Cubans and Dominicans, despite being at polar extremes among Hispanics, have some traits in common. They are both moderately to highly segregated from non-Hispanic groups, and they are very likely to live in neighborhoods where Hispanics are a majority or near-majority. This is especially true in Miami and New York, given the magnitude of immigration in both parts of the country in the last several decades. Regardless of the differences in their socioeconomic background, both Cubans and Dominicans manifest the same process of spatial assimilation. Living in a Cuban or a Dominican neighborhood—as do more than half of group members in these two metropolises—implies not only a particular ethnic character but also substantial socioeconomic disadvantages. When they move to mainstream neighborhoods, members of both groups continue to have high exposure to immigrants, but they achieve greater integration with people of other racial and ethnic backgrounds in addition to improved residential surroundings. The project of assimilation, manifested in the labor market or in space, may be the most significant common denominator of the Latino experience in the United States.

Appendix
Estimates of Hispanic-Origin Populations

The adjustment procedures described here are analogous to standard techniques employed by the Census Bureau to deal with incomplete census forms. The bureau routinely "imputes" information from other household members or from neighbors to fill in missing data. The difference is that our adjustment is done at the level of the census tract. To the extent that we believe the tract's Other Hispanics population has been overstated, we impute specific national origins to the "excess Other Hispanics" based on the distribution of responses of others in the tract.

Estimates for 1990

We first describe our approach to 1990. The Public Use Microdata Sample (PUMS) from the 1990 Census provides individual-level information for a large national sample on Hispanic origin, country of birth, and ancestry. In the PUMS sample, 8.7 percent of Hispanics are classed as Other Hispanics. If we also use country of birth and ancestry as a basis for determining individuals' specific Hispanic origin, we can reduce Other Hispanics to 7.5 percent. For some specific states or metropolitan areas, however, we can do much better, reducing Other Hispanics to less than 1.5 percent of Hispanics in New York, Los Angeles, and Miami.

We treat these estimates of the "real" size of the Other Hispanics category as targets, setting a specific target for every census tract. For tracts in metro areas with more than 100,000 Hispanics (39 metro areas), we calculate the target from data for the metro area itself. In other cases, we apply statewide figures. For the thirty-one states with fewer than 100,000 Hispanics, we apply the national target of 7.5 percent.

We then turn to the figures from the 1990 Census, comparing our target for every census tract with the number of Other Hispanics reported by the census. If the reported number is equal to or below the target, we make no adjustment. If it is larger than the target, we allocate the number of "excess" other Hispanics to specific national-origin categories based on the reported figures in the tract for those categories.

Analysis of 1990 PUMS data reveals that people of Mexican, Puerto Rican, or Cuban birth or ancestry were much less likely (by a factor of 1:4) to fail to indicate an origin than were Hispanics of other backgrounds, a result that we attribute to the questionnaire format. It is appropriate to allocate some Other Hispanics to these listed groups, but not in the same proportion as for unlisted groups. In allocating Other Hispanics, therefore, we weight members of the listed groups in each tract at .25; this procedure generates national totals that are consistent with the national group populations found in the PUMS.

Estimates for 2000

Our procedure for 2000 follows the same logic but draws on a different source for calculating targets. We use the Current Population Survey, pooling together the samples from March 1998 and March 2000. As a national average, information on the person's country of birth and both parents' country of birth from the Current Population Survey allows us to reduce the target to 3.3 percent—well below the 17.3 percent reported in the decennial census. These targets also vary by state and metro area. For Consolidated Metropolitan Statistical Areas (CMSAs) with more than 400 sampled Hispanics, we use CMSA figures to calculate targets (this covered 67 Primary Metropolitan Statistical Areas, or PMSAs). For other cases, we employ statewide figures or, where a state has fewer than 400 sampled Hispanics, we use the national target. In some cases, the targets are even lower than 3.9 percent: they are 2.4 percent in New York, and 1.1 percent in

Los Angeles. This procedure reallocates a very large share of people who were reported as Other Hispanics in Census 2000.

As in 1990, we allocate a substantial number of Other Hispanics to Mexican, Puerto Rican, and Cuban. The weighting factor for these groups is .10, calibrated to yield national totals that are consistent with the Current Population Survey. Substantively, this weight means we are estimating that members of other groups were ten times more likely to fail to indicate their origin, a greater discrepancy than in 1990. The difference reflects the fact that the Census 2000 questionnaire provided no examples to guide respondents from the unlisted groups, examples that proved helpful in 1990.

References

Anselin, Luc. 1995. "Local Indicators of Spatial Association—LISA." *Geographical Analysis* 27: 93–115.

Cresce, Arthur R., and Roberto R. Ramirez. 2003. "Analysis of General Hispanic Responses in Census 2000." Working Paper 72. Washington, D.C.: U.S. Bureau of the Census. Available online at www2.census.gov/census_2000/datasets/Sim_Hispanic_Totals/General_Hispanic_Working_Paper_%2372.pdf (accessed April 29, 2005).

Grasmuck, Sherri, and Patricia R. Pessar. 1991. *Between Two Islands: Dominican International Migration.* Berkeley: University of California Press.

Logan, John R. 2001. "The New Latinos: Who They Are, Where They Are." Lewis Mumford Center for Comparative Urban and Regional Research, September 10. Available online at http://browns4.dyndns.org/cen2000_s4/HispanicPop/HspReport/HspReportPage1.html (accessed April 29, 2005).

Logan, John R., Richard D. Alba, and Brian J. Stults. 2003. "Enclaves and Entrepreneurs: Assessing the Payoff for Immigrants and Minorities." *International Migration Review* 37 (Summer): 344–388.

Logan, John R., Richard D. Alba, and Charles Zhang. 2002. "Immigrant Enclaves and Ethnic Communities in New York and Los Angeles." *American Sociological Review* 67 (April): 299–322.

Logan, John R., Brian Stults, and Reynolds Farley. 2004. "Segregation of Minorities in the Metropolis: Two Decades of Change." *Demography* 41: 1–22.

Martin, Elizabeth. 2002. "The Effects of Questionnaire Design on Reporting of Detailed Hispanic Origin in Census 2000 Mail Questionnaires." *Public Opinion Quarterly* 66, no. 4: 582–593.

Massey, Douglas. 1985. "Ethnic Residential Segregation: A Theoretical Synthesis and Empirical Review." *Sociology and Social Research* 69: 315–350.

Pessar, Patricia. 1995. *A Visa for a Dream: Dominicans in the United States.* Boston: Allyn and Bacon.

Portes, Alejandro, and Robert L. Bach. 1985. *Latin Journey: Cuban and Mexican Immigrants in the United States.* Berkeley: University of California Press.

Portes, Alejandro, and Alex Stepick. 1993. *City on the Edge: The Transformation of Miami.* Berkeley: University of California Press.

■ Reading 3.1

Define the following concepts/phrases:

"other Hispanics"   female-headed household
enclave economy   human capital resources
national origins of Hispanics   ethnic neighborhoods
Hispanic segregation   spatial assimilation
residential pattern   socioeconomic disparities

Answer the following question:

Write a short essay explaining the reasons for the Cuban and Dominican migration to the United States and compare them to the reasons for the migration of Mexicans and Puerto Ricans.

Divergent Latino Immigrant Stories
Salvadorans and Peruvians in America

María E. Verdaguer

T HIS CHAPTER PROVIDES A CONTEXTUAL OVERVIEW of Salvadoran and Peruvian immigrants in the United States, including a brief description of their distinct demographic, economic, and settlement patterns. Equally important, it offers a snapshot of Latino small businesses in the Greater Washington and national economy.

The chapter is organized in three parts. First, it explores nationwide population demographics for Salvadorans and Peruvians, including divergent socioeconomic indicators and self-employment rates. Next, it provides a close up look at Washington Salvadorans and Peruvians, including the social, political, and economic forces that have fueled their migration to the area. Last, it explores Washington's unique features as a new immigrant receiving gateway, outlining the economic and social changes that have affected the region over the last three decades.

National Demographic Overview
Salvadorans and Peruvians in the United States

Salvadorans constitute the fourth largest Latino population in the United States after Mexicans, Puerto Ricans and Cubans.[1] According to 2000 Census data, there are 655,000 Salvadorans in the US, which shows a modest increase of 100,000 above the 1990 census figure of 565,081. More realistically, the recent 2006 American Community Survey estimates the national Salvadoran population as high as 1,371,666. Underlying these disparate figures is the fact that Latinos have been, and still remain, historically undercounted by the census,[2] a situation which is particularly acute for undocumented migrants who are reluctant to participate for fear of deportation. Thus, an accurate number is clouded by thousands of Salvadorans awaiting approval of their applications for legal permanent residency under various US immigration programs.

María E. Verdaguer, "Divergent Latino Immigrant Stories: Salvadorans and Peruvians in America," *Class, Ethnicity, Gender, and Latino Entrepreneurship*, pp. 31-49, 194-195, 199-210. Copyright © 2009 by Taylor & Francis Group. Reprinted with permission.

The US Salvadoran community is popularly referred to as Salvador's "15th Department"[3] given that over 15 per cent of the total Salvadoran population of seven million now reside in US territory. Salvadorans are concentrated geographically in metropolitan areas such as Los Angeles, Washington DC/Northern Virginia, Houston, Phoenix and the Greater New York region. These Salvadoran settlements, however, differ in important ways. While the Los Angeles metropolitan area has a larger concentration of Salvadorans in absolute terms, Washington Salvadorans constitute a much larger percentage of the Latino population in the metropolitan area. In fact, with the exception of the Washington region, most Salvadoran settlements are embedded in areas characterized by different racial and ethnic landscapes where either Mexicans, Puerto Ricans or Cubans predominate among Latinos.

Peruvians also tend to settle in a few select metropolitan areas. By 2000, the vast majority was concentrated in the Greater New York area, including New Jersey and its suburbs (US Census Bureau 2006). With the exception of a handful of recent studies, there is a dearth of research on Peruvians in the US, and none at all on Washington Peruvians. Although we know that they are the third largest South American national origin group in the US after Colombians and Ecuadorians, their precise numbers are, again, debatable given the historical undercount of Latinos in censuses. According to 2006 American Community Survey data, there are currently 435,368 Peruvians in the United States. Yet, Peruvian official sources claim there are over a million Peruvians in the United States, which is the top country of destination for emigrants from that country (US Census Bureau 2006; Organización Internacional para las Migraciones 2008).

Table 3.2.1 shows notable socioeconomic differences among both groups. In fact, one of the few early studies of Peruvian and Salvadoran migration to the New York/New Jersey area confirms a class divide between Peruvians and Salvadorans (Mahler 1995). Although both Salvadorans and Peruvians are newcomers with as many as 82 per cent of their total US population being foreign born, Peruvians include more recent arrivals given that 61 per cent of their newcomers arrived to US shores over the past two decades. Instead, over half of the Salvadoran immigrant population arrived to the US before 1990. Salvadorans are also younger than Peruvians, and least likely to have attained high school education and beyond (41 per cent). Furthermore, Table 3.2.1 shows Salvadoran median household income is lower than that of their Peruvian counterparts (US Census Bureau 2004). Conversely, Peruvians are one of the Latino national origin groups most likely to have attained high school education and beyond (89 per cent), showing one of the highest median household incomes among Latinos in the US.

Everywhere Salvadorans have settled, they have concentrated in the low-wage service sector of the urban and suburban economy. In fact, a disproportionate number of Salvadorans are concentrated in private service occupations such as maids, domestics, and babysitters (99 per cent of whom are females), sewing operators, construction workers, gardeners, and painters (primarily

TABLE 3.2.1 Social Characteristics of Salvadorans and Peruvians in the United States, 2004 (National Average Values, Survey and Interview Data).

	Salvadorans			Peruvians		
	2004 ACS	Survey Population N = 49	Inter-views N = 23	2004 ACS	Survey Population N = 58	Inter-views N = 22
Male/Female ratio (adults, age 16+)	51/49	53/47	45/54	49/51	58/42	47/52
Median Age	29	40	39	35	44	43
Median Family Income	$36,789	—	—	$42,956	—	—
Per cent Foreign Born	67.7%	100%	100%	72.2%	100%	100%
Education (over age 25)						
% less than high school	58.7%	34.9%	22.7%	10.9%	03.4%	00.0%
% high school graduate or more	41.3%	59.1%	63.6%	89.1%	34.5%	36.9%
% bachelor's degree or more	06.2%	06.0%	09.0%	30.0%	46.5%	47.5%

Source: US Department of Commerce, Bureau of the Census, 2004 American Community Survey, Selected Population Profiles; survey and in-depth interview study participants.

male occupations). Further, a sizable share of the Salvadoran population resorts to self-employment in the informal and/or formal economy either as primary or secondary sources of income.

Table 3.2.2 shows that Peruvians' occupational distribution in the United States is less concentrated in the low-wage service sector than that of Salvadorans'. Recent American Community Survey data indicate that as many as 22.7 per cent of Peruvians are in the managerial and professional specialty categories, 25 per cent in the technicians, sales, and administrative support occupations, 26.5 per cent in service categories, 11.9 per cent in construction trades, and only 0.2 per cent in agricultural occupations (US Census Bureau 2004). Salvadorans, instead, have as much as 73.8 per cent of their population (over 16 years old) concentrated in the service and manual labor categories; only 9.8 per cent are in the managerial and professional specialty occupations.

Based on recent census data and on my personal observations, surveys, and interviews, it is clear that the Washington Peruvian community has as much as a fourth of its population in higher-wage professional occupations, particularly in service and high tech industries such as communications, marketing, and information technology. Simultaneously, however, they can be found in the low tech and lower wage sector of the formal and informal economy. Males are concentrated in construction and service industries in areas such as home remodeling, residential and commercial painting, janitorial services, restaurants, and professional specialty occupations.

TABLE 3.2.2   Occupational Distribution of Peruvians and Salvadorans in the United States, 2004

Occupations	Peruvian	Salvadoran
Managerial and professional specialty	22.7%	9.8%
Technical, sales, and office occupations	24.9%	16.4%
Service occupations[a]	26.5%	33.5%
Construction, extraction and maintenance[b]	11.9%	16.1%
Production, transportation, and material moving	13.7%	23.7%
Agricultural, farm-related[c]	0.2%	0.5%

Source: US Department of Commerce, Bureau of the Census, 2004 American Community Survey, Selected Population Profiles, S0201.
Notes:
a This category includes workers in personal service, private household service, food preparation, restaurants, cleaning, building and protective services, and in childcare.
b This category includes mechanics, repairers and workers in construction trades, such as carpenters, electricians, and painters.
c This category includes workers in farming and in forestry, including groundskeepers and gardeners.

Women, instead, work as childcare providers, hairdressers, caterers, and secretaries, as well as in professional categories. Very much like Salvadorans, Peruvians resort to self-employment in formal and informal settings and there is a growing entrepreneurial class among both populations. Yet, neither group reaches the level of economic dynamism, job generation, and co-ethnic employment that are pre-requisites to become an economic ethnic enclave. Miami Cubans' or Los Angeles Koreans' are the quintessential models of successful ethnic enclaves where ethnic-owned businesses that employ and market to co-nationals are salient features of the immigrant community (Portes and Manning 1986).

In contrast to Salvadorans, Peruvian immigrants have fewer peasants or poor among them; this fact that can be easily explained because poor Peruvians migrate primarily from the Peruvian countryside to the cities. The Peruvian upper and lower middle classes, and most recently some segments of the working class, seem to be those most likely to engage in international migration. Instead, Salvadoran migrants, because of their closer proximity to the US, the push effect of the civil war at home, and the momentum reached by the chain migration process that started in the 1970s, have a more heterogeneous class base, including the upper-middle and middle segments of society, the urban poor, and rural peasants. Salvadoran migration networks to the Washington DC area are younger than those of other Salvadoran settlements and have been largely restricted to the unregulated service sector. As will be examined later on, this together with the fact that Washington Salvadorans are less educated than both Salvadoran national averages and other Salvadoran-American communities suggests that, as a whole, Washington Salvadorans are less diverse and heterogeneous in their class composition.

A great deal of research has been conducted on the success stories of Cuban and Dominican businesses in Miami and New York, while there is virtually no data on the entrepreneurial activities of Salvadorans and Peruvians. Captured in the census aggregate category of "Other Spanish/Hispanic/Latino," they have the second largest share of Hispanic -owned small businesses in the US.[4] This lack of data is even more striking considering that, from 1992 to 2002, the only Latino ethnic groups that have increased their share of Hispanic-owned business have been "Other Spanish/Hispanic/Latino" (US Census Bureau 1992, 1997, 2006).[5] Because of the lack of national origin disaggregated economic data beyond Cubans, Mexicans, and Puerto Rican-owned businesses, official figures fail to capture nuances among South and Central Americans' business experiences.

During the 1990s, Latino small businesses became the nations' fastest growing business population, after enjoying a phenomenal growth rate of 83 per cent from 1985 to 1992 (US Small Business Administration 1998). This figure is particularly striking when compared to the average small business growth rate of 26 per cent during that same period. By 2002, there were 1.6 million Latino small businesses in the US, up from 1.2 million only a decade earlier. Mexican, Mexican-American, and Chicano-owned businesses were at the lead, constituting 43.8 per cent of all Latino businesses, followed by Other Spanish/Hispanic/Latino businesses, which included Salvadoran and Peruvian-owned firms, and made up 37.2 per cent of all Latino businesses. Cuban and Puerto Rican businesses followed respectively with 9.4 and 6.8 per cent of all Latino businesses (US Census Bureau 2006).

Nationwide Hispanic-owned businesses operate primarily in the retail, construction, administrative and support services, concentrating disproportionately in business and personal services. Most of them operate as individual proprietorships and, although they own the largest share of firms owned by US minorities, Asian-owned businesses reap the largest share of minority-owned business revenues. This is indicative of the relatively lower profit margin of most Hispanic small businesses, a fact which is confirmed by their underrepresentation in the more profitable wholesale trade and manufacturing industries (US Census Bureau 2006).

During the 1990–2000 decade, the growing presence of Latinos other than Mexican, Cuban, and Puerto Rican in southern states strikingly diversified the Latino immigrant population across a wider range of American communities. Census data show that, during this time period, the proportion of Central and South Americans living in the Northeast decreased from 30 per cent to 25 per cent whereas that of those living in the South (including Washington DC and Miami and Orlando metropolitan areas) rose from 17.6 per cent to 18.5 per cent. In northern Virginia, in particular, by 2000, "Other" Latinos (Central and South Americans) accounted for 62.5 per cent of all Latino residents in the region (Vazquez et al. 2008).

Naturally, this new pattern of immigrant dispersion beyond traditional destinations reshaped the geographic concentration of Hispanic-owned businesses in traditional immigrant receiving states. Thus, by 2002, it was not only California, New York, Florida, and Texas that had the largest numbers of Latino-owned firms. Urban areas across the Washington DC region, North and South Carolina, Nevada, and the New York-New Jersey corridor welcomed important concentrations of Other Spanish/Hispanic/Latino-owned small businesses. Most notably, in all other geographical settings where there is an important concentration of Central and South American businesses, Other Spanish/Hispanic/Latino are second in numbers to more numerous Latino national origin groups such as Mexicans in California or Cubans in Florida. Only in the greater Washington DC and New Jersey areas do Hispanic Latin American-owned businesses acquire numerical prominence without being eclipsed by other Latinos.

Salvadoran and Peruvian Self-Employment

Because the foreign-born have been traditionally over-represented in US small businesses since the 1880s, it has long been perceived that immigrants are distinctly entrepreneurial. Scholars largely attribute the survival and success of ethnic business ventures to group specific resources and, to determine which immigrant groups are more or less entrepreneurial than others, they have computed immigrants' self-employment rates. As with census data, exact self-employment rates for Salvadorans and Peruvians are elusive and figures vary from one source to the next. Yet, while there are discrepancies in the various figures used, the differential national and gender patterns remain the same.[6]

In analyzing 1990 census data on the foreign born, Light and Gold (2000) argue that even the smallest ethnic economies of American ethnic groups—which they define as the sum of co-ethnic self-employed, employers and their co-ethnic employees—merit more attention than what they have received thus far. Table 3.2.3 presents some of their sex disaggregated data on self-employment rates[7] of selected immigrant groups categorized by the level of significance of their ethnic economies. To evaluate the importance of individual ethnic economies, they establish that threshold significance is reached when an ethnic economy occupies 5 per cent or more of any group's civilian labor force, high significance when it occupies 10 to 19 per cent, and extreme significance when it occupies 20 per cent or more. Men, women, total self-employed, and unpaid family workers of each national group are shown as a percentage of that group's labor force in 1990. Adding the ethnic economy's co-ethnic employees at one half the self-employed, they arrive at an estimate of individual ethnic economies in 1990. Their analysis yields an immigrant median ethnic economy of 10.4 per cent of the total labor force.

Thus, the data in Table 3.2.3 shows that Peruvian's ethnic economy not only coincides with the median ethnic economy for all foreign born but reaches high significance since it occupies over 10 per cent of Peruvians' labor force. Meanwhile, Salvadoran's 7.4 per cent ethnic economy falls below the median but easily surpasses Light and Gold's 5 per cent threshold of significance. Hence, while Peruvians seem to be more entrepreneurial than Salvadorans, both groups have

TABLE 3.2.3 Self-Employment Rates and Ethnic Economies for Selected Immigrant Populations, Census 1990.

Birthplace	Self-employed and unpaid family workers			Estimated Employees	Ethnic Economy
	Men	Women	Total		
Extreme Significance					
Korea	23.5	18.3	20.9	10.5	31.4
High Significance					
Cuba	10.1	4.5	7.7	3.9	11.6
Peru	7.2	6.5	6.9	3.5	10.4
Significant					
Vietnam	6.1	7.1	6.5	3.3	9.9
Dominican Republic	7.1	3.7	5.6	2.8	8.5
El Salvador	4.1	6.2	4.9	2.5	7.4
Below Significance					
Guyana	3.4	2.6	3.0	1.5	4.5

Source: This table was published in Ethnic Economies, Ivan Light and Steven J. Gold, Table 2.4, 34-35, Copyright Academic Press (2000). Data computed from 1990 Census of Population and Housing, The Foreign-Born Population in the United States.

ethnic economies important enough to merit attention. Remarkably, Salvadoran women exhibit much higher rates of self-employment than men. In contrast, Peruvian women show rates of self-employment lower than their men but almost as high as Salvadoran women. As we will see in chapter eight, the dynamics of Washington Salvadoran women's networks might help explain their higher levels of entrepreneurship relative to Salvadoran men.

Washington Salvadorans and Peruvians: A New Latino Presence

Salvadorans and Peruvians are certainly newcomers to the Washington area, although their presence in other regions of the United States traces back many generations. Salvadoran migration to the Bay area, for example, was fueled by the commercial trade between San Francisco and Central America in the early 1900s. California's burgeoning shipping industry attracted a pioneer wave of Salvadorans to the area in the 1940s, which paved the way for subsequent migration networks heading to the West coast (Menjivar 2000). Similarly, Peruvian presence in the US traces as far back as 1848, when experienced miners and Andean women migrated to California for the gold rush (Julca 2001; Monaghan 1973). Almost a century later, beginning in the 1930s and 1940s, both working class Peruvians and members of the elite settled in the New York and New Jersey areas (Altamirano 2003). It would take until the second half of the 20th century for either Salvadorans or Peruvians to establish a presence in the Greater Washington region.

Salvadoran's first significant contingent arrived to Washington during the 1960s, when an informal gendered labor recruitment cycle brought thousands of Salvadoran women to work in the houses of international civil servants to fill childcare, cleaning and other social reproduction jobs (Repak 1995). This first wave of pioneer immigrants built the initial network that would attract the subsequent chain migration (spouses, children, relatives, friends and acquaintances) that would follow. Thus, the Greater Washington area contains the nation's largest Salvadoran community outside of Los Angeles. Official counts estimate 168,119 Washington Salvadorans, however, officials of the Embassy of El Salvador and others say the number of Salvadoran immigrants in the region may be as high as 600,000.[8]

Also recent newcomers, Peruvians comprise the largest South American population in the area.[9] Peruvians first significant contingents arrived, together with a sizable population of Bolivians, during the early 1970s when severe Andean droughts expelled many of them from their homelands. Back in 2000, census figures estimated that roughly 30,000 Peruvians lived in the Washington D.C metro area. Yet, according to the Peruvian Consulate, there are roughly 300,000 Peruvians in the Washington DC metropolitan area alone.

As discussed earlier, Washington Salvadorans differ substantially from their Peruvian counterparts. Most Washington Salvadorans trace their roots to the country's eastern provinces of La Unión, San Miguel, and Usulután, coming either from secondary cities or small rural towns. Incidentally, the Intipucá-Washington DC route is one of the oldest and most publicized Salvadoran 'transnational migrant circuit' (Rouse 1991), linking that small town at the southern tip of La Unión Department with migrant settlements in specific neighborhoods across Washington DC and suburban Maryland and Virginia. Over 20 per cent of Salvadorans from Intipucá have resettled in the Washington metropolitan area, moving back and forth between the town and the nation's capital since the 1960s (Levitt 2001; Pedersen 2001).[10]

Instead, exceedingly large numbers of Washington Peruvians come from Peru's capital city of Lima, where they had always lived or temporarily settled after migrating from the countryside. An exception is the less ubiquitous migrant circuit between the Andean town of Cabanaconde, in the Peruvian Andes south of Arequipa, and the Washington DC region. Since the early 1970s, roughly 400 Cabaneños have settled in the area, regularly traveling back to their hometown to partake in religious and cultural celebrations (Gelles and Martinez 1992). In general, Peruvians predominantly come from Lima or secondary cities like Trujillo and Arequipa.

Likewise, the largest Salvadoran influx arrived to the Washington metropolitan area after the 1970s, when Central American migration escalated as a result of political and economic turmoil back home. Despite the fact that most Salvadorans were fleeing from persecution and violence amidst the bloodshed of civil war, US immigration policy did not recognize them as political refugees. Hence, their "official" categorization as economic rather than political migrants made them ineligible to receive state-sponsored resettlement assistance, including programs to support and strengthen community building and social service efforts.

The following decade provided the backdrop for the migration of thousands of Peruvians to European and North American destinations as the Maoist guerrillas-based Sendero Luminoso (Shining Path) unleashed a fierce terrorist campaign against the government. Guerrilla warfare, the violence resulting from State efforts to combat the insurgency, and the economic downfall that ensued during Alan Garcia's presidency fueled the migration of large numbers of Peruvians to the United States. Such was the economic chaos during those years that hyperinflation reached 2,350 per cent in 1989 (Julca 2001). Fleeing primarily from economic recession and, to a lesser degree, from political chaos, the Peruvian's exodus was nowhere as dramatic or as massive as that of Salvadoran refugees. While Peruvians did not enjoy the welcoming reception Cubans were given either, US immigration policies proved coldly neutral towards them and far less hostile as towards Salvadorans.

Reflecting national occupational patterns, Washington Salvadorans are mostly employed in construction, landscaping, restaurants, cleaning and maintenance, and as domestic workers (Repak 1995). Many of them also make ends meet in the informal economy as survivalist micro-entrepreneurs. It has been estimated that approximately 10 per cent of the Salvadoran population in the DC metro area receives its primary income from self-employment (Landolt 2000).

In contrast, Peruvians show a bimodal occupational distribution with a considerable share of its population in higher-wage professional occupations in service industries, most notably in communications and marketing. At the other end of the spectrum, Washington Peruvians concentrate in the low tech and lower wage sector of the formal and informal economy in the construction and retail industries. In fact, Peruvian entrepreneurs have a strong presence across the Washington area Latino immigrant business landscape together with Salvadorans and smaller number of Bolivians.

In terms of educational achievement levels, Table 3.2.4 presents socio-demographic census data for Washington Salvadorans. These figures highlight their lower levels of educational attainment since 61 per cent of its population has not completed high school studies, just 32.3 per cent having completed high school or more, and only 6.5 per cent reporting completion of college and beyond. Notably, a quick glance at demographic indicators of other populous Salvadoran communities across the country reveals that Washington Salvadorans show lower educational levels relative to fellow Salvadorans in Los Angeles or New York. This confirms that the Washington metro area has received a larger proportion of Salvadorans of lower working class and/or peasant background than might be the case in other Salvadoran settlements.

TABLE 3.2.4   Social Characteristics of Salvadorans, Census Figures 2006

	Greater Washington	Greater Los Angeles	Greater New York	Survey Population (N = 49)
Median age	28.0	30.9	28.4	40
Male	54.7%	48.1%	55.0%	53%
Female	45.3%	51.9%	45.0%	47%
Median household income	$54,637	$39,131	$49,724	—
Educational Attainment (age 25+)				
Less than high school	61.5%	52.1%	51.5%	34.9%
High school graduate or more	32.3%	41.2%	41.2%	59.1%
Bachelor's degree or more	6.5%	6.8%	7.4%	6.0%

Source: US Department of Commerce, Bureau of the Census, 2006 American Community Survey; survey study.

In contrast, Washington Peruvians show higher levels of educational attainment. Accordingly, 10 per cent of Washington Peruvians have not completed high school studies, 52.6 per cent have graduated from high school and beyond, and 37.4 per cent have completed college and a graduate or professional degree. In fact, findings from a poll conducted across the Washington metropolitan area in 2000 confirmed the differential human capital endowments of both populations.[11]

Furthermore, it showed that one in four Latino immigrants in the region was of South American descent, making the Washington metro area one of the few American cities with a large concentration of South American residents. The data also showed that most South American families came from urban middle-class origins, thus being better educated and more prosperous than other Latino immigrants in the area. Finally, findings corroborated that large portions of particular Salvadoran rural villages resettled in the Washington metro area, thereby confirming that Washington Salvadorans include a disproportionate number of peasants among their population.

In contrast to traditional immigrant receiving destinations, Washington immigrants do not tend to cluster in immigrant neighborhoods in the city, but are scattered throughout suburban areas (Singer et al. 2008). Notwithstanding, there are key urban and suburban neighborhoods where Salvadorans and Peruvians settle selectively. While Salvadorans are likely to reside in both urban and suburban areas, Peruvians tend to settle almost exclusively in the suburbs. In fact, there are populous Salvadoran settlements in the areas of Mount Pleasant, Petworth/Brightwood Park and Columbia Heights in the Northwest quadrant of the District of Columbia, in South Arlington, Culmore, Arlandria[12] and Landmark in Northern Virginia, in the Langley Park/Hyattesville area of Prince George's County and in the Silver Spring/Takoma Park area of Montgomery County.

Conversely, Peruvians settle in largest numbers across Northern Virginia suburbs such as Annandale, South Arlington, Bailey Crossroads, and Landmark. A study based on INS data for legal immigration to the Washington region between 1990–98 showed that 51 per cent of

TABLE 3.2.5   Social Characteristics of Peruvians, Census Figures 2006

	Greater Washington	Greater New York	Survey Population (N = 58)
Median age	33	35.4	44
Male	49%	48.7%	58%
Female	51%	51.3%	42%
Median household income	$62,033	$50,712	—
Educational Attainment (age 25+)			
Less than high school	10.0%	10.3%	3.4%
High school graduate or more	52.6%	65.4%	34.5%
Bachelor's degree or more	37.4%	24.2%	46.5%

Source: US Department of Commerce, Bureau of the Census, 2006 American Community Survey, Selected Population Profiles; survey study.

Washington Peruvians lived outside the Capital Beltway[13] whereas only 33 per cent of Salvadorans resided in the outer suburbs (Singer et al. 2001). These differential settlement patterns further suggest that Peruvians come to the area endowed with more financial resources and transferable skills than their Salvadoran counterparts. Regardless of differentiated residential settlement patterns, Salvadoran and Peruvian small businesses can be found across a wide array of urban and suburban locations in the Washington metropolitan area.

Latino Small Businesses in the Greater Washington Area

Over the last couple of decades, Latino small businesses have experienced a boom across the Greater Washington region, which is now listed among the top metropolitan areas with largest number of Hispanic-owned firms, ranking 7th among a total of fifty (US Census Bureau 2006). From an estimated 3,000 Latino-owned businesses in 1988, the number skyrocketed to 12,703 by 1992, to 27,000 by 1997, and to 32,419 by 2002 (US Hispanic Chamber of Commerce 1988; US Census Bureau 1996, 2001, 2006). Specifically, Washington "Central and South Americans" (including Salvadorans and Peruvians) own more firms than Mexicans, Cubans, and Puerto Ricans, and those of European Spanish descent (Economic Census 2002). In fact, in 2002, 67 per cent of all Hispanic-owned businesses were Central and South American-owned.[14]

As described earlier, the flux of Central and South American immigrants to the area in the 1970s fueled the reconfiguration of its Latino commercial landscape which, until then, had been dominated by Cubans and Dominicans. Thus, a dynamic Salvadoran, Peruvian, and Bolivian business community quickly emerged to respond to the market needs of co-ethnics, who painstakingly

TABLE 3.2.6   Small Businesses across the Washington D.C. Metro Area by Ethnicity, 2002

	Non-Minority Owned	Latino- Owned	African-American Owned	Asian-American Owned
District of Columbia	64.0%	4.6%	25.8%	5.1%
Alexandria, VA	71.8%	7.3%	12.4%	8.3%
Arlington County, VA	73.0%	9.9%	6.3%	9.9%
Fairfax County, VA	71.6%	7.7%	5.4%	15.2%
Loudoun County, VA	83.0%	5.6%	4.6%	6.2%
Prince William County, VA	71.3%	12.0%	9.4%	7.1%
Montgomery County, MD	69.7%	7.5%	11.5%	11.0%
Prince George's County, MD	40.2%	5.5%	47.7%	6.3%

Source: US Department of Commerce, Bureau of the Census, 2002 Economic Census, Survey of Business Owners.

attempted to recreate a familiar environment in their new surroundings. A host of ethnic stores carrying a wide variety of Latino products and offering a variety of services, from translation and international couriers, to notaries and apparel retail, mushroomed throughout the area.

Simultaneously, a different but complementary type of Latino business emerged, formally or informally, to cater to the needs of Washington American and international clients: home-remodeling contractors, family childcare providers, construction and janitorial sub-contractors, and ethnic restaurants located in gentrified upscale neighborhoods. In fact, a close look at Central and South American-owned firms in the area reveals that they are primarily concentrated in service industries, followed by construction and retail. Such polarized Latino commercial landscape with immigrant business owners at both ends of the spectrum well fits the Washington metro area post-industrial economy with dual demand for higher tech/skilled and lower wage/skilled workers.

The racially and ethnically diverse demographic profile of the Washing-ton region translates into a small business metroscape where Latino businesses are uniquely embedded in urban and suburban neighborhoods with distinct racial and ethnic configurations (Singer et al. 2008). Clearly, Washington Salvadoran and Peruvian small businesses respond to local structural forces such as active market competition from non-Hispanic white, minority, and other immigrant entrepreneurs, discriminatory practices that curtail Latino business creation and development, and marginalization from institutional mainstream agencies.

Table 3.2.6 presents findings from the latest economic census. Prince William and Arlington Counties in Northern Virginia have the largest concentration of Latino-owned firms, whereas Maryland's Prince George's County and the District of Columbia have the highest concentration of African-American businesses. In fact, during the last decade, Latino small business growth has been modest in Prince George's County relative to growth in either Prince William, Fairfax, or Montgomery Counties. Notwithstanding, Virginia has become fertile terrain for Latino-owned businesses, ranking 10 among states with the largest numbers of Hispanic-owned businesses. As important, the data show that, without exceptions, Asian-American small businesses are a growing force in the area's minority commercial landscape, primarily concentrated in Fairfax and Montgomery Counties (US Census Bureau 2006). Therefore, Latino immigrant settlements and small businesses in the Washington metro area remain uniquely embedded in settings with distinct racial and ethnic landscapes.

Greater Washington as a New Immigrant Gateway

The Greater Washington area provides a strikingly distinct economic and social landscape than other Latino immigrant receiving US metropolitan areas. This is so because, historically, the Washington economy has been dominated by federal government services, and not by an industrial sector which rapidly absorbs immigrant workers in garment factories such as those in New York or Los Angeles. Because of this, most immigrants to the area did not have access to the local labor market until the beginning of the 1970s (Manning 1998). The most important exception to this exclusion were international civil servants employed by multilateral institutions such as the International Monetary Fund, the World Bank, and others, who started settling in the area after the 1950s.

Beginning in the 1960s and 1970s, the region underwent a major transformation as small businesses proliferated, and a growth of service industries, biomedical firms, research-and-development, defense, and consulting companies skyrocketed. As professionals and government technocrats settled in the area, Washington DC underwent a simultaneous and complementary process of gentrification. Thus its labor market expanded with a growing demand for low-wage personal services such as child-care and domestic workers for the two-career families residing in the area (Repak 1995). This economic growth peaked during the 1980s with the employment growth rate ranking the 6th most rapid among the nation's 25 largest metropolitan areas (Kingsley et al. 1998). Such expansion was largely driven by the dynamic creation of jobs in high-end service industries, such as information technology, biomedical industries, and business services. In fact, between 1980 and 1996 employment in information technology in private industries grew by 178 per cent in the metro area (Henry 2000; Friedman 2000).

Socially, the ethnic and racial composition of the Washington area has traditionally included a large presence of African-Americans and non-Hispanic whites at the expense of other ethnic groups. Further, since the 1970s, the region has had a strong African-American working and middle-class dominating government institutions both in the District of Columbia and Prince George's County. Starting in the 1990s, however, such dichotomous racial and ethnic landscape began to diversify as the area's increasing minority population, including Latino immigrants, accounted for most of the region's 16 per cent growth. Table 3.2.7 shows 2000 census data on population demographics in the Greater Washington area.

It is a well known fact that the region is racially segregated and the District itself has been traditionally perceived as a southern city. Sixteen Street, NW marks the racial divide with most whites living in western neighborhoods and most blacks living on the east side of the city, only recently separated by a growing belt of Hispanic newcomers. Precisely because of this black and white dichotomous landscape, Latino immigration to the area went largely unnoticed during the fifties and sixties when a few Cubans and Dominicans opened the first Latino businesses in the neighborhood of Adams Morgan in the District. Therefore, the changes in the local economy throughout much of the seventies and eighties coincided with a massive population gain in the area that included documented and undocumented immigrants from developing countries.

Following this trend, by the mid-1980s, the area had become home to one of the largest concentrations of Central Americans, the fourth largest settlement of Koreans in the US, and the largest Ethiopian community outside of Africa (Landolt 2000). Such massive population growth translated into a dramatic increase of Latinos. In fact, during the 1980s and 1990s, Washington Latinos grew by 96 and 90 per cent respectively (US Census Bureau 1990, 2000). As highlighted earlier, Central and South Americans remain the fastest growing segment of Latinos nationwide, and they are major contributors to the Washington metro area growth. Approximately 70 per cent of all Washington Latinos are of South and/or Central American origin and Salvadorans, Peruvians, and Bolivians show numerical dominance with the largest numbers of businesses in the area (US Census Bureau 2006; Economic Census 2002; Pessar 1995).[15] In fact, certain suburban areas show exceedingly high proportions of Central and South Americans. Such is the case of Langley Park in Maryland, or Culmore, Arlington, and Alexandria in Northern Virginia, where Central and South Americans predominate within the Latino population.[16]

Strikingly, most of the population growth in the region has taken place in the suburbs. From 1950 to date, the District of Columbia has been consistently loosing residents while the suburbs have been expanding at an unabated pace. From 1970 to 2007 the area's population has almost tripled, increasing from nearly 3 million to over 8 million residents with the suburbs experiencing all of the area's growth. Official estimates show that nine out of ten immigrants choose to settle in the suburbs first and not in the city, and that over 85 per cent of Latino businesses concentrate in the Northern Virginia and Maryland suburbs (US Census Bureau 2006).

Undisputedly, over the past two decades, the Greater Washington region has acquired prominence as an "emerging immigrant gateway"; a term that Singer et al. have coined to describe metropolitan areas which, over the past twenty-five years, have shown rapidly growing immigrant populations (2008). According to 2005 ACS data, Greater Washington ranks seven in the number of foreign born residents with a total of 1,016,221 immigrants. Specifically, the area is home to a highly diverse immigrant population, partly because of refugee resettlement in the region starting in the 1980s. Thus, this wide range of immigrant diversity gives place to pockets of Latino settlements and businesses embedded in multi-ethnic/racial urban and suburban neighborhoods.

TABLE 3.2.7 Racial and Ethnic Composition of the Population in the Washington Metro Area, 2000.

	Non-Hispanic Whites	Latinos	African-Americans	Asian-Americans
District of Columbia	30%	8%	61%	1%
Virginia	70%	5%	20%	4%
Fairfax County	64%	11%	9%	14%
Arlington County	60%	19%	9%	10%
City of Alexandria	58%	15%	22%	6%
Loudoun County	80%	6%	7%	6%
Prince William County	65%	10%	19%	5%
Maryland	64%	4%	28%	4%
Montgomery County	63%	11%	15%	11%
Prince George's County	27%	7%	62%	4%

Source: US Department of Commerce, Bureau of the Census, 2000 Census of Population and Housing, Summary File 1 (SF1).

Adding complexity to the picture, Greater Washington also presents a uniquely "fragmented" Latino community with many national origin groups despite the numerical preponderance of Salvadorans. Likewise, because of its decentralized suburban/urban metropolitan landscape, including its fragmented governance structure, the region presents special challenges for, and uneven responses to, immigrant integration. Social tensions and uneven responses towards immigrants has become increasingly noticeable after the 9/11 terrorist attacks. The following chapter will examine the opportunity structure and business environment the region offers to Latino entrepreneurs.

Endnotes

1. Central Americans constitute 8.2 per cent of the total US Hispanic population and Salvadorans make up 41 per cent of this share. Mexicans lead the way with 65.5 per cent of the total U.S. Hispanic population, Puerto Ricans make up 8.6 per cent, and South Americans make up 6.0 per cent, with Peruvians representing as much as 18 per cent of this share. Latest Census data show that Mexicans, Central and South Americans are gaining numerical dominance in detriment of Cubans and Puerto Ricans who are decreasing their share because of lower levels of new migrants.
2. Early queries on 2000 Census data showed that information on Latino populations was skewed. In fact, officials in various cities claimed the bureau had significantly

underestimated the size of several groups, including Dominicans and Colombians. It seems that large numbers of Latinos failed to identify themselves as belonging to any specific Latino group. Demographers traced the problem to the rewording of a census question about Hispanic ethnicity.

3. Salvadorans use the term 'Department' to convey the idea of municipality or province.

4. Economic Census categories for Latino-owned small businesses have changed through the years. Whereas the 1997 Economic Census included Mexican, Hispanic Latin American (previously called Central or South American), Cuban, Puerto Rican, Other Spanish/ Hispanic and Spaniard (previously European Spanish), the latest 2002 Census only distinguishes between four categories: 1) Mexican, Mexican-American, and Chicano; 2) Puerto Rican; 3) Cuban; and 4) Other Spanish/Hispanic/Latino.

5. Several changes to the economic census survey methodology make the data for 2002 not directly comparable to previous survey years, and thus exact estimates of change are not available. Yet, trends shown at the aggregate level seem reliable. Hispanic Latin American's share has grown from 21 to 24 per cent and Other Hispanics from 7 to 15 per cent respectively. Cubans', Mexicans', Puerto Ricans', and Spaniards' share has decreased, although such data should be used with caution because of the methodological limitations described before.

6. Based on 1990 Census data, Barkan estimates Salvadoran women and men's self-employment rate to be 5.9 and 3.8 per cent, respectively. In a different analysis, based on March 2000 CPS data, Camarota reports Salvadorans' self-employment rate to be as low as 2.4 per cent and Peruvians' as high as 13.5 per cent. Somewhat in the middle, based on 1990 Census data on the Foreign-Born population, Light and Gold estimate Salvadorans' self-employment rate at 4.9 per cent and Peruvians' at 6.9 per cent.

7. Self-employment rates depict self-employed individuals of a particular ethnic group as percentage of total employed. To calculate self-employment rates for particular ancestry groups, analysts divide the number of self-employed persons in the group by the total size of the group, and multiply it by 1,000. The total self-employment rate is partly a function of the sex ratio of the group and, therefore, it can be subject to slight variations. If the group were female-dominated, then it would have a slightly lower self-employment rate than if male-preponderant.

8. Even back in the early 1990s, Repak's research claimed that 200,000 Central Americans alone resided in the Washington DC area (Repak, 1995:33).

9. El Salvador, Mexico, and Peru are the leading Latin American source countries in the Washington metropolitan region. Further, El Salvador ranked number one among the top 10 immigrant-sending countries to the area. See Singer, A. et al. (2008).

10. Journalists brought Intipucá to public attention as early as 1979. In 1986, Salvadoran sociologist Segundo Montes conducted survey research in Intipucá and among Salvadorans in

DC and, throughout the 1980s and 1990s, journalists from all over the world reported on Intipucá and its unique ties to DC.

11. The Washington Post, Harvard University, and the Kaiser Foundation conducted a phone survey of Washington Latinos between the months of June and August of 2000. 603 Latino adults were interviewed in either Spanish and/or English across the metro area and compared to a control group of 309 Washington non-Latinos and to a national sample of 1,814 Latinos and 1,888 non-Latinos. See the Washington Post, January 2000.

12. "Arlandria" is the geographical area where Alexandria and Arlington converge. This neighborhood is home to one of the Latino communities with highest density of Salvadoran residents and businesses.

13. Interstate 495 encircles Washington DC and is commonly referred to as the Capital Beltway.

14. In Virginia, Other Spanish/Hispanic Latinos own 67.3 per cent of all Latino businesses while in Maryland and in the District of Columbia they own 74.6 and 66.6 per cent, respectively (Economic Census, 2002).

15. In her research on Latino-owned businesses in the DC area, Pessar's ethno-survey indicated that Salvadorans, Peruvians, and Bolivians remained the top three groups with higher representation in the area's small business community. El Salvador is the indisputable top country of birth for immigrants to the District of Columbia as well as to the Northern Virginia and Maryland suburbs. Peru figures as the only other South American nation among the top ten countries of birth for immigrants to Virginia, the District of Columbia, and Maryland.

16. South and Central Americans constitute 90 per cent of the Langley Park, 88 per cent of the Bailey Crossroads, 87 per cent of the Arlington County, 83 per cent of the Alexandria, 81 per cent of the Fairfax and Montgomery Counties, and 81 per cent of the District of Columbia Latino population (2000 Census).

References

Altamirano, T. 2003. *El Perú y el Ecuador: Nuevos Paises de Emigración*. Universidad Andina Simón Bolivar 2003 [Accessed June 20 2008]. Available from http://www.uasb.edu.ec/padh/revista7/articulos/teofilo%20altamirano.htm.

Friedman, S. 2000. Behind the Monuments: Taking a Sociological Look at Life in the Nation's Capital. *Footnotes*.

Gelles, P., and W. Martinez. 1992. Transnational Fiesta. Berkeley, CA: University of California Extension, Center for Media and Independent Learning.

Henry, S. 2000. Digital Capital: Bear this in Mind: Domain is Destiny. *Washington Post*, May 8.

Julca, A. 2001. Peruvian Networks for Migration in New York City's Labor Market, 1970–1996. In *Migration, Transnationalization, and Race in a Changing New York*, edited by H. Cordero-Guzmán, R. Smith and R. Grosfoguel. Philadelphia: Temple University Press.

Kingsley, T., K. S. Pettit, and C. Hayes. 1998. *Washington Baseline: Key Indicators for the Nation's Capital*. Washington, DC: The Urban Institute.

Levitt, P. 2001. *The Transnational Villagers*. Berkeley: University of California Press.

Light, I., and S. Gold. 2000. *Ethnic Economies*. San Diego: Academic Press.

Mahler, S. 1995. *American Dreaming: Immigrant Life on the Margins*. Princeton: Princeton University Press.

Manning, R. D. 1998. Multicultural Washington, DC: The Changing Social and Economic Landscape of a Post-Industrial City. *Ethnic & Racial Studies* 21:328–355.

Marticorena, P. A. Landolt. 2001. The Causes and Consequences of Transnational Migration: Salvadorans in Los Angeles and Washington, DC. *Ph.D. diss.* Balti-more: Johns Hopkins University.

Menjivar, C. 2000. *Fragmented Ties: Salvadoran Immigrant Networks in America*. Berkeley: University of California Press.

Monaghan, J. 1973. *Chile, Peru, and the California Gold Rush of 1849*. Berkeley: University of California Press.

Organización Internacional para las Migraciones. 2008. DIGEMIN. Perú: Estadísticas de la Migración Internacional de Peruanos, 1990–2007: Dirección General de Migraciones y Naturalización, Instituto Nacional de Estadísticas e Información, Lima.

Pedersen, D. 2001. In Pursuit of American Value: Credibility, Credulity and Credit in El Salvador and the United States (Unpublished Manuscript).

Pessar, P. 1995. The Elusive Enclave: Ethnicity, Class and Nationality among Latino Entrepreneurs in Greater Washington DC. *Human Organization* 54 (4):383–392.

Portes, A., and R. D. Manning. 1986. The Immigrant Enclave: Theory and Empirical Examples. In *Competitive Ethnic Relations*, edited by S. Olzack and J. Nagel. FL: Academic Press.

Repak, T. 1995. *Waiting On Washington: Central American Workers in the Nation's Capital*. Philadelphia: Temple University Press.

Rouse, R. 1991. Mexican Migration and the Social Space of Postmodernism. *Diaspora: A Journal of Transnational Studies* 1 (1):8–23.

Singer, A., S. Friedman, I. Cheung, and M. Price. 2001. The World in a Zip Code: Greater Washington DC as a New Region of Immigration. In *The Brookings Institution Survey Series*. Washington, DC: Center on Urban & Metropolitan Policy, Brookings Greater Washington Research Program.

Singer, A., S. W. Hardwick, and C. B. Brettel, eds. 2008. *Twenty-First-Century Gateways: Immigrant Incorporation in Suburban America*. Washington, DC: Brookings Institution Press.

US Bureau of the Census. 2007. The American Community—Hispanics: 2004. American Community Survey Reports: Washington DC: US Department of Commerce.

———. 2006. American Community Survey. Selected Population Profile in the United States. S0201 Washington, DC: US Government Printing Office.

———. 2000. Census of Population and Housing. United States: Summary Tape File 1 (SF1).

———. 1992, 1990. Census of Population, General Social and Economic Characteristics, DC Report: Washington, DC: US Government Printing Office.

———. 2003, 2000. Census of Population: The Foreign-Born Population in the United States. 2000 CP-3-1: Washington, DC: US Government Printing Office.

———. 2000. Current Population Report, March: Washington, DC: US Government Printing Office.

———. 1996, 1992. Survey of Minority and Women-Owned Business Enterprises, Hispanics: Washington, DC: US Government Printing Office.

———. 2001, 1997 Survey of Minority and Women-Owned Business Enterprises, Hispanics: Washington, DC: US Government Printing Office.

———. 2006, 2002 Survey of Minority and Women-Owned Business Enterprises, Hispanics: Washington, DC: US Government Printing Office.

US Dept. of Commerce, Bureau of the Census. *Census of Population and Housing, 1990*. United States: Summary Tape File 4B. Computer File. ICPSR version. Washington, DC: US Government Printing Office.

Vazquez, M. A., C. E. Seales, and M. Friedmann Marquardt. 2008. New Latino Destinations. In *Latinas/os in the United States: Changing the Face of America*, edited by H. Rodriguez, R. Saenz and C. Menjivar. Secaucus, NJ: Springer.

◼ Reading 3.2

Define the following concepts/phrases:

cash remittances

transnational migration

transnational migrant circuit

self-employment rate

Answer the following questions:

1. Describe the demographic estimates for the Salvadorian and Peruvian populations and compare them with other immigrant groups.
2. Identify the settlement areas for Salvadorians and Peruvians.
3. Using Table 3.2.1, compare the median family incomes for both groups and compare them with white median family income.
4. Using Table 3.2.2, compare educational attainment and male/female ratio in both communities.
5. Analyse the self-employment rates of four Latino immigrant groups using Table 3.2.3, and discuss the importance of this variable.
6. Why did the greater Washington, D. C. area become a magnet for Peruvian and Salvadorian immigrants?
7. Analyzing the data from Tables 3.2.1–3.2.4, describe the socio-economic profiles of Salvadorians and Peruvians.

Part IV

Asserting Their Rights: Latinos and Their Quest for Inclusion

Viva la Raza

Urban Latinos and the Chicano Movement

Steven W. Bender

Every man who comes to the picket line is our brother, immediately, regardless of color.

—César Chávez[1]

H ISTORIAN IGNACIO GARCÍA DOCUMENTED THE VIVA Kennedy campaign at the start of the 1960s that prompted Mexican Americans throughout California, the Southwest, and the upper Midwest to form Viva Kennedy clubs in aid of John Kennedy's 1960 presidential campaign.[2] As García observed, Mexican American activists had not yet looked within the barrio for inspiration for their reformist ideals—their 1960 dream was in search of Camelot, not a separatist Aztlán.[3]

During the 1960s, César Chávez's farm labor movement was a class-based struggle that aimed beyond the Mexican American community in attracting membership and support. Among the workers represented by Chávez were Filipinos and Anglos; moreover, Anglo supporters of the farm workers union included the Kennedys as well as Hollywood entertainment notables such as Steve Allen. The farm labor struggle engaged a broad coalition but with its rural foundation did not resonate as much with urban youth.[4] By contrast, urban Mexican American youth in large part propelled the so-called Chicano Movement that emerged in the late 1960s.

The Chicano Movement was an urban-based awakening of activists and youth channeled through such events as protests of urban school conditions and the Vietnam War, and by the political uprising that formed a separatist Chicano political party. The movement was marked by a nationalist orientation toward self-determination and anti-assimilationism that sometimes was hostile toward Anglos. For example, the movement's manifesto from 1969, "El Plan Espiritual de Aztlán," declared:

> Brotherhood unites us, and love for our brothers makes us a people whose time has come and who struggles against the foreigner "gabacho" [Anglo] who exploits our riches and destroys our culture. ... We are a bronze people with a bronze culture.

Before the world, before all of North America, before all our brothers in the bronze continent, we are a nation, we are a union of free pueblos, we are Aztlan....

Nationalism as the key of organization transcends all religious, political, class, and economic factions or boundaries. Nationalism is the common denominator that all members of La Raza [the Mexican race] can agree upon.[5]

By the late 1960s, Mexican Americans made up 67 percent of California's farm workers, with only 12 percent of the farm labor force Anglos.[6] In leading the United Farm Workers union, Chávez often invoked Mexican American influences—for example, the union flag portrayed an Aztec eagle, the farm worker theme song was *De Colores*, a religious song in Spanish, and the union's rallying calls were in Spanish: "¡Viva La Huelga [strike]!," "¡Viva La Causa [the movement for farm worker justice]!" and "¡Sí Se Puede [we can do it]!" Still, Chávez lamented about the budding nationalism of the Chicano Movement in contrast to the colorblind aspirations of the farm labor struggle:

[I]f we wanted civil rights for us, then we certainly had to respect the rights of blacks, Jews, and other minorities.... That's why today we oppose some of this La Raza business [in the Chicano Movement] so much. When La Raza means or implies racism, we don't support it. But if it means our struggle, our dignity, or our cultural roots, then we're for it.... [W]e can't be against racism on the one hand and for it on the other....

[At the time of my earlier involvement with the Community Service Organization,] the constitution of most [barrio-based] groups said members had to be Mexican, but our [union] constitution had no color, race, religion or any other restrictions, and we stuck to it."[7]

Expressing his movement goals in broader terms than the struggles of just Mexican American workers, Chávez also questioned: "La Raza? Why be racist? Our belief is to help everyone, not just one race. Humanity is our belief."[8]

Harboring fear that nationalism eventually would splinter opportunities for coalition as well as fracture the Mexican American community itself, Chávez explained: "I hear about *la raza* more and more. Some people don't look at it as racism, but when you say *la raza*, you are saying an anti-gringo thing, and our fear is that it won't stop there. Today it's anti-gringo, tomorrow it will be anti-Negro, and the day after it will be anti-Filipino, anti–Puerto Rican. And then it will be anti–poor-Mexican, and anti–darker-skinned Mexican."[9]

Chávez faced the pressures of nationalism in his own movement—particularly when the Mexican American–dominated union he led, the National Farm Workers Association, united in 1966 with the Filipino union, the Agricultural Workers Organizing Committee, to form a single union with greater clout. Chávez held his ground that Filipinos must be represented in union leadership, despite some Mexican Americans who were ready to leave the union in protest. As one author explained, Chávez from the beginning "had not thought of La Causa as a movement that would be motivated primarily by appeals to race or nationality."[10]

The Chicano Movement peaked between 1968 and 1973.[11] Although I do not contend that the assassination of Robert Kennedy prompted the heyday of the Chicano Movement, I nonetheless suggest that some of the nationalism that emerged in that movement was a reaction to the sentiment that the potential for Mexican Americans to find Camelot with other Americans died with Kennedy in 1968. This change in attitude was captured best in a memorial procession for Kennedy at dusk through the streets of East Los Angeles. Members of the Brown Berets, a Chicano youth group described unflatteringly by the *Los Angeles Times* as "militant," marched in the procession and sang "We Shall Overcome." As night overtook the marchers on their way to the East Los Angeles Junior College Stadium, Brown Beret members lit flaming torches to guide the journey. At the Stadium mass, leader of the Brown Berets David Sánchez lamented "It is a time of real mourning. He was our last hope. There will be no more outside help for us."[12] While serving a jail term in early 1968 for unlawful assembly, Sánchez struck chords of nationalist contempt, warning the Brown Berets to avoid "Anglos," and commanding "Do not talk to the [Anglo] enemy, for he is either a dog or a devil."[13]

Despite the potential for coalition with African Americans, at times the Chicano Movement excluded black participation as well. For example, in announcing that Martin Luther King, Jr. was invited to attend his land rights convention, Chicano Movement icon Reies López Tijerina cautioned "[W]e are only going to admit the Negroes when Martin Luther King speaks. After that they have to get out, because the convention belongs to our *raza*."[14]

* * *

A defining episode of the Chicano Movement was the 1968 school "blowouts" in East Los Angeles. By that time, almost every East Los Angeles resident was Mexican American—87 percent bore Spanish surnames and of those an estimated 95 percent were Mexican American.[15] In early March 1968, thousands of mostly Mexican American students walked out of Garfield, Roosevelt, Lincoln, and other barrio high schools, voicing demands that included bilingual education, more Mexican teachers, and reduced class sizes.[16] In the same days that Chávez fasted in rural Delano to aid the struggle of farm worker equality, Chicano students were leading their own urban strike against inequality in the classrooms. While in California to celebrate the end of Chávez's fast in March 1968, Robert Kennedy bridged these urban and rural struggles of Mexican Americans by meeting in East Los Angeles with the student leaders of the blowouts and expressing his support for their cause: "He knew all about the walkouts.... He had a list of our demands ... and he told us that he supported everything that we did."[17]

Kennedy's embrace of the organizers of the East Los Angeles school blowouts in 1968 reflected his imperatives of educating youth effectively and creating opportunities for them. It is unclear, however, what tools the federal government could wield in relieving the conditions that led to the blowout. The impetus for school reforms was a grassroots movement intended to assert community control over localized issues of cultural competency and educational funding, and federal law would have little influence here. Further, the concurrent move to establish Chicano Studies programs and Mexican American support networks at colleges was far removed from federal prerogatives. But the federal government played a role in bilingual education, funding these programs in legislation cosponsored by Robert Kennedy, and presidential leadership intersected with the Chicano Movement in other respects such as the war in Vietnam and economic programs and policies for the inner cities.

As the Chicano Movement blossomed, student activism followed a nationalist path, evidenced best by the genesis of the above-quoted "Plan Espiritual de Aztlán" at the Chicano Youth Liberation Conference, held in March 1969 in Denver, and the production of the blueprint for college Chicano Studies programs, "El Plan de Santa Barbara," drawn at a conference held in Santa Barbara in April 1969.[18] Historian Juan Gómez Quiñones asserted the significance of the Denver student conference as signaling "a break at a national level from the assimilationist 'Mexican American' consciousness and politics of the previous decades,"[19] instead substituting a new nationalist ideology. Similarly, the "Plan de Santa Barbara" expressed an anti-assimilationist ideology for the Chicano community by stating: "Cultural nationalism is a means of total Chicano liberation."[20]

* * *

In addition to the nationalism that marked the Chicano Movement, the occasional punctuations of violence that accompanied events loosely grouped within the movement were contrary to principles espoused by Chávez and the farm labor movement. Although there was no organized agenda of violence in the Chicano Movement, its galvanizing document, "El Plan Espiritual de Aztlán," invoked a Malcolm X–like message of community defense in advocating "[s]elf defense against the occupying forces of the oppressors at every school, every available man, woman, and child." The Brown Beret group also mirrored the philosophy of Black Power leaders by calling for use of "any and all means necessary ... to resolve the frustrations of our people."[21] Among the episodes of violence that erupted in the movement were those of the fringe group Chicano Liberation Front that took credit for bombing government targets in Los Angeles in 1971, and the land grant movement, led in New Mexico by Reies López Tijerina, that triggered the kidnapping of law enforcement officers and later a jailhouse shooting in a failed effort to make an armed citizen's arrest of a reticent district attorney.[22] Rioting also flared occasionally in East Los Angeles in 1970 and 1971, leading to several confrontations with local police. As a Los Angeles television station editorialized critically about one of these episodes:

About a thousand angry youth, perhaps inflamed by [antiwar] rally speeches, certainly frustrated by the ghetto conditions in which they live, turned to meaningless destruction and violence....

The Mexican American community is a vitally important part of our Southern California society. But such immature displays by a minority of the citizens there are major obstacles in keeping it from gaining the position of respect it deserves.[23]

As discussed previously, Chávez adhered steadfastly to the nonviolence principles of Gandhi. Robert Kennedy also preached a nonviolent ethos, declaring flatly that "violence will bring no answer" while addressing farm workers at the end of Chávez's 1968 hunger fast. In his 1967 book *To Seek a Newer World*, Kennedy similarly condemned violence as a means of social change:

[Urban violence] is the most destructive and self-defeating of attempts. This is no revolution. The word means to seize power, but the advocates of violence are not going to overthrow the American government; when Rap Brown threatens "to burn America down," he is not a revolutionary, he is an anarchist. The end is not a better life for Negroes, but a devastated America; as William Pfaff has said, "a program of death, not life." So it has already proven, all over the face of America.[24]

Although it is hard to pinpoint its precise date of birth,[25] the late 1960s and particularly the early 1970s saw the rise (and rapid fall) of La Raza Unida (the united race) Party, another defining facet of the Chicano Movement. La Raza Unida is said to be the first political party to have represented a single ethnic group,[26] as its membership was almost exclusively Mexican American. Although evolving over time and varying locally in California, Texas, and the other states of its presence, La Raza Unida's party platform tended to advocate national health care, immediate withdrawal from Vietnam (where Latino soldiers were dying in disproportionate numbers), bilingual/bicultural education, abolition of the death penalty, and reform of the tax system, including repealing regressive sales taxes.[27] La Raza Unida Party counted successes primarily in Texas, where it achieved local victories, gained control of the Crystal City school board, and placed two members on the five-member Crystal City council.[28] In two other Texas towns, La Raza Unida party members won election to the mayor's office.[29]

Conflicts emerged quickly within La Raza Unida Party over its nationalism and its relationship to the Democratic and Republican parties. At a 1972 party conference in California, for example, membership rejected a proposal to convert La Raza Unida into a multiracial "people's party."[30] Generally the party's positions followed themes of anti-assimilationism and self-determination.[31] At La Raza Unida's national convention in 1972, party organizer Rodolfo "Corky" Gonzales (the former head of the 1960 Viva Kennedy Club in Colorado)[32] reflected the distance from the two national mainstream parties in describing them as "a monster with two heads [Republican and Democrat] that feed from the same trough."[33] In late December 1969, a co-organizer of the party, José Angel Gutiérrez, declared that "Democrats and the Republicans are all alike. They are all Gringos ... neither party has ever delivered for the Chicano ... both parties have promised a hell of a lot, but neither has delivered. Now we as Chicanos are calling their bluff.... [T]he only viable alternative is to look into political strategies which will yield maximum benefits for la Raza."[34]

The northern California chapter of La Raza Unida ultimately passed a motion that "La Raza Unida will not support any candidate of the Democratic or Republican Party or any individual who supports these parties."[35] The tension of whether La Raza Unida would function as a bona fide third party or instead would lend its support to mainstream party candidates who best served its platform existed throughout La Raza Unida's brief political life in the early 1970s. Representing this tension was the uneasy relationship between La Raza Unida and César Chávez. Chávez had a history of alliance with the Democratic Party, highlighted by his support of Robert Kennedy but also evidenced by his endorsement of other local, state, and national Democratic candidates, such as George McGovern's 1972 presidential campaign. Further, Chávez had distanced himself from the nationalistic advocacy of the Chicano Movement. To the organizers of La Raza Unida, then, Chávez must have represented the old guard assimilationist Mexican American with close ties to the Democratic Party "monster."

The strained relationship between Chávez and La Raza Unida party leadership became national news during the late summer 1972 campaign for the presidency between incumbent Nixon and Democrat George McGovern. Holding the party's national convention in El Paso in early September 1972, La Raza party leaders invited Chávez, along with Nixon and McGovern, to address the convention; none ultimately attended. Party leaders imposed conditions on Chávez that led him to decline; among them was that Chávez could only discuss the Chicano Movement and not McGovern's candidacy.[36] The *Washington Post* reported that "La Raza Unida Party leadership apparently has severed its loose ties with farm labor leader Cesar Chavez over Chavez's announced support for presidential candidate George McGovern and over his longtime connection with the Democratic Party."[37] One party leader attacked Chávez, singling out his alleged failure to assist young Chicanos, while others in the party accused Chávez of being a "one-issue" leader more relevant to the rural labor struggle than the more comprehensive Chicano Movement.[38]

Democratic Party leaders were attacked along with Chávez. During the 1972 presidential campaign, La Raza Unida members heckled Senator Edward Kennedy when he came to an East Los Angeles College rally for McGovern. They carried signs such as "Kennedy and McGovern are carpetbaggers and political pimps," "What have we gained from the Democrats?" and "Raza, sí, Kennedy no."[39] As author Tony Castro opined:

It is significant that the brother of President Kennedy and Robert Kennedy, both of whom had been revered and elevated to a kind of sainthood by Mexican Americans, should be so harshly treated by even a small segment of that same minority group. For if anyone represented the unfulfilled hopes of the Chicanos during the past dozen years [the 1960s and early 1970s], it was the Kennedys, whose own tragedy had served only to magnify the despair and frustrations of the Chicanos and others who had attached their own aspirations to the promise the Kennedys extended.[40]

La Raza Unida Party criticism of Chávez reflected the growing divide between the causes of urban and rural Latinos, particularly within the Mexican American community. Nixon's campaign exploited the rift, with Nixon's top Latino campaigner contending that Chávez represented only the small percentage of Mexican Americans who were field workers, and challenging Chávez: "He speaks for only 5 percent of the Spanish-speaking people in the country. I'm concerned about the other 95 percent. He's not. I'm concerned about the Mexican Americans in East Los Angeles and other urban areas. When has he ever done anything for the urban Mexican American?"[41]

Chávez avenged the hostility directed at him by La Raza Unida Party organizers by helping to defeat La Raza Unida candidates in Los Angeles in the 1970s. Dolores Huerta explained the union's position as stemming from the acceptance of money by La Raza Unida candidates from the Nixon campaign in order to attack the farm workers union.[42] McGovern also accused La Raza Unida of accepting money from Republicans in exchange for its neutrality in the 1972 race.[43] A McGovern representative contended that Nixon promised Crystal City, Texas, officials a medical clinic in exchange for votes.[44] Nixon campaign strategy documents boldly suggested that the Republicans assist the nationalist Mexican American party in order to pull votes from the Democrats.[45] Allegations of support from the Nixon campaign are not surprising given that at the time that La Raza Unida was formed as a predominantly Mexican American party, 85 percent of Mexican American voters were registered as Democrats. The Republican Party clearly stood to gain the most from La Raza Unida votes that likely otherwise would have gone to Democratic candidates. Still, La Raza Unida posed no real sustained threat to the Democratic Party, "declining rapidly"[46] after 1973 from its internal power struggles, having managed only a few years of localized political viability from perhaps 1970 until 1973.

* * *

The Chicano Movement faded as the Chicano political party flickered out. By the mid-1970s, the Vietnam War finally ended, La Raza Unida Party lost favor, and New Mexico land movement icon Reies López Tijerina was jailed, all contributing to derailment of the struggle. As the urban-based Chicano Movement lost momentum, so too did the rural organizing of farm workers. Ironically, as the Chicano Movement and the farm worker La Causa movement separated over such fault lines as urban nationalism and Chávez's support for the Democratic Party, the lack of cohesion accelerated their declines. The urban-rural Latino divide became even more pronounced in the 1980s. Perhaps, though, in the mid-1990s, California's divisive anti-immigrant initiative, Proposition 187, helped to restore a galvanizing pro-immigrant and pro-farm worker consciousness among Latinos that helped unite urban and rural interests. By that time, undocumented Latino workers dominated the agricultural workforce, and were the target of this backlash initiative attacking their health and education. Many urban Latinos came to realize that no matter how separated they were from their migrant worker backgrounds of past generations, the voting public viewed all Latinos as a work force to be exploited, then discarded if they caused trouble, needed services, or tried to forge a culture or community in the United States. This consciousness connecting the urban Latino to the rural farm worker offers the possibility of political unity on issues of crucial relevance to Latinos—immigration, health care, fair labor laws, education, recognition of culture, and the other building blocks of community and dignity [...].

Endnotes

1. Hammerback and Jensen, *Rhetorical Career*, 84. Nevertheless, César Chávez did employ symbols of Mexican pride, such as the Virgen de Guadalupe, in his organizing efforts. Ian F. Haney López, *Racism on Trial: The Chicano Fight for Justice* (Cambridge, MA: Belknap Press, 2003), 158.
2. García, *Viva Kennedy*.
3. Ibid., 84.
4. See Carlos Muñoz, Jr., *Youth, Identity, Power: The Chicano Movement* (New York: Verso, 1989), 60.
5. Mario Barrera, *Beyond Aztlan: Ethnic Autonomy in Comparative Perspective* (Notre Dame, IN: University of Notre Dame Press, 1988), 37–38.
6. Carlos Ynostronza, "The Farm Worker—The Beginning of a New Awareness," 20 *American University Law Review* (1970): 39, 40–41.
7. Levy, *Cesar Chavez*, 123.
8. Del Castillo and Garcia, *Triumph of Spirit*, 154.
9. Matthiessen, *Sal Si Puedes*, 143.
10. Richard W. Etulain ed., *César Chávez: A Brief Biography with Documents* (Boston: Bedford/ St. Martin's, 2002), 93 (also noting that Chávez had confronted nationalism in fighting doggedly for inclusion of blacks in the CSO, where he started his organizing career).
11. Barrera, *Beyond Aztlan*, 45.
12. Doug Shuit and Dial Torgerson, "Southland Observances Pay Final Respects to Kennedy," *Los Angeles Times*, June 9, 1968, B1.
13. Chávez, *Raza Primero*, 46.

14. Suzanne Oboler, *Ethnic Labels, Latino Lives: Identity and the Politics of (Re)Presentation in the United States* (Minneapolis: University of Minnesota Press, 1995), 63.

15. López, *Racism on Trial*, 16 (observing that by 2000, 97 percent of residents in East Los Angeles were Latino). The white flight from the East Los Angeles area took off in earnest during the years I resided there—in 1960, its Spanish-surname population was 66 percent, but by 1965, the Spanish-surname population had increased to 76 percent as the overall area population declined. Progress Report, Mexican American Study Project, Division of Research Graduate School of Business Administration, University of California, Los Angeles, June 1996.

16. López, *Racism on Trial*, 20–21; the Garfield High School Student Demands, printed on March 7, 1968, included:

    1. Class size will be reduced so that teachers can be more effective in the classroom and devote more time to each student....
    2. New high schools in the area to be built immediately. The present local schools should be renamed to help establish community identity.
    3. All counselors should be able to speak Spanish.
       ...
    12. Teachers should become more aware of the social and economic problems of the community. (Gerald Paul Rosen, *Political Ideology and the Chicano Movement: A Study of the Political Ideology of Activists in the Chicano Movement* [San Francisco: R and E Research Associates, 1975], appendix 2, 139).

    Although California schools later implemented bilingual education programs, California voters in 1998 passed an anti–bilingual education initiative to eradicate bilingual programs absent a carefully prescribed parental waiver allowance.

17. Chicano! History of the Mexican American Civil Rights Movement (NLCC Educational Media, 1996), part 3. A Chicano scholar reacted negatively to Kennedy's visit as reflecting more unfulfilled promise in the barrio: "Oh, joy! Oh, happiness! Oh Nirvana! One more person listened.... Let's see now, that makes the U.S. Commission on Civil Rights ... the secretaries of the Interior, Housing, Agriculture ... and President Johnson have listened ... police departments have listened, etc., etc." García, *Chicanismo*, 41 (letter to editor by scholar Octavio Romano). One writer claims that Kennedy contributed $10,000 to the legal defense fund of thirteen students and activists charged a couple months after the East Los Angeles walkouts with the felony of conspiring to disturb the peace (Burton Moore, *Love and Riot: Oscar Zeta Acosta and the Great Mexican American Revolt* [Mountain View, CA: Floricanto Press, 2003], 39–40), charges that were later dropped when these defendants prevailed on First Amendment grounds in their appeal; see López, *Racism on Trial*

and *Castro v. Superior Court*, 9 Cal. App. 3d 675, 88 Cal. Rptr. 500 (1970). Despite Kennedy's affinity for these students, any contribution seems unlikely given the timeline in which the leaders were arrested—late night Friday, May 31—and that Kennedy was killed a few days later. Carlos Muñoz, one of those arrested, remembers that Senator McCarthy did make a sizable contribution to the defense fund. Interview with Dr. Carlos Muñoz, Jr., Oct. 1, 2005.

18. In 1968 the first campus Chicano Studies department, at California State College in Los Angeles, was founded, in response to the Mexican American student protest. Rosales, *Chicano!*, 253.

19. Quiñones, *Chicano Politics*, 123.

20. Barrera, *Beyond Aztlan*, 42.

21. Chávez, *Raza Primero*, 46 (statement of jailed Brown Beret leader David Sánchez).

22. Steven W. Bender and Keith Aoki, "Seekin' the Cause: Social Justice Movements and LatCrit Community," 81 *Oregon Law Review* (2002): 595, 610–611.

23. See Armando Morales, "The 1970–71 East Los Angeles Chicano-Police Riots," in *La Causa Politica*, 401–402 (also containing Morales's response to the editorial, which explained the "point" of the violence in addressing institutional violence in the barrio in the form of police brutality and other roots of the response).

24. Robert F. Kennedy, *To Seek a Newer World* (Garden City, NY: Doubleday, 1967), 27.

25. Ignacio M. García, *United We Win: The Rise and Fall of La Raza Unida Party* (Tucson: University of Arizona, 1989), 20 (suggesting the first La Raza Unida conference took place in El Paso in 1967 with a follow-up conference in San Antonio in 1968, although other sources suggest the political party was unnamed until 1970, including Chávez, *Raza Primero*, 82).

26. Armando Navarro, *La Raza Unida Party: A Chicano Challenge to the U.S. Two-Party Dictatorship* (Philadelphia: Temple University Press, 2000), 263; but see John C. Hammerback, Richard J. Jensen, and José Angel Gutierrez, *A War of Words: Chicano Protest in the 1960s and 1970s* (Westport, CT: Greenwood Press, 1985), 149 (detailing early Mexican American political party efforts in 1890 to form El Partido del Pueblo Unido, and in 1904 to organize the Mexican Liberal party in Missouri).

27. Navarro, *La Raza Unida*, 44; López, *Racism on Trial*, 20.

28. Navarro, *La Raza Unida*, 90.

29. Chávez, *Raza Primero*, 82.

30. Muñoz, *Youth, Identity, Power*, 121.

31. Barrera, *Beyond Aztlan*, 40.

32. García, *Viva Kennedy*, 175.

33. García, *United We Win*, 89.

34. Navarro, *La Raza Unida*, 31.

35. Muñoz, *Youth, Identity, Power*, 107; although La Raza party leaders invited both Nixon and McGovern to address their 1972 national convention, neither attended and at the

convention party members voted for political independence from both party candidates rather than to endorse either candidate. "Raza Unida Won't Back Candidate," *Salinas Californian*, Sept. 4, 1972.

36. Tony Castro, "Chavez, Chicano Party in Split," *Washington Post*, Sept. 3, 1972.
37. Ibid.
38. Ibid.
39. Castro, *Chicano Power*, 24–25.
40. Ibid., 26.
41. Ibid., 103.
42. Rosales, *Chicano!*, 244.
43. Castro, *Chicano Power*, 19.
44. Santillan, *Chicano Politics*, 162.
45. Castro, *Chicano Power*, 19, 202; see also José de la Isla, *The Rise of Hispanic Political Power* (Los Angeles: Archer Books, 2003), 25–26.
46. Muñoz, *Youth, Identity, Power*, 122.

◼ Reading 4.1

Define the following concepts/phrases:

Viva Kennedy club	Chicano movement
farm workers union	Urban movement
political alliance	rural movement
Raza Unida Party	Proposition 187

Answer the following questions:

1. Why did César Chavez and the farm workers union decide to organize a political alliance with the Democratic Party?
2. Why did the Raza Unida Party and the Republican Party establish a temporary political alliance?
3. How did the farm workers union and the Raza Unida Party develop different points of view regarding the organizations of the Mexican American community?
4. What are the main points of the Raza Unida Party agenda?
5. How does Proposition 187 (1990) impact the Mexican American community in California?

New York, Puerto Ricans, and the Dilemmas of Integration

Madeleine E. López

La segregacíon escolar no es constitucional, dice la Corte.

—La Prensa, 18 May 1954

The Supreme Court Rules School Segregation Unconstitutional.

—New York Times, 18 May 1954

T HE IMPACT OF *BROWN V. BOARD of Education* was greater than the justices of the U.S. Supreme Court or the American public could have possibly imagined. Almost immediately, the scope of the ruling expanded beyond the American South and the dismantling of legalized segregation in tax-supported institutions. New York offers a fascinating example. On 24 December 1954 the New York City Board of Education issued a response to the Supreme Court decision, noting: "the board is determined to accept the challenge implicit in the language and spirit of the decision. We will seek a solution to these problems and take action with dispatch."[1] Jim Crow and public school segregation were not simply a southern problem, and educational officials invoked the city's tradition of liberalism to take action.[2]

The doctrine of "separate but equal" did not solely affect African Americans. People of color across the racial spectrum endured segregation in both de facto and de jure forms throughout the country. To date, scholars have devoted little attention to the issue of segregation and the meaning of *Brown* beyond the black–white and southern parameters of traditional civil rights historiography.[3] This bias has marginalized the experiences of other racial and ethnic communities in relationship to Brown and left unexplored the decision's broader ramifications in battles over the desegregation of public schools.

The experience of Puerto Ricans in New York City reflects the multifaceted nature of *Brown* and its broad reach in American life and politics. Puerto Ricans brought new meaning to the struggle for desegregation and the historical implications of the landmark ruling. In this chapter I discuss how Puerto Ricans, at the public policy and grassroots levels, reshaped *Brown* to emphasize the centrality of language, an essential part of their cultural and political identity, in the struggle for educational equality. Puerto Rican educators and community activists interpreted *Brown* on their own terms. Defined by their historical and cultural experiences, Puerto

Ricans made the marker of language, not race, their site of action. This effectively challenged the black–white conception of segregation in New York and forced city education officials to include Puerto Ricans in municipal desegregation efforts. Simultaneously, the reinterpretation of *Brown* revealed the determination of the Puerto Rican community to demand equal educational opportunity for their children. Examining *Brown* from the perspective of New York City and its Puerto Rican community demonstrates how a complete assessment of the decision's full impact has only begun.

Neighborhood Schools

The Second World War and its aftermath brought forth two of the largest demographic changes in the history of the northern United States: the African American Great Migration from the South and the Puerto Rican Great Migration from the island.[4] Because of wartime employment opportunities, between 1940 and 1950 the population of African Americans in New York rose from 328,000 to 750,000.[5] Similarly, 58,500 Puerto Ricans had migrated to the city by 1954, bringing the size of the community to 254,880. A decade earlier, Puerto Ricans numbered in the city only 61,463, and any movement from the island was negligible in official census records.[6] As many European immigrants once had, African Americans and Puerto Ricans arrived in New York City sharing dreams of economic opportunity.[7] Like earlier immigrants, both groups settled into racial and ethnic enclaves, sometimes by choice but most often because institutionalized housing discrimination provided no alternative.[8] As a result, racial and ethnic residential segregation became further entrenched in New York's demographic fabric.

Neighborhood segregation inevitably translated into segregated public schools. To address this situation, city educators and urban planners organized neighborhood schools with four goals in mind: cheap, safe transportation of children; a small school population; learning in a familiar environment; and a close relationship between school and community,[9] a notion strongly supported by the New York State Education Department.[10] State administrators believed that neighborhood schools promoted important educational values, which in turn led to more effective participation by parents and other supportive citizens.[11] Commenting on the importance of neighborhood schools to the life of the city, the state's commissioner of education, James Allen, wrote: "The present difficulty is in the changing character of many neighborhoods, not in the concept itself…. It will take time to correct this situation, to restore racial balance in these areas. In the meantime, the school is the agency that can do something about the problem, which can be modified to overcome the injustices caused by segregation and achieve the educational and social values inherent in integration."[12] Likewise, parents saw neighborhood-based schools as an integral part of community networks and thus fiercely protected their continued existence.

Despite their usefulness, neighborhood schools obviated any implementation of proposed integration efforts in New York City. New York State offered little help in this area, placing all the responsibility on individual school districts.[13] In response, the city took steps to promote educational initiatives rather than address segregation as a systemic issue. For a decade after the *Brown* decision, special service programs such as the "Demonstration Guidance Program" and "Higher Horizons" preoccupied school administrators. While these programs attempted to equalize city schools through additional funding, remedial instruction, counseling, and other special services, little was done to actually desegregate schools.[14] At the heart of the matter were different understandings among administrators and parents of the place that neighborhood schools occupied in the integration process.

While administrators understood neighborhood schools as traditional, safe, and convenient, African American and Puerto Rican parents also expected educational quality. They were keenly aware that such schools tended to be available only outside their own neighborhoods. While parents laid great stress on improving their local schools, they nevertheless reserved the option of placing their children elsewhere until this improvement took place. Such action, however, remained a last resort. African American and Puerto Rican parents would have preferred improvements in their neighborhood schools to transfers and busing. This is why integration plans like Open Enrollment and free transfer plans, or one-way busing, did not work. Instead they exacerbated tensions and were seen by parents as an attempt to circumvent real change.

Parents eventually turned to school boycotts.[15] Pockets of chaos erupted as parents and administrators clashed over which changes needed to take place and how. In 1958 African American parents in Harlem withdrew their children from public schools and created their own freedom school. They rejected busing, the Board of Education's only proposed remedy for inferior, overcrowded facilities. As the movement for integration grew in the early 1960s, boycotts became a powerful negotiating tool.[16] The largest occurred in February 1964, when nearly 500,000 students stayed away from school.[17]

As African American and Puerto Rican parents fought on their children's behalf, school administrators began to criticize the increasing rate of de facto segregation in the ten years following *Brown*. In early 1965 Irving Anker, principal of Benjamin Franklin High School and later the city's schools chancellor, wrote: "The implications for northern public school de facto segregation are most serious because there appears to be a population pattern forcing changes in the schools quite independent of the policies of any one board of education."[18] Recognizing the declining number of white students, administrators increasingly saw the futility of the Board of Education's integration efforts. As Anker stated, "It becomes more and more apparent that each new plan is but a new act of desperation. Failure to recognize this as the central issue—keeping a reasonable proportion of whites in the public schools—will result in continuing school segregation."[19]

In the midst of these disputes, Commissioner Allen ordered the city's superintendent of schools, Calvin Gross, to assume all accountability in matters of school desegregation. In 1963 Allen wrote to Gross, "At this stage the initiative for planning the means for eliminating imbalance is in your hands." He also noted, "Few problems facing the schools in our State and elsewhere have ever given local school officials the opportunity to use their imagination, initiative, leadership and resources in the way this one does."[20] Allen presented desegregation to Gross as an opportunity rather than a problem for local school officials. He ordered the school board to reflect on its progress toward integration. However, Allen continued to define an integrated school as one that that was more than 50 percent white, an impossibility in a racially heterogeneous New York City. Calvin Gross and the Board of Education struggled with this task. This period of confusion marked the beginning of a new regional discussion on racial classification within a black–white dichotomy. Puerto Ricans, like Mexican Americans in Texas who also confronted a narrow racial classification system in the wake of *Brown*, listened to this discussion: despite attempts to marginalize them they took it upon themselves to develop a system for defining racial groups and how they fit into the city's desegregation efforts.[21]

Race and Puerto Ricans

In 1963 the New York City Board of Education published a report entitled "Progress Towards Integration and Plans for the Immediate Future." This report divided school integration goals into two categories: equality of educational and vocational opportunities and the promotion of ethnic integration.[22] Significantly, the report discussed Puerto Ricans and African Americans as one group without distinction. For Gross, the report proved inconclusive because it did not provide clear data; one could not tell which group—Puerto Rican or African American—benefited from the proposed solutions.

Seeking clarification, Gross inquired about the data, which in the past had been collected and reported only for African Americans. Allen replied: "Although my request contemplated information on schools with 50% or more Negroes only, in order to have the total picture for New York City, data on Puerto Rican pupils is also necessary. For each of the schools, report the number and percent of each category, namely Negro, Puerto Rican, Other."[23] His response illustrates several key points: the confusion caused by the city's racial classification system; the difficulty of factoring Puerto Ricans into the state's integration plans; and the slow pace at which the city's demographic reality was officially recognized. That noted, the situation in New York City had compelled Allen to alter his previous request by including Puerto Ricans. This marked the beginning of an effort at the administrative level to effectively address the city's diverse population and was a sign that the black–white parameters of the desegregation debate were beginning to expand.

Simultaneously, Puerto Rican officials in the Migration Division Office of Puerto Rico in New York internally inquired about the steps toward integration. Ralph S. Rosas, who worked in the office, questioned the data given for Puerto Ricans in the "Progress Towards Integration" report. Though he believed in the importance of the report, particularly on the instructional front, he still found the data insufficient, as Puerto Ricans and African Americans remained grouped together. In December 1963 Rosas asked the director of the Migration Division Office, Joseph Monserrat, to inquire about the data and find out which programs specifically targeted and assisted Puerto Rican children. There was apparently no response to this memo.[24]

In the following years, internal debates continued regarding Puerto Ricans and their place in many of the city's proposed projects. Throughout the highest levels of the New York State Education Department, the difficulty of distinguishing between Puerto Ricans and African Americans remained a troubling one. As late as 1968 Lorne H. Woollatt questioned the categorization of Puerto Ricans. Seeking to comply with a data request from the Office of Civil Rights, Woollatt asked which of the five categories described Puerto Ricans: Negro, American Indian, Oriental, Spanish Surnamed American, and Other.[25] In a handwritten note, James Allen himself questioned whether the state should classify Puerto Ricans as "other." After further investigation, Allen wrote to Woollatt on 31 May 1968, explaining that according to the U.S. Department of Health, Education and Welfare the category "Spanish Surnamed American" included "persons considered in school or community to be of Mexican, Central American, South American, Cuban, Puerto Rican, Latin American or other Spanish speaking origin."[26] The Spanish-surnamed category, which ultimately encompassed Puerto Ricans, was not an automatic choice for a group that had previously been classified within rigid black–white racial categories. This process of self-reflection slowly pushed education officials in New York to realize that the problem of desegregation existed within a more complicated matrix that included blacks, whites, and Puerto Ricans.

Articulating a Space for Puerto Ricans

City education officials prepared the Allen report after the first major school boycott in February 1964. Its publication promoted ethnic integration, rather than racial integration, as the focal point of desegregation discussions. "We prefer, however, to speak of desegregation rather than integration or ethnic balance," its author noted, "since the segregated school is the evidence of the difficulty and must therefore be the target of the corrective effort."[27] The report defined a public school as ethnically segregated in New York City if in 1963 less than 10 percent of its enrollment was African American, Puerto Rican, or belonging to some other group. The debate of the preceding year over categorizing Puerto Ricans framed the awareness of the administrators. Researchers reached an understanding that racial classification could not encompass whites, African Americans, and Puerto Ricans, and past efforts to classify Puerto Ricans within a black–white binary had proved ineffective. The researchers even cast doubt on their own past data collection—data on which they based their recommendations. In a report entitled *Desegregating the Public Schools* (1964), the New York State Board of Education observed: "The terms, Puerto Rican and White are most doubtful, since most Puerto Ricans were classified as Whites in the 1960 Census. Nevertheless, we employ the three terms, Negro, Puerto Rican, and White on the ground that they are fairly accurate and commonly understood."[28] Nevertheless, uncertainty continued over how to factor Puerto Ricans into the city's integration plans. An outmoded system of racial classification continued to hold sway, even as dramatic demographic changes rendered it increasingly inadequate to the tasks at hand.

The Allen report was marked by a very pessimistic tone regarding the city's desegregation progress. It concluded that Open Enrollment, a plan that offered African American and Puerto Rican students the opportunity to transfer to designated receiving schools which were predominately white, had no significant effect on integration and that at the elementary level it actually increased segregation. The report concluded that this program failed because it depended entirely upon the voluntary choice of African American and Puerto Rican parents.[29] Parents had good reason to hesitate in sending their children into potentially hostile environments. The Free Choice Transfer Policy, a program initiated in 1963 which allowed children in schools with a "high" percentage of African Americans and Puerto Ricans to transfer to any school where space was available, was also considered incapable of reducing the city's level of segregation.[30] The report ended by expressing little hope for future success: "We must conclude that nothing undertaken by the New York City Board of Education since 1954, and nothing proposed since 1963, has contributed or will contribute in any meaningful degree to desegregating the public schools of the city. Each past effort, each current plan, and each projected proposal is either not aimed at reducing segregation or is developed in too limited a fashion to stimulate even slight progress toward desegregation."[31] Nearly a decade after *Brown*, efforts to desegregate New York remained stagnant.

For Puerto Ricans, the turmoil surrounding the efforts of city bureaucrats to create and successfully implement integration plans had an unintended consequence. It created a space for Puerto Ricans to formulate an agenda of their own in support of the needs of their children. Previous studies of ethnic groups in New York have erroneously assumed that Puerto Ricans had no interest in mobilizing around desegregation issues and no influence over the process.[32] Because integration was largely framed in black–white terms, the parameters of the debate did mute the voice of Puerto Ricans. It did not, however, stop their participation. Puerto Ricans remained highly involved in the education of their children and took advantage of every opening, no matter how small, to demand a say in how and under what conditions they would be taught.

A pivotal moment in the efforts of Puerto Rican parents and activists to insert themselves into debates over school integration occurred during the Conference on Integration in the New York City Public Schools, held in 1963 at Columbia University.[33] This event provided Puerto Ricans with a rare public opportunity to voice their own perspective on integration struggles. The goal of the conference was to offer tangible solutions for school integration to the city of New York. Together, the participants advanced the following propositions: the government at all levels must commit itself financially to education so that schools can have flexible policies; foundations need to bear the cost of research; and total community involvement is necessary.[34] Puerto Rican involvement at the Columbia conference was limited in scope. The Office of the Commonwealth of Puerto Rico Migration Division stood as the lone Puerto Rican representative out of twenty participating organizations. Two staff members from the Office of the Commonwealth of Puerto Rico, Max Wolff and Rosa Estades, sat on the thirty-one-person conference planning committee. Until the 1960s New York City viewed this office as the official spokesperson for the Puerto Rican migrant community. However limited, its presence at least ensured that the perspective of Puerto Ricans would be represented at the conference.

Born in Puerto Rico, Joseph Monserrat was one of the conference's eight principal speakers. Like thousands of other Puerto Ricans, Monserrat migrated to New York City after the Second World War. He graduated from Benjamin Franklin High School and later studied social work at the New School for Social Research and Columbia University. An active member of the Puerto Rican political leadership, he led the Migration Division Office and sat on the New York City Board of Education. Monserrat promoted active participation in the city's pluralistic ethnic culture.[35] In his conference presentation, he confronted the ambiguous place of Puerto Ricans in the city's racial classification system. "I welcome this opportunity to discuss with you what has been called a 'Puerto Rican View of School Integration,'" he began. "This title would seem to imply that Puerto Ricans view the question of school integration somewhat differently from others. As a matter of fact—we do."[36] This introduction initiated a discussion that distinguished between two minority communities in New York City: Puerto Rican and African American. Monserrat inserted a Puerto Rican view of race into the desegregation debate that until then discussions had sorely lacked.

As his first goal, Monserrat demonstrated the varied historical experiences of African Americans and Puerto Ricans. "In a multi-cultured democratic society such as ours," he noted, "integration must not and cannot mean submerging or forgetting the specific content and values of one's own past, whether as an individual or as a member of a group."[37] Puerto Ricans did not and could not conform to America's existing conceptions of race: "In discussing the issues of integration in New York City schools, Negroes and Puerto Ricans are referred to constantly almost as if they were one and the same. They are not. Unlike the Negro, we Puerto Ricans are not a race. We are, at most, an ethnic group. As such, some of us are 'white,' some of us are 'Negro' and some of us are so-called 'mixed.'"[38] The grouping of Puerto Ricans with African Americans marginalized the Puerto Rican voice in discussions of school integration.

As Monserrat explained, categorizing Puerto Ricans as a race was the product of the postwar migration to New York City and the resulting efforts to "fit" Puerto Ricans into state bureaucrats' integration plans for the city's schools. He explained: "It was not until after 1946 that we became a 'race,' that an identifiable descriptive stereotype had been created for us. In 1954 we discovered that our children, along with Negro children, were being described as 'X' children who attended 'X' schools. There also were some other children who were called 'Y' children and they attended 'Y' schools. We also learned at that time, that when the 'X' schools were compared with the 'Y' schools it was discovered that the 'X' school buildings were older and somewhat less well-equipped than the 'Y' school buildings; also, that there were fewer regular teachers in the 'X' schools."[39]

The racial identity ascribed to Puerto Ricans by state officials, according to Monserrat, proved not only inadequate to addressing the particular needs of Puerto Ricans in school debates. Like Mexican American activists in Texas, Monserrat found that the classification also led to a fundamentally flawed strategy for confronting segregation. "From a 'racial' point of view," he noted, "the all-Negro school is in fact completely segregated. On the other hand, because of the racial background of the Puerto Rican child, an all–Puerto Rican school may well be, from a 'racial' point of view, the most integrated of schools."[40] Acknowledging the distinctiveness of Puerto Rican racial ideology was necessary for *Brown* and school integration to be truly effective.

Monserrat's discussion foreshadowed those of recent scholars of Puerto Ricans in articulating and historicizing Puerto Rican conceptions of race. Once in New York City, Puerto Ricans encountered a system of racial classification that differed in substantive ways from the system they lived with in Puerto Rico. As Clara Rodriguez explains in her seminal essay "The Rainbow People," "in Puerto Rico, racial identification was subordinate to cultural identification, while in the U.S., racial identification, to a large extent, determines cultural identification. Thus Puerto Ricans were first Puerto Ricans, then *blanco/a* (white), *moreno/a* (dark), and so on, while Americans were first white or black, then Italian, West Indian or whatever. This is not to say that Puerto Ricans did not have a racial identification but rather that cultural identification superseded it."[41] For Monserrat, the privileging of race in debates over public school education submerged the broader concerns of Puerto Ricans that flowed not from their understanding of themselves as a race, but from their understanding of themselves as a distinctive people, with a distinctive culture tied closely to their language.

As Juan Flores has argued, the Great Migration was a defining historical event in the shaping of Puerto Ricans' consciousness of themselves as a people and a nation. Homage to Taino (indigenous) and African roots and a reverence for the island of Puerto Rico as a homeland played important roles in the shaping of this consciousness. Flores maintains, however, that the Spanish language was the foremost cultural symbol and theme in organizing the community in New York City.[42] Although African Americans and Puerto Ricans had much in common—the experience of migration, ties to a real and imagined African past, as well as rampant discrimination in access to adequate housing and schooling in New York City—Puerto Ricans' particular identification with and desire to preserve the Spanish language in their new geographic setting marked a significant point of departure. In New York City, loyalty to the Spanish language became an important marker of Puerto Rican identity. Through the issue of language, more so than race, Puerto Ricans began to assert themselves in city politics, particularly in relationship to debates about equality in public school education.

Puerto Ricans' emphasis on language marked a key difference in how they understood and defined the struggle in the city's public schools in relationship to African Americans. At the practical, day-to-day or grassroots level, however, Puerto Ricans and African Americans found much in common. The renowned Puerto Rican author Piri Thomas recalls in his memoir how white New Yorkers: "couldn't decide whether I was a nigger or a spic so they called me both."[43] Thomas, who like many Puerto Ricans shared physical characteristics with African Americans, still identified himself as Puerto Rican, even when others failed to do so. Despite clear cultural differences, the shared social positions of Puerto Ricans and African Americans led to cooperative efforts that informed Puerto Rican activism in significant ways. In 1964, for example, when the chairman of the education committee of the Brooklyn NAACP, Milton Galamison, and other black leaders led a boycott against the city's public schools, a handful of Puerto Rican leaders, including the community activist Evelina Antonetty, joined them. The experience of participating in the African American civil rights struggle, as Juan Gonzalez has recently argued, played an important role in the development of Puerto Rican leadership.[44]

Such participation also sharpened the perception among Puerto Ricans that they needed to create their own sociopolitical vehicles to address concerns specific to their community. In the mid-1960s, as debates over school integration and equality continued, Puerto Rican parents and community leaders confronted the herculean task of forming their own educational and political agenda for progress. They began to build neighborhood institutions with the aid of federal anti-poverty funds, joining other grassroots organizers in challenging racial and class injustice.[45] When Monserrat spoke at Columbia, he challenged Puerto Ricans to join a crusade for improving their children's educational opportunities. Puerto Rican parents responded and in doing so came into their own as a political force, articulating their own political agenda out of the turmoil surrounding debates over school integration.

A Community in Action

Examining the efforts of the United Bronx Parents, Inc. (UBP), demonstrates how a migrant community emerged as a viable political force. Established in 1965 by Puerto Rican parents in the South Bronx, the UBP was a grassroots, self-help organization that focused specifically on correcting the unresponsiveness of the city's public schools to the needs of Puerto Rican children, who had been neglected by the various and ineffective integration plans launched by the city. Since 1957 the number of African Americans in public schools had risen by 53 percent and of

Puerto Ricans by 38 percent, while whites' share of the total student population had decreased from 68 percent to 53 percent in 1964.[46] Despite an increase in enrollment numbers, city schools failed to meet the needs of Puerto Rican children.

The UBP responded to this neglect by formalizing its service agenda and increasing membership through a grant from the Department of Health, Education and Welfare. By 1967 increased funding allowed for expanding UBP services into the areas of health care, housing, welfare, and juvenile justice, although schools remained the primary focus. These additional funds enabled the UBP to establish satellite offices throughout New York. Through its Parent Leadership Training Program, each branch remained focused on the needs of children and parental empowerment.[47] As its founder Antonetty explained it, the UBP was created to address the concerns of parents and provide the community with "expertise, insight, new information, resources, criticism and contacts."[48] Keenly aware of the fragility of the impoverished, migrant community being served, Antonetty stressed the flexibility of the group. The continued arrival of migrants from Puerto Rico necessitated an accommodating approach to community issues and a respectful adherence to their cultural norms and language. Like many grassroots organizations during the War on Poverty, the UBP focused on alleviating immediate needs while working toward long-term improvement.

The UBP's plan for improving the education of Puerto Rican children was to create an effective monitoring system involving knowledgeable parents. As a result, the UBP concentrated on training parents to advocate, even agitate, for their children in schools. While it served the varied needs of Puerto Ricans, its principal work involved class and case advocacy.[49] Antonetty emphasized to parents and community activists the significance of education to unlocking upward social mobility.[50] The UBP placed the responsibility of raising educational standards on the parents themselves. One organizational flyer, "Homework: How Can It Help Your Child Learn," advised parents to participate in their children's homework and to be aware of the assignments their children received. Antonetty encouraged parents to demand that their children have the best educational experience and that the schools set the highest standards for their children.[51] Among other activities, Puerto Ricans openly criticized sociological studies that had labeled their children as "disabled learners" and "culturally deprived."[52] Through her writing, Antonetty challenged presumed notions of Puerto Rican inferiority and inability to learn. The UBP encouraged parents to expect equal opportunity and a good education as the standard for their children. In this sense the UBP resembled educational advocacy groups for African Americans, which used educational reform as a mechanism for larger political objectives. By the late 1960s the UBP was getting results.

A principal component of the UBP's effort was empowering parents within the public school buildings themselves. Too often, school buildings were a bastion of intimidation. The UBP encouraged parents to view themselves as the equal of their children's teachers and to assume ownership of their community schools. Bilingual organizational flyers instructed parents on

"How to Prepare for a Good Parent-Teacher Conference" and pushed them to view schools as a community institution. "A Good School Involves Its Students in the Life of Their Community," read one flyer, and "[t]he community gives life to the school." Antonetty worked to formalize the process of getting Puerto Rican parents involved in schools and helped to inform schools of community expectations for them. As the UBP understood it, "Parents and the general community should have major decision-making, not merely advisory, power on all levels—from local school policy decisions to national legislation and regulation."[53]

The UBP pressed for change in New York City public schools on a number of fronts. A critical concern was that teachers treat students with respect and sensitivity and that schools meet their particular needs, especially with respect to language. In addition to urging parents to become more deeply involved in the life of the schools, to question teachers' methods, and to intervene on their children's behalf, the UBP charged parents with protecting their children from ill-fitting desegregation policies. More specifically, the UBP supported efforts to ensure bilingual education and attention to Puerto Rican culture in the public school curriculum. The UBP directed parents to confront the learning barriers faced by their children. This effort centered on the preservation of Spanish as an essential component of Puerto Rican cultural identity. The UBP called on parents to demand bilingual and bicultural programs in the city's schools. It also called attention to the lack of Puerto Ricans in school administrative and teaching posts. Taking a page from the African American civil rights movement, the UBP encouraged parents to pressure the federal government for funds and the local government for representation in decisions concerning their children's schooling.[54]

The UBP saw the law as a means to educate and mobilize the community. It actively monitored developments in the courts and legislatures that affected the educational future of Puerto Rican children. It set out to train its staff and the community on their rights in the new legal environment after the U.S. Supreme Court held in *Lau* v. *Nichols* (1974) that the absence of remedial language assistance denied a meaningful education to Chinesespeaking students in San Francisco and after ASPIRA, a prominent Puerto Rican political and educational organization in New York City, in 1974 won a consent decree from the New York City Board of Education which established standards for bilingual education.[55] Antonetty took the lead in training parents in their legal rights and those of their children. By emphasizing the significance of these cases, the UBP instilled in Puerto Rican parents a sense of legal rights consciousness that translated into demands for an educational system reflective of their social and cultural needs.

Like the Student Nonviolent Coordinating Committee in the South, the UBP trained parents to help each other rather than depend on the agency to advocate on their behalf. As a result, parent organizers did the majority of the advocacy work as volunteers rather than as paid professionals. The UBP provided the environment of trust and the knowledge necessary to empower parents on behalf of their children, while community members learned to work together to protect their children in the city's educational system. By the late 1970s not only did the UBP advocate bilingual and bicultural education for its community, but it also campaigned for community control of schools, easier access by parents to their children's school records, a reduction in suspension cases so that more children would remain in school, and an increase in educational options, including a more liberal transfer policy and free bus passes.[56]

Three decades after the mass arrival of Puerto Ricans to New York, the UBP helped Puerto Rican parents to develop a stance in educational politics. The demand of Puerto Rican parents—the right to determine and secure the best educational experience for their children—did not differ from those of other parents. As Puerto Ricans entered the schools, bilingual education became the vehicle through which to express ethnic identity and particular concerns. It was the cornerstone in their fight for educational equality because they believed it guaranteed the best schooling experience possible for their children, who had limited English proficiency. Bilingual education also guaranteed that the Spanish language and Puerto Rican culture would not be viewed as a hindrance to success in the broader life of the community. In part, it was a matter of recognition and cultural validation. Parents saw Spanish as "their language." The teaching of that language was viewed as a connection between their homes and the public schools. To be fully recognized in the system of public education, the Spanish language had to become part of the dialogue between teachers, administrators, schools, and parents. More importantly, for a child to succeed, to be educated in a supportive and productive learning environment, Puerto Rican parents felt that the home language had to be introduced as an educational tool. For many Puerto Ricans, empowerment in schools and the broader political life of New York City required that the Spanish language be a central part of their children's educational experience. It was a matter of educational quality and cultural inclusiveness.[57]

As Puerto Ricans migrated in growing numbers to New York City after the Second World War, they arrived in a city that like the nation as a whole was grappling with a long history of racial exclusion and discrimination. In 1954 *Brown v. Board of Education* elevated the question of Jim Crow segregation and equality in public schools to a new level of debate and conflict. The debate was too often couched in uniquely southern terms and the problem viewed too frequently through the lens of white and black. Puerto Ricans soon found themselves deeply immersed in questions of integration and equality in the public school system in New York City. Because of the confining terms of the debate, Puerto Ricans battled to make themselves heard and to develop a political agenda that addressed their specific concerns as a community. Through the UBP Puerto Ricans worked to personalize the debate and reform efforts that flowed from *Brown*. They worked to liberate themselves from the black–white binary which regulated debates about school reform in the early 1960s. More importantly, they worked to liberate their own children from discriminatory practices. Members of the UBP addressed the need for school integration on their own terms, eschewing the racially polarized strategies of the city's education officials. Instead, they worked to persuade parents to advocate on their children's behalf by focusing on the specific cultural needs of the Puerto Rican community, especially the need for bilingual and bicultural education. Puerto Rican participation in the early integration battles of New York was a learning experience. In a short time, community groups, such as the UBP, became full-fledged participants in the educational politics of the country. Through the UBP, parents demanded cultural recognition and demanded that their children receive the best education possible.

The UBP is an example not only of Puerto Rican creativity and activism in New York City but of the multifaceted impact of *Brown*. The significance of the decision transgressed both regional and racial boundaries. While *Brown* dismantled Jim Crow segregation in public schools, a highly visible manifestation of structural inequality, it simultaneously provoked a more wide-reaching debate about education and equality in America at large. It brought to the surface a whole range of issues of concern to racial and ethnic communities in addition to southern African Americans. Though this chapter focuses on New York City, the battles that took place there demonstrate the importance of rethinking *Brown* and its legacy in light of the demographic diversity of every American city. The issues of segregation and desegregation, education, access, and equality have touched the lives of many. Contrary to previous popular and academic assumptions, Puerto Ricans were active in struggles around school integration in the wake of *Brown*. If the terms of the debate muted their voices or marginalized their concerns, they battled in myriad ways to change these terms and influence outcomes. They formed their own political and cultural organizations, raised their voices, and participated in educational politics less than thirty years after their mass arrival in the continental United States. While unique, the Puerto Rican experience reminds us of the need to broaden our geographic and race-based conceptualizations of the meaning and consequences of *Brown*. Only in doing so will we come to a full appreciation of the historic decision.

Endnotes

I would like to thank Jeremy Adelman, Carlos Decena, Sarah Igo, Kevin Kruse, Peter Lau, Felix Matos Rodríguez, Elizabeth Todd, and Chad Williams for their assistance and encouragement throughout the writing of this chapter.

1. *New York Times*, 24 December 1954.
2. Diane Ravitch, *The Great School War: A History of the New York City Public Schools* (Baltimore: Johns Hopkins University Press, 2000), 252.

3. The startling exception has been the work on Mexican American children in public schools. See: Guadalupe San Miguel, *"Let All of Them Take Heed": Mexican Americans and the Campaign for Educational Equality in Texas, 1910–1981* (Austin: University of Texas Press, 1987); Benjamin Marquez, LULAC: *The Evolution of a Mexican American Political Organization* (Austin: University of Texas Press, 1993); George Sánchez, *Becoming Mexican American* (New York: Oxford University Press, 1993); David Gutiérrez, *Walls and Mirrors: Mexican Americans, Mexican Immigrants, and the Politics of Ethnicity* (Berkeley: University of California Press, 1995).

4. Oscar Handlin, *The Newcomers: Negroes and Puerto Ricans in a Changing Metropolis* (Cambridge: Harvard University Press, 1959); Virginia Sánchez-Korrol, *From Colonia to Community: The History of Puerto Ricans in New York City* (Berkeley: University of California Press, 1994).

5. Ravitch, *The Great School War*, 242.

6. Sánchez-Korrol, *From Colonia to Community*, 224. The period between 1946 and 1964 is known as the Great Migration. During these years the largest number of Puerto Ricans migrated from the island. Their communities grew in East Harlem, the South Bronx, and the Lower East Side. For more on this see Clara Rodriguez, *Puerto Ricans: Born in the USA* (Winchester, Mass.: Unwin Hyman, 1989).

7. While other European immigrants have been able to go through a whitening process and integrate themselves according to their whiteness, this has not happened en masse for Puerto Ricans. For a concise summary on all that is white see Peter Kolchin, "Whiteness Studies: The New History of Race in America," *Journal of American History* 89 (June 2002): 154–73; Noel Ignatiev, *How the Irish Became White* (New York: Routledge, 1995); David R. Roediger, *The Wages of Whiteness: Race and the Making of the American Working Class* (New York: Verso, 1991); Matthew Frye Jacobson, *Whiteness of a Different Color: European Immigrants and the Alchemy of Race* (Cambridge: Harvard University Press, 1998).

8. For early accounts on housing discrimination see Leonard Covello, "A Community-Centered School and the Problem of Housing," *Educational Forum* 7 (January 1943): 133–43; Oscar Handlin, *The Newcomers: Negroes and Puerto Ricans in a Changing Metropolis* (Cambridge: Harvard University Press, 1959); Robert W. Peebles, "Interview with Leonard Covello," *Urban Review* 3 (January 1969): 13–18.

9. For more on neighborhood schools see Allan Blackman, "Planning and the Neighborhood School," *Learning Together: A Book on Integrated Education*, ed. Meyer Weinberg (Chicago: Integrated Education Associates, 1964), 49–56.

10. After making a commitment to integration in 1955 the New York City Board of Education created a Commission on Integration to investigate zoning and teacher assignments. As the commission began hearings, the Public Education Association launched a census on the student population. Board of Education of the City of New York, *Toward Greater*

Opportunity: A Progress Report from the Superintendent of Schools to the Board of Education (New York, June 1960), 1.

11. State Education Commissioner's Advisory Committee on Human Relations, "Guiding Principles for Dealing with Defacto Segregation in Public Schools" (Albany, N.Y., 17 June 1963), 3.

12. James E. Allen Jr. to Calvin E. Gross, 2 August 1963, transcript in Allen's files at the State Archives, Albany, N.Y.

13. In 1963 the Board of Education wrote: "Participation by the local communities themselves in developing and working out the pattern to accomplish these objectives will give strength to our program. If the proposals for progress come from the communities themselves, they will then have ample reason to see that these proposals work and will find satisfaction in their accomplishments. Therefore, every opportunity will be given to the communities to work out their own destinies without premature action from central headquarters." Board of Education of the City of New York, *Progress toward Integration* (New York, December 1963), 3.

14. In 1956 Dr. Kenneth Clark's subcommittee of the Commission of Integration initiated the Demonstration Guidance Program. This program sought to equalize schools by providing additional services that would improve academic achievement. The Higher Horizon program began in 1959. Seen as a tool to equalize educational opportunities, this program offered remedial instruction, cultural activities, and extra counseling to all children beginning in the third grade. However, because of insufficient funds few students benefited. For more on this see Ravitch, *The Great School War*, 260–61.

15. Nathan Glazer and Daniel Patrick Moynihan, *Beyond the Melting Pot: The Negroes, Puerto Ricans, Jews, Italians, and Irish of New York City* (Cambridge: MIT Press, 1963), 46–47.

16. Meyer Weinberg, *A Chance to Learn: A History of Education in the United States* (Cambridge: Cambridge University Press, 1977), 114.

17. Leonard Buder, "Schools in City Will Open Today Despite Boycott," *New York Times*, 14 September 1964, 1.

18. Irving Anker, "Our Northern Cities: Toward Integration or Segregation?," *Strengthening Democracy* (New York: Board of Education of the City of New York, February 1965).

19. *Id.*

20. James E. Allen Jr. to Calvin E. Gross, 2 August 1963, New York State Education Department, Albany, 4.

21. The Mexican American struggle in Texas was multifaceted and changed over time. From early efforts by the League of United Latin American Citizens (LULAC) to classify their children as "white" to a radical grassroots switch in the early 1970s seeking a "nonwhite" racial status, their struggle is not so much about identity as it is a continual battle against discrimination. A discussion on the shift in consciousness as well as historical insight can

be found in Guadalupe San Miguel's *Brown, Not White: School Integration and the Chicano Movement in Houston* (College Station: Texas A & M University Press, 2001).

22. Board of Education of the City of New York, *Progress toward Integration*, 1.

23. James E. Allen Jr. to Calvin E. Gross, 2 August 1963, New York State Education Department, Albany, 1.

24. Subsequent reports do not distinguish between the groups. Memo from Ralph S. Rosas to Joseph Monserrat, Commonwealth of Puerto Rico Migration Division Office, New York, 19 December 1963.

25. Memo from Lorne H. Woollatt to James E. Allen Jr., New York State Education Department, Albany, 10 May 1968, James E. Allen Papers, New York State Archives, Albany.

26. Memo from James E. Allen Jr. to Lorne H. Woollatt, New York State Education Department, Albany, 31 May 1968, Allen Papers, New York State Archives, Albany.

27. New York State Board of Education, *Desegregating the Public Schools* (Albany, N.Y., 1964), 1.

28. *Id.* at 2.

29. For example, in September 1964 about 110,000 elementary pupils were offered the opportunity to transfer yet only 2,000 applied and only 1,800 ultimately transferred, or less than 2 percent of those eligible. The authors of the report found that the number of segregated, predominantly African American and Puerto Rican schools in New York City increased over five years, from 12 percent to 22 percent at the elementary level, from 10 percent to 19 percent at the junior high level, and from 0 to 2 percent at the senior high school level. About three-quarters of the city's schools showed no change in their percentage of Negro and Puerto Rican students. *Id.* at 4–5.

30. *Id.* at 7.

31. *Id.* at 8.

32. Glazer and Moynihan, *Beyond the Melting Pot*, 47.

33. Gordon J. Klopf and Israel A. Laster, *Integrating the Urban School: Proceedings* (New York: Teachers College, 1963).

34. *Id.* at 10–11. This was very unlike the many other academic conferences held in New York City throughout the 1960s. See Proceedings of the Invitational Conference on Northern School Desegregation (New York: Yeshiva University, 1962); Hubert H. Humphrey, *School Desegregation: Documents and Commentaries* (New York: Thomas Y. Crowell, 1964).

35. For more on Joseph Monserrat see Michael Lapp, "Managing Migration: the Migration Division of Puerto Rico" (diss., Johns Hopkins University, 1990).

36. Joseph Monserrat, "School Integration: A Puerto Rican View," *Integrating the Urban School: Proceedings*, 60.

37. *Id.* at 64.

38. *Id.* at 66–67.

39. *Id.* at 65.

40. *Id.* at 13.

41. Rodriguez, *Puerto Ricans,* 52.

42. Juan Flores, "'Qué assimilated, brother, yo soy asimilao': The Structuring of Puerto Rican Identity," *Divided Borders: Essays on Puerto Rican Identity* (Houston: Arte Publico, 1993); Juan Flores, "Broken English Memories: Languages in the Trans-Colony," *From Bomba to Hip-Hop: Puerto Rican Culture and Latino Identity* (New York: Columbia University Press, 2000), especially 57.

43. Interview with Piri Thomas, cited in Clara E. Rodriguez, "The Rainbow People," *Puerto Ricans Born in the USA* (Boulder: Westview, 1989), 272.

44. David Rodgers, *New York City and the Politics of School Desegregation* (New York: Center for Urban Education, 1968), 139–40; Juan Gonzalez, *Harvest of Empire* (New York: Penguin, 2000).

45. Another example of mobilization by Puerto Rican parents is documented in Tom Roderick's *A School of Our Own: Parents. Power, and Community at the East Harlem Block Schools* (New York: Teachers College Press, 2001).

46. Anker, "Our Northern Cities," 1.

47. Evelina Antonetty, "History of United Bronx Parents, Inc.," 5–6, United Bronx Parents Records, Center for Puerto Rican Studies in New York City, box 2, folder 14 (hereafter cited as "UBP Records").

48. Antonetty, "History of United Bronx Parents, Inc," 7.

49. See Sánchez-Korrol, *From Colonia to Community.*

50. *Id.* at 10.

51. United Bronx Parents, Inc., "Homework: How Can It Help Your Child Learn," UBP Records, box 2, folder 11.

52. National Conference of Puerto Ricans, Mexican-Americans, and Educators on the Special Educational Needs of Urban Puerto Rican Youth, *"Hemos trabajado bien": A Report* (New York, 1968).

53. United Bronx Parents, Inc., "How to Prepare for a Good Parent-Teacher Conference" and "A Good School Involves Its Students in the Life of Their Community," UBP Records, box 2, folder 11; Emile Schepers, *Law and Community Advocacy: A Case Description of the Use of the Law by United Bronx Parents* (Chicago: Center for New Schools, 1978), UBP Records, box 2, folder 14.

54. Schepers, *Law and Community Advocacy.* For more on the efforts of Puerto Ricans in reforming public schools see Melissa Rivera and Pedro Pedraza, "The Spirit of Transformation: an Education Reform Movement in a New York City Latino/a Community," *Puerto Rican Students in U.S. Schools,* ed. Sonia Nieto (Mahwah, N.J.: Lawrence Erlbaum, 2000), 223–45.

55. Schepers, *Law and Community Advocacy,* 9.

56. *Id.* at 22–25.

57. Catherine E. Walsh, *Pedagogy and the Struggle for Voice: Issues of Language, Power, and Schooling for Puerto Ricans* (New York: Bergin and Garvey, 1991); Ana Celia Zentella, *Growing Up Bilingual* (Oxford: Basil Blackwell, 1997). For more on the language and public schooling for Latinos see Antonio Darder, Rodolfo D. Torres, and Henry Gutiérrez, eds., *Latinos and Education: A Critical Reader* (New York: Routledge, 1997).

■ Reading 4.2

Define the following concepts/phrases:

"separate but equal"

Brown v. Board of Education

white and black racial binary

Spanish surname category

desegregation in public school

open enrollment program

free choice transfer policy

racial identification

cultural identification

integration

desegregation

Answer the following questions:

1. Summarize the state of the public school system in New York City.
2. What were the public schools not offering to Puerto Rican students?
3. How did Puerto Rican activists articulate their demands for an inclusive system?
4. Enumerate the demands of parents and activists.
5. What did Puerto Rican activists learn from African American counterparts?
6. What is the role of ASPIRA in the success of advocates' demands?
7. What is the role of Evelina Antonetty and United Bronx Parents in this period?
8. Assess the legacy of Puerto Rican public school activism today.

■ Reading 4.3

Latina Activism

Iris Morales

T ODAY LATINA ACTIVISTS AND ARTISTS ARE leading dynamic campaigns, projects, and grass-roots movements to end systems of poverty and racism that are crushing the working poor, immigrants and families, LGBTQ and women of color. They are part of a growing political consciousness shaping a network of alliances among Latinxs, African Americans, Native Americans, Asians, Arab Americans, and progressive whites in the United States. Their demands challenge state and corporate power, broaden our vision of justice, and create possibilities for societal transformation. Yet struggles for economic and racial justice are largely invisible in the public discourse and generally ignored in the mainstream fight for women's rights.

Immediately after the results of 2016 U.S. presidential election were announced, women united to protest the anti-women politics promoted during the campaign. Latinas and other women of color assumed key leadership roles to organize a Women's March in Washington D.C. held on January 21, 2017. It was one of the largest political mobilizations in U.S. history galvanizing millions of women, men, and children of all ages to protest misogyny and the anti-immigrant, racist, and militarist direction of the new administration. At the massive gathering, prominent Latinas took center stage delivering fiery speeches and energizing cultural performances. Among them, actress America Ferrera set the tone in her opening remarks: "Our dignity, our character, our rights have all been under attack and the platform of hate and division assumed power yesterday … we march today for our moral core." Sister marches and rallies also mobilized in cities across the U.S. and around the world with crowds surpassing projected numbers. An estimated 2.6 million people participated in all 50 states and 32 countries,[1] displaying an exceptional outpouring of support for the rights of women, and for the rights of immigrants, African Americans, Muslims, LGBTQ persons and others targeted for hate by the administration.

Iris Morales, "Introduction," *Latinas: Struggles & Protests in 21st Century USA*, pp. 1-10. Copyright © 2018 by Red Sugarcane Press. Reprinted with permission.

Latinas turned out in big numbers. Not only to protest but also to articulate a vision of what we aspire to see in the world. This idea is at the heart of *Latinas: Struggles & Protests in 21st Century USA*, a collection of poetry and prose reflecting on women's lived experiences and the ways that Latinas address the relationship between gender and social change. The contributors are poets and activists, educators, artists, and journalists engaged in a variety of work from community organizing to university teaching. The selections illustrate how Latinas understand and resist the gendered conditions of their lives. They expose inequities that Latinas face as women but also by class; race, ethnicity, and national origin; immigration status; social location; and the legacy of history. The volume is most closely aligned with the view of feminism as "a movement to end sexist oppression, both its institutional and individual manifestations."[2]

Latinas: Struggles & Protests in 21st Century USA includes a mix of genres: poems, personal narratives, blog posts, letters, scholarly essays, artwork, mission statements, excerpts from plays, lyrics, and herstories looking across time, generational, and geographic boundaries. Each piece is unique. Together they open a window that reveals a range of Latina perspectives on important contemporary socio-economic-political and cultural issues, and imaginings for a more humane world.

Who Are Latinas?

At the outset, it is important to emphasis that "Latina" is a "socially constructed" concept. In the 1960s, Chicana/Chicano and Puerto Rican activists in the U.S. used the terms "Latino/Latina" to signify similar histories and express solidarity with each other's social justice struggles. Later advocacy groups pressured to include a separate category in the U.S. Census to identify Latinos/Latinas, and the government settled on the term "Hispanic" in 1973 to recognize persons with origins in Latin America and the Spanish-speaking Caribbean.[3] (Until then, they had been assigned to the same category as "Whites.") The new classification—"Hispanic"—was, and continues to be, vigorously debated regarding the term itself as well as who is, or is not, included, and who decides. (The term Latino/a/x is used in this essay instead of Hispanic.) Nonetheless, the umbrella designation has served to recognize a national constituency that continues to evolve and represents a source, or a potential, for political power.

In 2015, more than 26 million Latinas lived in the United States.[4] This diverse population shares histories, cultural values, and languages but also has greatly different experiences based on social class, race, and immigration status. Several distinguishing characteristics are outlined here. For example, Latinas have lived in the U.S. for varying durations. They may be descended from immigrants who came to this country many generations ago, or they may be recent arrivals. Latinas are also descendants of the Native peoples who lived in the Americas before the European colonizers invaded—they are *not* immigrants. Puerto Ricans as U.S. citizens since 1917 also are not immigrants.

Generally, Latinas, documented or undocumented, migrate to the U.S. searching for economic opportunity or seeking refuge from political instability and violence in their home countries. In recent years, even thousands of unaccompanied children, including girls, have arrived at the U.S.-Mexico border. They make the journey alone fleeing horrific poverty, and political and drug-related violence.[5]

Latinas in the United States have roots in every Latin American country; the largest group is of Mexican descent followed by Puerto Ricans, Salvadorians, Cubans, Dominicans, Guatemalans, Colombians, and others in lesser numbers.[6] Latinas may identify as natives of their home country or as Latina, or both. For example, the contributors to this book identify as Latina, but also as Chicana, Dominican, Mexican, Puerto Rican, San Salvadoran, Argentinian, Afro-Latinx, Afromexicana, and Boricua.

According to a 2014 study, the majority of Latinas in the United States were born in the U.S.,[7] spoke English and were fluent in Spanish.[8] Latinas may speak only English and Spanglish, a mix of English sprinkled with Spanish words. Latinas who speak only Spanish face steep language barriers and discrimination in getting jobs, education, housing, healthcare, and other vital needs.

While Latinas can be of all social classes, most are workingwomen. Disproportionately in the ranks of the poor and working class, they live within a complex set of pressures both as workers and as women. Of approximately 11.1 million Latinas in the labor force in 2015,[9] more than one-third worked low-paying jobs in the service sector in hotels, restaurants, casinos, household services, and childcare settings, and another third in sales and office occupations. About 25% held management, professional and related positions. Note that at every socioeconomic level, Latinas were paid substantially less than men.[10] Even Latinas with masters, professional, and doctoral degrees had the lowest median earnings of all racial and ethnic groups in the U.S.[11]

Racial differences and skin colors among Latinas span the human spectrum. The race dynamics in the Latinx community are multilayered and complex, and challenge the prevailing "white-black" racial binary of U.S. society. In general terms, Latinas confront systemic and individual racism and colorism (preference for lighter over darker skin color) as well as discrimination by ethnicity, class, and immigration status. Black Latinas are subjected to racism as Latinas, Afro-Latinas, and African Americans. Brown-skinned Latinas also confront racism based on skin color. Light-skinned Latinas face discrimination as an oppressed national, ethnic group. Because "whiteness" is promoted, both across Latin America and in the U.S., those who are seen as "white" have more advantages and benefit from "white skin" privilege. Latinas who can pass as "white" might choose to adopt whiteness and reject Latinidad altogether. The impact of racism, both in U.S. society as a whole and among Latinx people, is a central theme of the anthology.

Colonization, Slavery, and Women's Resistance

Our shared histories as Latinas began the moment the Spanish conquistadores set foot on Caribbean beaches in 1492. There began the massacre of Native people that continued into South America. "The Indians of the Americas totaled no less than 70 million when the foreign conquerors appeared on the horizon; a century and a half later they had been reduced to 3.5 million."[12] The colonizers slaughtered an estimated 60 to 80 million Native people from the Indies to the Amazon,[13] and then they declared the Indigenous people *extinct*.

The European colonizers perpetuated another holocaust. They enslaved and exported Africans to every South American country from Brazil to Bolivia, from the Caribbean Islands to Honduras and North America. Though the precise number is unknown, scholars believe that the slave traders shipped 12.5 million Africans to North America, the Caribbean, and South America. 10.7 million men, women, and children survived the Atlanta Ocean crossing; but approximately 2 million did not.[14]

The invaders committed mass murder and genocide. They seized the lands and looted its vast resources. They raped Indigenous and African women. Picture women running, screaming and crying in terror, trying to get away, fearing and pleading for their lives, fighting their attackers—millions of women over time. Desperation and despair drove some women to commit suicide and infanticide rather than suffer, or have their children suffer, the sadism and tortures of men.[15]

African and Native women were not passive victims. They fought back from carrying out acts of insubordination and destroying property, to poisoning the slaveholders and participating in uprisings and slave rebellions.[16] They also preserved and protected Indigenous and African cultures, passing on community values, traditions, and customs to their children.[17] Remembering and retelling stories from generation to generation was curative and healing, and is so to the present day. The horrors of colonization endure in our collective memory as the anthology's writers affirm.

By the 1800s, newly emerging nations in the Americas fought for independence from the Europeans. Women joined these struggles and expected that the triumphant leaders would grant basic rights to women; but they didn't. From then to the present, Latin American women have had to fight for access to education, labor laws, the right to vote,[18] and gender equality in all arenas. They have battled sexual violence and high rates of femicide.[19] Black, Native, and poor women relegated to the bottom of class and social hierarchies, suffered, and continue to suffer, most of all.

With the Monroe Doctrine of 1823, the U.S. government declared the Western Hemisphere closed to further European colonization, and the U.S. corporate elite took over. They exploited the laboring people, and financed dictators and regimes of savagery and torture to quash opposition. The resulting poverty and terror compelled Latinx people to seek escape and migrate from their home countries. In the case of Puerto Rico, U.S. colonial policies since 1898 have caused waves of mass migration so that today more Puerto Ricans live in the United States than in Puerto Rico.

Latinx arrivals find greater economic opportunities in the U.S. than back home, but they also suffer severe exploitation, language and racial barriers, and relentless police and state violence.

Women of Color Feminism

In the United States, the women's movement has its roots in the early resistance and rebellion of Native and African women. This long history is only briefly reviewed here.

By the 1800s, opponents of slavery were vigorously organizing for the immediate emancipation of slaves, and the end of racial discrimination and segregation. Out of this struggle also emerged a women's equal rights movement. Sojourner Truth, a former slave, an abolitionist, and a women's rights advocate, was a leading spokesperson addressing the inequalities facing both Blacks and women. In her famous *"Ain't I a Woman?"* speech delivered at the Ohio Women's Rights Convention in 1851,[20] Truth underscored the power of women: "If the first woman God ever made was strong enough to turn the world upside down all alone, these women together ought to be able to turn it back and get it right-side up again."[21] At the same time, she emphasized the racial divide and differences in the treatment of women, contrasting the chivalry afforded White women with the brutalization inflicted on Black women.

The 1960s opened a new chapter for women's rights in the U.S. African American feminists were again at the forefront fighting racism, sexism, and exploitation. Neither the Black Liberation struggle nor the women's movement responded to specific issues concerning Black women's lives. Black male activists refused to recognize and address the "double jeopardy"[22] of racial and gender inequality, and the woman's movement focused primarily on the concerns of white middle-class women, failed to deal with both their class privilege and racism.

Like African American women, Latinas confronted similar experiences and barriers in the Latino and white women's movements. To fight for women's rights and social justice, Latinas mobilized in communities, workplaces, and schools, and led campaigns for economic and racial justice, affordable housing and healthcare, safe and legal abortions, and an end to experimentation with women's bodies. Puerto Rican feminists fought sterilization policies in Puerto Rico, which, by the mid-1960s, had resulted in more than 35% of women unable to bear children.[23] Across the United States, women of color joined in solidarity to stop sterilization of Native American, African American, Chicana, and Puerto Rican women.

Feminists of color also developed revolutionary ideas and frameworks that analyzed how systems of power operated. Identifying capitalism as the main oppressor, they described the multiple and intersecting dominations affecting women's lives by gender, class, race, and ethnicity—today known as intersectionality. Black feminists expanded on these ideas in the Combahee River Collective Statement written in 1977:

"We believe that sexual politics under patriarchy is as pervasive in Black women's lives as are the politics of class and race. We also often find it difficult to separate race from class from sex oppression because in our lives they are most often experienced simultaneously. We know that there is such a thing as racial-sexual oppression which is neither solely racial nor solely sexual, e.g., the history of rape of Black women by white men as a weapon of political repression.[24]

The women's movements of the 1960s and 1970s fought for the radical transformation of society and pinpointed the ways in which patriarchy and forms of male privilege were embedded in the practice of every political, economic, and cultural institution. These movements successfully challenged and transformed views about women, opened new opportunities, initiated groundbreaking laws, and introduced a broad range of social, cultural, and political rights enjoyed by women in the United States today.

Latina Activism in the 21st Century

Despite the tremendous gains women have achieved, the struggle for gender and racial justice has not progressed far enough. Women still face violence, discrimination, and institutional barriers to equal participation in society. Zealous anti-women crusades have re-emerged that are eroding legal rights won in the courts, reducing workplace protections, decreasing women's health services, and minimizing claims of sexual violence. This well-financed backlash seeks to turn back the clock on women's rights.

Critically impacted by these politics, Latinas have mobilized and are organizing campaigns for economic and racial justice, affordable, quality education and health care, LGBTQ rights, an end to sexual violence, and other urgent social justice demands. With a clear stake in the outcome, they are striving to build organizations that include participation of women most affected by the issues—rather than the top down leadership structures of the status quo. Like prior generations, Latina activists are finding it essential to reclaim herstories for survival, develop collective strategies, and create coalitions to fight back. As the Combahee River Collective declared decades ago, "The most profound and potentially most radical politics come directly out of our own identity and oppression."

Latinas: Struggles & Protests in 21st Century USA reflects on themes emerging from women's lived experiences, and "on how gender has mattered and continues to matter—politically."[25] The collection shows Latina activists expanding the feminist agenda, emphasizing the transnational nature of women's exploitation, and reaching out to women who have too often been ignored. Latinas are organizing women in low-paid, non-union jobs, linking women's and workers' rights, and recruiting new members into the labor movement. They are battling for improved workplace conditions and the end of the gender wage gap that pays Latinas an average of 54 cents to the dollar paid to white male workers.[26] Afro-Latinas are leading the fight against racism in Latinx communities in the U.S. and in Latin America. Inspired by, and in solidarity with, the Black Lives Matter movement, Latina activists are fighting police and other forms of racial violence. LGBTQ Latinas are at the frontlines responding to hate crimes and defending the rights of undocumented women and transgender immigrants. Latinas are exposing high incidences of sexual assault and violence in detention centers and prisons. They are also directing campaigns to safeguard reproductive health options for low-income women and families. Across the United States, Latinas are leading grassroots struggles for climate justice, immigrant rights, and decolonization.

Latinas: Struggles & Protests in 21st Century USA reaffirms the important role of Latina activism in the human rights struggle. The writings share dreams of a just world, the break down of hierarchies, and ideals of sisterhood. They imagine a different kind of future, of ways of living and relating to one another, and of organizing societies that are in harmony with the Earth and the needs of the people.

Endnotes

1. Heidi M. Przybyla and Fredreka Schouten, "At 2.6 million strong, Women's Marches crush expectations." *USA Today*, January 22, 2017. https://www.usatoday.com/story/news/politics/2017/01/21/

2. "The Combahee River Collective Statement," http://circuitous.org/scraps/combahee.html

3. U.S. Census Bureau. Equal Employment Opportunity. https://www.census.gov/eeo/special_emphasis_programs/hispanic_heritage.html

4. Department of Education. *"Fulfilling America's Future: Latinas in the U.S., 2015"* https://sites.ed.gov/hispanic-initiative/files/2015/09/Fulfilling-Americas-Future-Latinas-in-the-U.S.-2015-Final-Report.pdf. 7.

5. Ian Gordon, *"70,000 Kids Will Show Up Alone At Our Border This Year. What Happens To Them?" Mother Jones*, July/August 2014. http://www.motherjones.com/politics/2014/06/child-migrants-surge-unaccompanied-central-america/

6. Antonio Flores, *"How the U.S. Hispanic Population is Changing."* September 18, 2017. www.pewresearch.org/fact-tank/2017/09/18/how-the-u-s-hispanic-population-is-changing/

7. Tanzina Vega, *"Most Latino Workers Born in U.S., Study Says." New York Times*, June 19, 2014. https://www.nytimes.com/2014/06/20/us/majority-of-latino-labor-force-now-born-in-us-study-finds.html?r=0

8. Flores, *"How the U.S. Hispanic Population is Changing."*

9. United States Department of Labor, Women's Bureau. *"Hispanic Women in the Labor Force."* https://www.dol.gov/wb/media/Hispanic_Women_Infographic_Final_508.pdfJ.

10. *"Fulfilling America's Future: Latinas in the U.S., 2015"* 12.

11. Ibid.

12. Eduardo Galeano, *Open Veins of Latin America, Five centuries of the Pillage of a Continent.* (New York: Monthly Review Press, 1973, 1997), 38.

13. David E. Stannard, Ph.D. *"Genocide in the Americas."* The Nation, October 19, 1992, 430–434 http://www.skeptic.ca/Genocide_in_the_Americas.htm

14. Henry Louis Gates Jr. *"How Many Slaves Landed in the US?"* The Root. January 6, 2014. http://www.theroot.com/how-many-slaves-landed-in-the-us-1790873989

15. Karen Viera, *Powers, Women in the Crucible of Conquest, The Gendered Genesis of Spanish American Society, 1500–1600,* (New Mexico: University of New Mexico Press, 2005), 178.

16. *"Women In Resistance."* Slave Resistance A Caribbean Study. http://scholar.library.miami.edu/slaves/womens_resistance/womens.html

17. Melanie Byam, *"The Modernization of Resistance: Latin American Women since 1500."* Undergraduate Review, 4, 145–150. Available at: http://vc.bridgew.edu/undergrad_rev/vol4/issl/26; p.1.

18. Julie Shayne. *"Feminist Activism in Latin America."* Encyclopedia of Sociology. Blackwell Publishing. Vol no. 4: 1685–1689. 2007. http://www.Julieshayne.net/Ency_FemActv.pdf 1685.

19. Virginia Sanchez Korrol. *"Women in Nineteenth and Twentieth Century Latin America and the Caribbean."* http://emsc32.nysed.gov/ciai/socst/ghgonline/units/5/documents/Korrol.pdf

20. Sojourner Truth. *"Ain't I a Woman?"* December 1851. Modern History Sourcebook. https://sourcebooks.fordham.edu/mod/sojtruth-woman.asp

21. Ibid.

22. Frances M. Beal, "Double Jeopardy: To Be Black and Female," in *Black Women's Manifesto* (New York: Third World Women's Alliance, 1969), 21–22.

23. Laura Briggs, *Reproducing Empire: Race, Sex, Science, and US Imperialism in Puerto Rico* (Berkeley: University of California Press, 2002), 83–87.

24. "The Combahee River Collective Statement," http://circuitous.org/scraps/combahee.html

25. *Women Imagine Change,* eds. Eugenia C. DeLamotte, Natania Meeker, and Jean F. O' Barr (New York and London: Routledge, 1997), 3.

26. National Women's Law Center and Labor Council for Latin American Advancement (LCLAA). "Fact Sheet: Equal Pay for Latinas." http://lclaa.org /images/Trabajadoras_Campaign_2016/latinaequalpay _2016_ english.pdf

Reading 4.3

Define the following concepts/phrases:

Latinas

women resistance

activism

intersectionality

network of alliances

misogyny

LGBTQ

feminism

women of color feminism

Answer the following questions:

1. What are the reasons for Latina migration to the United States?
2. Describe characteristics of Latina women activism.
3. What is the meaning of the concept "double jeopardy" (Briggs) in reference to African American women?
4. How was male privilege embedded in the everyday practices of political, social, and cultural institution?
5. How did Sojourner Truth's life inspire Latina Activism?
6. Who is Dolores Huerta and how did her life inspire Latinas?
7. How did the system of power operate in a capitalist society at the individual and societal levels? How did the system impact women in regards to class, race, and ethnicity?
8. What are the twenty-first-century movements and campaigns that Latina women are organizing?

Part V

Migration and Transnationalism: Opportunities and Challenges

The Political Economy of Transnational Labor in New York City
The Context for Immigrant Workers Militancy

Immanuel Ness

AFTER YEARS OF WORKING IN OBSCURITY in the unregulated economy, transnational workers in New York City catapulted themselves to the forefront of labor activism in November and December 1999 through three separate organizing drives among low-wage workers. Immigrants initiated all three drives: Mexican immigrants organized and struck for improved wages and working conditions at greengroceries; Francophone African delivery workers struck for unpaid wages and respect from labor contractors for leading supermarket chains; and South Asians organized for improved conditions and a union in the for-hire car service industry.

This chapter argues that the militancy of immigrant workers arises from their distinct position within the political economy of New York City. Immigrant workers occupy specific economic and social niches characterized by exploitation and isolation that nurture class consciousness and militancy. These niches are the result of local and international economic processes and policies. Delineating the parameters of immigrant life on the job and in the community clarifies why seemingly invisible workers rise up to contest power in their workplaces and why immigrant workers are currently more prone to self-organization and unionization than are native-born workers.

Transnational Migration and New York City's Industrial Restructuring

During the decades on either side of the turn of the twentieth century, New York City's ethnic composition changed dramatically with the influx of Southern and Eastern European immigrants. They came to work in the city's burgeoning apparel, fur, printing, construction, and transportation industries. Many of these immigrants formed the backbone of the city's labor movement. By building the International Ladies Garment Workers Union, the Furriers Union, the International Brotherhood of Teamsters, and other unions, they made New York City a leading union center even before the passage of major federal labor legislation in the 1930s (Tichenor 2002).

Immigration to the United States and New York City declined dramatically with World War I and the passage of the Quota Act of 1921. The Immigration Act of 1924 (Johnson–Read Act) virtually shut the door to immigrants, especially from outside Northern Europe. As a result, it was the children of those earlier immigrants who launched the wave of industrial unionism in the 1930s. After World War II, most immigrants were Europeans displaced by war and Mexican agricultural workers.

Passage of the Hart–Celler Act in 1965 transformed immigration by eliminating country-of-origin quotas that had restricted immigration from non-European countries. The new legislation contributed to the expansion of immigration from Latin America, Asia, Africa, and the Caribbean, creating what sociologist Roger Waldinger (1996) calls "the new immigrants" (44–47). However, U.S. immigration policy since the 1980s has been incongruent with economic reality. On the whole, migration to the United States is growing with the demand for low-wage labor in manufacturing, services, and agriculture. The Immigration Reform and Control Act (IRCA) of 1986 intended to restrict unauthorized immigration but did almost nothing to stem the tide, as migration grew even faster. Ten years later, the Immigration Reform and Immigrant Responsibility Act of 1996, passed by the right-wing Republican majority in Congress, placed harsh restrictions on undocumented immigration. It, too, failed to halt the flow of immigrants. The failure of recent immigration restriction has been intentional, as economic priorities trumped political preference. In effect, there are two national immigration policies: the official policy of restricting immigration passed to satisfy anti-immigrant political constituencies and the actual policy of allowing a steady flow of immigration to satisfy the demands of corporate constituencies in search of cheap labor. This creates the best of both worlds for employers. On the one hand, low-wage immigrant labor is readily available. On the other, immigrant workers' illegal status increases employers' leverage in all aspects of the employment relationship.

As it did a century ago, the influx of immigrants at the turn of the twenty-first century has once again rearranged the ethnic mix of New York City. Many of the descendents of European immigrants have left the city for the suburbs, and their places have been taken by immigrants from Asia, Latin America, the Caribbean, Africa, and a new wave from former Communist countries in Eastern Europe. In the 1990s, New York State's officially documented foreign-born population—the vast majority of whom live in New York City—grew by nearly one million (Camarota and McArdle 2003, 10). The city's 2.9 million foreign-born residents make up 35.9 percent of the population. More than half the city's immigrants are from Latin America. A quarter is from Asia, a fifth from Europe, and 3.2 percent from Africa (United States Census Bureau 2000). Table 5.1.1 provides statistics on the country-of-origin breakdown of New York City immigrants.

TABLE 5.1.1 Legally Admitted Immigrants: Top 20 Source Countries to New York City Primary Metropolitan Statistical Areas, Fiscal Years 1992–2002

	Total Number Counted		New Arrivals 1992–2002		Adjustments*	
1	Dominican Rep.	179,596	Dominican Rep.	156,922	Former USSR	121,705
2	Former USSR	140,016	China	71,043	China	31,261
3	China	102,304	Jamaica	51,000	Dominican Rep.	22,674
4	Jamaica	68,070	Guyana	45,283	Jamaica	17,070
5	Guyana	54,488	Haiti	29,693	Trinidad & Tobago	14,992
6	India	39,382	Bangladesh	29,122	Philippines	14,099
7	Haiti	38,885	India	28,663	India	10,719
8	Ecuador	38,064	Ecuador	28,627	Korea	9,640
9	Poland	32,981	Poland	24,786	Ecuador	9,437
10	Bangladesh	32,828	Pakistan	23,106	Colombia	9,260
11	Trinidad & Tobago	32,173	Colombia	18,497	Guyana	9,205
12	Philippines	29,047	Trinidad & Tobago	17,181	Haiti	9,192
13	Pakistan	27,849	Former USSR	18,311	Poland	8,195
14	Colombia	27,757	Philippines	14,943	Mexico	8,342
15	Korea	16,606	Ireland	13,875	Former Yugoslavia	6,820
16	Ireland	14,897	Peru	11,307	United Kingdom	5,360
17	Peru	15,509	Ghana	9,185	Pakistan	4,743
18	Mexico	15,570	El Salvador	8,246	Israel	4,442
19	El Salvador	13,431	Honduras	8,112	El Salvador	5,185
20	Ghana	12,519	Mexico	7,228	Peru	4,202
	Total:	**931,972**		**615,130**		**326,543**

Source: Minnite, Lorraine. 2004. "Legally Admitted Immigrants: Top 20 Source Countries to New York City Primary Metropolitan Statistical Areas, Fiscal Years 1992–2002." Tabulation. New York.

*Adjustments represent immigrants overlooked in original enumeration.

Unlike their counterparts a century ago, many newcomers to New York City are now here illegally. Immigration restrictions have led to the creation of an underground population of transnational immigrants (See Basch Glick Schiller, and Szanton Blanc. 1993). Workers from Latin America typically migrate illegally without proper documentation; those from Africa, Asia, and Europe commonly arrive with business, worker, student, or tourist visas, which they overstay. In the wake of the events of September 11, 2001, the U.S. Bureau of Citizenship and Immigration Services (BCIS), a component of the new Department of Homeland Security, replaced the Immigration and Naturalization Service (INS) and cracked down on immigrants who overstay their visas by arresting and deporting many of them. BCIS has singled out southern and southwestern Asians for deportation because they tend to be on the Department of Homeland Security émigré watch list. Undocumented workers from the West Indies, Latin America, Eastern Europe, and East Asia—though frequently harassed—are less likely to be deported.

Whether they are in New York City legally or not, most recent immigrants work. In some cases, they do virtually the same work immigrants did a century ago. For example, just as Russian and Italian women sewed garments in sweatshops on the Lower East Side in the early twentieth century, today women from China and Latin America do the same thing in sweatshops in Chinatown and Sunset Park. Other new immigrants work in new or vastly altered industries, such as greengrocery, transportation, health care, domestic service, communications, delivery, and construction. Between 1990 and 2000, the percentage of immigrants in New York City increased from 28.4 percent to 35.9 percent. The 2000 Census reported that immigrants comprised nearly 2.9 million of the city's total population of just over eight million. Due to a high labor force participation rate, immigrants comprise 47 percent of the city's workforce. According to data compiled by the Fiscal Policy Institute based on the 2000 Census and 2003 Current Population Survey, immigrants represent 62 percent of the low-wage workforce earning between $5.15 and $7.10 an hour (Parrot 2004). Officially, workers from Latin America and the Caribbean (Dominican Republic, Haiti, and Trinidad and Tobago) comprise a large share of low-wage immigrants (see Table 5.1.2).

From 1970 to the present, the primary occupational trend in New York City's workforce has been the shift away from manufacturing to service industries. As the garment and printing trades have shrunk, retailing, personal services, and business services sectors of the economy have expanded. On the whole, native-born whites have gravitated to high-paying professional service jobs, African Americans and native-born Latinos have occupied jobs that rely on public sector funding. Meanwhile, over the past thirty years, immigrants tend to fill many of the low-wage jobs created in the new sectors of the economy. Low-end jobs in the service sector pay low wages and provide few, if any, benefits. These new jobs include private transportation, hotel and restaurant, delivery, security, building maintenance, and other low-wage services (Harris 1995; Kazis and Miller 2001).

TABLE 5.1.2   New York City's Low-Wage Immigrant Workforce by Place of Birth*

Country of Birth	Share of low-wage immigrants	Approximate number of low-wage immigrants	Share of foreign-born population, Census 2000
Dominican Republic	17.9%	90,000	12.9%
Mexico	13.7%	68,500	4.3%
China	6.0%	30,000	7.2%
Jamaica	5.7%	28,600	6.2%
Ecuador	5.4%	26,900	4.0%
Guyana	4.7%	23,700	4.6%
Haiti	3.5%	17,400	3.3%
Trinidad and Tobago	3.0%	15,000	3.1%
Russia	3.0%	15,000	2.8%
Colombia	2.5%	12,500	2.9%
Korea	2.2%	11,000	2.5%
India	2.0%	10,200	2.4%
El Salvador	2.0%	9,900	0.9%
Bangladesh	1.9%	9,600	1.5%
Poland	1.8%	8,900	2.3%
Total, 15 Countries	**75.2%**	**377,200**	**60.9%**

Source: Fiscal Policy Institute analysis of Current Population Survey Outgoing Rotation Group files provided by the Economic Policy Institute; Census 2000.

*Low-wage workforce defined as those earning less than $10/hour in inflation-adjusted 2003 dollars. The immigrant low-wage workforce numbered approximately 500,000 for the four-year period 2000 to 2003.

The recent influx of immigrant workers is the result of industrial restructuring and capital mobility that has eroded traditional industries and remade New York City's political economy in the last thirty years (Bronfenbrenner 2000). One very general aspect of this restructuring is the decline of manufacturing. Through the first three quarters of the twentieth century New York City was a center for small-scale, flexible manufacturing that employed skilled and semi-skilled workers who made a myriad of goods, including garments, printed matter, electrical equipment and supplies, non-electrical machinery, furniture, chemicals and allied products, leather and leather products, and food and beverage products. Today, with a few important exceptions such as apparel making and food service, most of these industries are either completely gone or marginal to the city's economy.

The loss of manufacturing jobs in New York City, like that elsewhere in the United States, has two basic sources: relocation and technological obsolescence. Neither process is particularly new, though they work at different paces in different periods. Manufacturing jobs have relocated out of New York City for many reasons, including the high cost of real estate, the difficulty and expense of transportation, and the relatively high rate of unionization. Rampant industrial closings have cut the city's manufacturing base from one million workers in 1950 to fewer than 200,000 today (Bureau of Labor Statistics 2002). In a typical recent example of job loss resulting from labor costs, the Swingline Stapler factory closed its doors in Long Island City in 2000, moving 450 manufacturing jobs to Nogales, Mexico, where workers earn a fraction of the wage earned in New York City. Often jobs can be moved because productivity has improved to the point where unskilled workers can replace skilled workers or jobs are rendered wholly redundant through advances in computerization (Levy and Murnane 2004, 31–54). In the middle of the twentieth century, as electrical equipment manufacturing grew more standardized production began to move from the city to New Jersey and Pennsylvania, and eventually to Mexico and China. Throughout the twentieth century, thousands of employers in chemicals, furniture, leather, and other industries made similar moves. Technological innovation eliminated many of the city's high-paying manufacturing jobs altogether. The most notable example of this is the printing and publishing industry, formerly home to one of the city's largest concentrations of unionized workers, where electronic publishing and computerized printing eliminated thousands of typesetters and pressmen. As standard jobs have been replaced by contingent work, a larger share of the labor market is falling into the informal sectors (Bailey and Waldinger 1991). Those industries in New York City that employ the greatest share of immigrants parallel the informalization of the industry in other large U.S. cities, as reflected in the Los Angeles data, where a large informal economy has grown in the low-wage service sector (see Table 5.1.3).

The decline of manufacturing has had manifold implications for the city's workforce. Most importantly, it has eliminated numerous possibilities for stable, well-paid employment and undermined some of the city's most powerful unions. The unemployment created by the shrinking, relocation, and closing of manufacturing establishments has put downward pressure on wages and working conditions in the rest of the city's economy. It has also freed up workers for employment in a whole new set of service industries. In these industries, specific strategies for corporate restructuring have led to the influx of immigrants from around the world.

None of the service industries that have risen to prominence in New York City's economy over the past half-century is particularly new. Finance, insurance, real estate, media, retail, and even technology have had long histories in the city. But these industries did not just get larger. They altered the way they did business. Most importantly, through subcontracting and outsourcing they have stimulated the development of highly competitive markets for various business and consumer services. Firms have broken down their work into smaller parts and farmed these parts out to weaker, marginal firms who compete on the basis of cheap labor. In the garment industry, one of the few remaining manufacturing industries, this age-old practice has seen a revival

TABLE 5.1.3 Informal Occupations—California

Occupational Category	Percent Informal
Private household services	42.82
Construction laborers	29.64
Cleaning and building	27.50
Food service	24.75
Construction trades	15.95
Motor-vehicle operators	13.68
Health technologists and technicians	5.18
Secretaries, stenographers, and typists	3.00
Teachers, elementary and secondary	1.91
Engineers	0.85
Police and fire fighting	0.71
Architects, mathematicians, and scientists	0.70

Source: Data derived from Marcelli, Pastor, and Joassart 1999, 586.

in recent decades as a network of small nonunion subcontractors employing immigrant workers in sweatshop conditions have popped up to undersell unionized apparel makers. The same phenomenon has occurred in construction and in the service sector. [...] New York City supermarkets contract out their delivery services to labor contractors who hire West African immigrants at below minimum wage. In an extreme form of this practice, firms do not actually hire their workers. Instead, they treat them as independent contractors, responsible for all the supplies and equipment needed to do their jobs. This was the case for South Asian black car drivers [...] before they unionized, and it is the case for immigrant and native-born telemarketing agents for banks, telephone companies, and retailers.

The decline of manufacturing and the rise of services altered the social geography of work in New York City. Service jobs tend to be dispersed in small firms throughout the city. Previous generations of immigrants who worked in small garment or printing shops benefited from the concentration of industries in specific areas of the city. As labor historian Joshua Freeman observes, mid-twentieth century New York City had a garment district, a printing district, a fur district, and a meatpacking district. The industrial geography of New York City, divided as it was into specialized economic zones, imparted a particular character to the city's economic life, labor relations, and even its culture. Areas like the garment district were swarming with local restaurants, cafeterias, bars, clubs, employment agencies, and union halls where employers and workers exchanged information, sought work or workers, socialized, organized, and developed shared ideas about life, work, and politics (Freeman 2000, 13–14). The immigrant social networks of the past established through these interchanges stimulated a class consciousness among employees at different companies that spurred the organizing of unions in various trades, crossing barriers of ethnicity.

That industrial topography is now extinct. This loss of manufacturing jobs has undermined the solidarity among workers that created strong unions. Since the 1970s, once-thriving industrial zones have been displaced by commercial and residential gentrification, which has made it almost impossible for small and medium-sized firms to remain. In the absence of commercial rent stabilization laws, rising real estate costs have uprooted entire trades from their old neighborhoods and dispersed them throughout the city and beyond. Only vestiges of the original industries remain. For example, between 1980 and 2000, Lower Manhattan's printing industry was displaced by commercial offices and residential housing. At the same time, technological advances enabled the publishing industry to outsource large segments of the production process to low-cost operators in the region. Service companies do not cluster, either. A growing number of low-wage services—domestic and janitorial work, for-hire vehicle services, restaurants, supermarkets, and retail stores—do not concentrate in a particular industrial zone, but are spread all over the city to meet customer needs.

The proliferation of geographically dispersed subcontractors who compete on the basis of low wages encourages a process of *informalization*—a term referring to a redistribution of work from regulated sectors of the economy to new unregulated sectors of the underground or informal economy. The result is a reduction of wages and a decline of working conditions below government-established norms. Although informalization is typically associated with underground economies in the developing world, there is growing recognition of the link between the regulated and unregulated sectors in advanced industrial regions. The regulated sector increasingly depends on unregulated economic activity through subcontracting and outsourcing of production to firms employing low-wage immigrant labor (Portes 1995; Portes and Castells 1991; Sassen 1991; 1999). Major corporations employ or subcontract to businesses employing transnational workers in what were once established sectors of the economy with decent wages and working conditions. Now the reliable jobs in the established labor market have been replaced by low wage jobs with substandard conditions commonly found underground. Thus, informalization does not represent industrial decline but horizontal restructuring, often done to maintain and increase flexibility and competitiveness in regional, national, and international markets.

Informalization requires government regulatory agencies to look the other way. For decades federal and New York State regulatory bodies have ignored violations of laws governing wages, hours, and workplace safety, leading to illegally low wages and declining workplace health and safety practices. The process of informalization is furthered by reduction and elimination of government wage protections such as disability insurance, Social Security, health care coverage, unemployment insurance, and workers compensation. Without these protections, workers—especially immigrant workers—are more dependent on their employers and more desperate for work.

The decline of union power and the process of informalization in New York City have been mutually reinforcing. On the one hand, the failure of unions to organize the newly established subcontractors in grocery, transportation, garment, construction, and other industries has allowed the subcontractors to flourish. On the other hand, the appearance of nonunion subcontractors has undermined the power of unions to win decent wages and working conditions from organized employers. In the regulated sector, between 1989 and 1999, jobs paying less than $25,000 per year increased by 81 percent; jobs paying $25,000 to $50,000 declined by 66.3 percent (Levitan 2000).

Creating a Pool of Low-Wage Workers

The informal sector is not limited to immigrant workers but also has grown to include a larger share of native-born workers employed in domestic services, personal services, and garment production. The size of the informal sector varies by occupation. For example, in 1999, the informal occupations in Los Angeles ranged from a low of 0.7 percent among architects, mathematicians, and scientists to 42.82 percent among domestic workers. Although no equivalent data breakdown of the informal economy is available for New York City, but because both cities have high numbers of new immigrants, one can extrapolate that the city's informal economy is equally large and growing at a rapid rate (see Table 5.1.4).

In essence, the growth of unregulated labor has dragged down wages in the regulated sector—in precisely the jobs where unions had been strongest. Some labor markets that had been under union control as late as the 1980s are now dominated by transnational workers. As a result, unions face something of a catch-22: They need to organize to increase their leverage against employers, but they need to demonstrate their ability to beat employers if they are to organize.

Still, unions are not helpless. While no labor market sector has been immune to informalization, worker organizing can sometimes reverse the trend, and labor markets can shift back and forth between standard and substandard. For example, in the building and construction industry a growing number of jobs formerly controlled by unions are now subcontracted to nonunion firms that perform an increasing proportion of construction work and hire marginal workers. Interior demolition and asbestos removal—the most strenuous, grimy, and dangerous construction work—is performed largely by Latin American and Eastern European immigrants. The nonunion firms have evaded state regulation, wages have fallen significantly below industry standards, and state and federal authorities have frequently ignored poor safety and health conditions. Even worse is that construction unions have been implicated in the mistreatment of transnational workers. In 1994, the New York City Mason and Tenders District Council of Greater New York of the Laborers' International Union of North America (LIUNA), which was dominated by

TABLE 5.1.4 New York City Industries Employing the Greatest Numbers of Immigrant Workers

Industry	Approximate number of immigrant workers	Immigrant share of industry's employment (%)	Median hourly wage of industry's immigrant workforce (2003 dollars)
Eating and drinking places	125,470	73	8.55
Construction	100,270	62	13.30
Hospitals	79,900	45	16.36
Health services	71,670	64	8.69
Apparel and accessories manufacturing	54,160	89	8.39
Elementary and secondary schools	45,840	26	15.34
Real estate	39,670	47	14.15
Grocery stores	38,670	64	8.01
Private households	38,360	85	7.96
Bus service and urban transit	33,680	46	14.69

Source: FPI analysis of CPS ORG files provided by EPI; Census 2000.

organized crime in the 1980s and 1990s, was placed into trusteeship by the federal government after it collected evidence that the union allowed firms to hire nonunion immigrant workers at a small fraction of normal union wages. However, only two years later, the union facilitated the organization of some 2,000 new members into LIUNA Local 78, a new local. Through the organization of immigrant workers within their communities and direct action at workplaces, the union again became a viable force in the building and construction industry (Kieffer and Ness 1999).

By the 1990s, substandard jobs employing transnational workers had become crucial to key sectors of the economy of New York City. Today, immigrants have gained a major presence as bricklayers, demolition workers, and hazardous waste workers on construction and building rehabilitation sites; as cooks, dishwashers, and busboys in restaurants; and as taxi drivers, domestic workers, and delivery people. Employers frequently treat these workers as self-employed. They have no union protection and little or no job security. With government enforcement shrinking, they lack the protection of minimum-wage laws and they have been excluded from Social Security and unemployment insurance. They are increasingly victimized by employers who force them to accept nineteenth-century working conditions and wages below the federally mandated minimum of $5.15 per hour.

Despite and because of industrial restructuring, New York City has become a nexus of international labor migration, with a constantly churning labor market. As long as there is a demand for cheap labor, immigrants will continue to enter the United States in large numbers. Stephen Castles (2002), an authority on immigration, challenges the conventional and parochial position that migration is caused solely by economic deprivation in the undeveloped world of the global South:

> Migration does not present an economic or social crisis for the North ... . [T]he main reason for the presence of economic migrants is that they are needed to fill jobs in industry and services. Undocumented entry of unskilled workers is seen as a problem, but is actually a result of Northern economic structures and immigration policies. Since there is a high demand for such workers in construction, manufacturing and services, the result is a burgeoning of undocumented workers in the informal sector. (188)

While many transnational workers migrate illegally and are treated inhospitably by employers and the general populace in their new countries, they have become crucial to corporate strategies that demand fluidity of capital, production, and labor (Michael Peter Smith 2001; Stalker 2001).

Although the *demand* for low-wage labor induces immigration from the global South, the *availability* of an immigrant work force enables employers in the urban centers of the global North such as New York City to pursue business strategies that rely on low-wage labor. New immigrants from the global South are crucial to the expansion of New York City's labor market [...]. The reserve army of immigrant worker labor provides an enormous incentive for larger corporations to create and use subcontracting firms. Without this workforce, employers in the regulated economy would have more incentive to invest in labor-saving technology, increase the capital–labor ratio, and seek accommodation with unions. As Guerin-Gonzalez and Strikwerda (1993) assert: "The international migration of workers is ... one element in a struggle for control over labor power and the conditions of work between industrial capitalists and workers (16)."[1]

Employers in restructured labor markets neglect native-born workers and recruit from among foreign immigrant workers [...]. In most cases, immigrants do not directly displace native-born workers. Instead, employers undermine established wage and working standards through industrial restructuring. This can take the form of union busting, relocation, outsourcing, the establishment of subsidiaries, or through the entrance of new capital and the creation of new firms. In each case, new jobs are created but at much lower wages and with worse working conditions precisely because the firms seek their competitive advantage through the use of low-wage labor. To meet this goal, they seek out workers who are willing to work for lower wages. New unauthorized immigrants residing and working in the U.S. are ideal: Their undocumented legal status makes them more tractable since they constantly fear deportation as 'illegals.' Undocumented immigrants understand less than do native-born workers about established labor standards, and even low U.S. wages represent an improvement over earnings in their home countries. The result of this interaction between supply and demand is a labor market segmented by race, nationality, and gender. For example, gender plays an important role among domestic workers in the Los Angeles labor market. The mostly female labor force has replaced some professional women in the household by performing domestic work, caring for children and the elderly, doing laundry, and running errands (Hondagneu-Sotelo 2001; Stafford 1985).[2]

The perception that new immigrants undermine the norms of the regulated labor market and threaten native-born workers by undercutting prevailing wage and work standards cannot be entirely dismissed. Immigrants in the underground economy reduce the labor market leverage of native-born workers and weaken government labor protections won by workers in the past century. But it is corporations—not immigrant workers—who benefit from this state of affairs. Rather than attributing the decline in working conditions to businesses that exploit immigrant labor and profit from lowered labor standards, some analysts blame immigration for the decline in native-born wages and working conditions (Briggs 2001; Buchanan 2001).

In the 1990s postindustrial era, the reduction of trade restrictions is driving consumer demand for low-wage goods and services. A large sector of this new growth is driven by expanding corporate and consumer dependence on informal goods and services. The postindustrial economic restructuring from goods production to services in the North and the growing impoverishment in the South is the impetus for growing migration. Notably, the informal economy is not isolated from the formal sector, but becomes integrated into the broader economy. Low-wage and low-skill service jobs are not isolated but vital to the formal sector as the need for domestic workers, delivery, retail, food services, transportation, hospitality, and other tasks becomes essential to the mainstream economy. While the informal sector is not regulated by the government, the formal sector remains dependent on workers for low-skill work.

The results of neoliberal policy and the legacy of colonization have undermined rural society and created unemployment and underemployment in many source countries. Without this process, most people would not leave those countries and would not provide the workforce necessary for the informalization process. Thus, undocumented migration is caused, on the one hand, by growing poverty conditions produced by neoliberal market reforms that eliminate social protection in the global South, and on the other hand, by demand for low-skill, low-wage labor in the global North creating the need for a pool of low-wage workers. Informal work is created through economic restructuring on a global and local level that fuels interdependency between formal and informal sectors.

Neoliberal policies have encouraged economic restructuring in the South that is the basis for the migration to the North. The availability of a large pool of low-wage migrant workers increases business reliance on low-wage and low-skill jobs in both formal and informal sectors. Indeed, foreign remittances from undocumented workers in the U.S. are an important source of revenue for countries of the global South. Deregulation of economic activity has displaced workers and rural peasants in Central America and the Caribbean through the creation of free-trade zones and the removal of government-sponsored social services for the poor. Long-established government subsidies provided by countries of the South that had sustained rural peasants and the urban working classes have been cut back significantly, precipitating the decline in food price supports, publicly subsidized housing, health care, and universal education. International migration is thus facilitated by the failure of governments of the South to support those with the fewest independent resources.

Forging Immigrant Solidarity

As a result of deliberate corporate and government policies that have transformed the New York City economy, myriad immigrant workers now occupy a range of employment niches at the bottom of the city's job hierarchy. They work under harsh conditions in unconventional work relationships. Because of restructured labor markets, outsourcing, nonenforcement of labor laws governing wages and working conditions, and the decline of union power, New York City businesses are engaging in exploitative labor practices not seen in nearly a century. [...] [E]mployers have frequently redefined immigrant workers as independent contractors, or even as entrepreneurs, while they actually resemble indentured servants. New low-wage transnational workers endure greater exploitation than did the workers who preceded them in similar occupations.

How then do new immigrants with tenuous ties to the organized labor movement and the state assert their interests? The answer lies in the character of immigrant work and social life. Both on the job and off, immigrants are concentrated by ethnicity, color, gender, language, religion, and nationality. As a consequence, they can draw on shared experiences and identities to create solidarity at work and in their communities.

New immigrants typically find jobs through social networks that are established in their home countries and reinforced in New York City. These networks usually point them to jobs in ethnic niches, creating what Foner refers to as the "ethnic division of labor" (2001, 1–31). But this division of labor actually includes a broader range of identities that goes beyond ethnicity. The "ethnic niche" hypothesis put forward by Waldinger suggests that employer–worker social networks create segmented immigrant labor markets. However, by focusing only upon country of origin, Waldinger misses the larger range of identities that funnels immigrants into certain industries. "Ethnic niches" can be expanded to include a broader range of distinctions—color, gender, language, religion, and nationality—that can collectively be called "identity niches." These niches are often reproduced outside the job in identity-defined communities.

Transnational workers bring social identities from their home countries, while new identities are shaped through socialization and work in this country. In New York City, the segmentation of immigrant workers from specific countries reinforces ethnic, national, and religious identities and helps to form other identities that may stimulate solidarity. For example, before arriving in the United States, Mexican immigrant workers often see themselves as peasants but not as "people of color," while Francophone Africans see themselves as Malian or Senegalese ethnics but not necessarily "black." Life and work in New York can encourage immigrants to adopt these new identities.

Isolated in their jobs and communities, immigrant workers have few social ties to unions, community groups, and public officials, and few resources to call upon to assist them in transforming their workplaces. Because new immigrants have few social networks outside the workplace, the ties they develop on the job are especially solid and meaningful—and are nurtured every day. The workers' very isolation and status as outsiders, and their concentration into industrial niches by employers who hire on the basis of identity, tend to strengthen old social ties, build new ones, and deepen class solidarity. Having few ties to well-established social organizations, immigrants' common bonds become stronger and more important (Foner, Rumbaut, and Gold 2000).

It is through these thick relationships developed on the job and frequently in the community that mutual resentment of the employer evolves into class consciousness and class solidarity. Typically, few workplace hierarchies exist among immigrant workers, since hardly any employees rise to supervisory positions. As a result, immigrant workers suffer poor treatment equally at the hands of employers. The interviews in this book show a gathering sense of collective exploitation that usually transforms individualistic activities into shared action. In the rare cases where there are immigrant foremen and crew leaders, recognizing this solidarity, many side with the workers, not with management. One former manager employed for a fast-food sandwich chain in New York City said: "We are hired only to divide the workers but I was really trying to help the workers get better pay and shorter hours" (interview, anonymous Mexican worker, October 2, 2003).

The timing of immigrant worker militancy is difficult to calculate, but it is usually based on a simultaneous process of workers realizing that they are treated in a disrespectful and worthless fashion, are paid unfair wages, and cannot make ends meet. Personal forms of abuse and discrimination are practiced every day in transnational immigrant work environments. But there is usually a trigger that sets workers off—nonpayment of wages or management verbal and physical abuse. Another important factor is the organizing that goes from workplace to workplace like wildfire. When workers realize that they *can* fight and prevail, it creates a sense of invincibility that stimulates militant action that would otherwise be avoided at all costs. This demonstration effect is vitally important, as was the case in past strikes among garment workers and coal miners.

Immigrant social networks established through ascriptive ties derived from heritage and through labor market niches provide the basis for worker militancy by solidifying and intensifying solidarities at the workplace. The concentration of immigrant networks at one job or labor market creates shared experiences on the basis of common exploitation that translate into more intense levels of resistance against employers and labor contractors. For example, over the last decade, concentration of Ecuadorian laborers in menial jobs as busboys and dishwashers in New York City's restaurant industry has consolidated labor solidarity on the basis of national origin. Because recent immigrant workers work all day and go home to neighborhoods, buildings, and even apartments in racially segregated communities, labor exploitation on the job is often the primary conversation on the street corner, soccer field, or at the dinner table. The fact that new immigrants work at subminimum wages under harsh conditions sets in motion labor resistance and worker militancy on the job.

Long days and nights spent working and living together give immigrant workers the opportunity to form ties that are thicker and more resilient than those of native-born workers who work shorter and fewer days and live separately. The typical immigrant in the informal sector can expect to work twelve-hour days, seven days a week. When arriving home, immigrant workers frequently share the same apartments, buildings, and neighborhoods. These employment ghettos typify immigrant communities in Harlem and Washington Heights, Manhattan; South Bronx; Woodside and Elmhurst, Queens; and Sunset Park and Brighton Beach, Brooklyn. Workers cook for one another, share stories about their oppressively long and hard days, commiserate about their ill treatment at work, and then go to sleep only to start the same day anew.

Immigrant social networks contribute to workplace militancy. Conversely, activism at work can stimulate new social networks that can expand workers' power. Evidence of the social interaction that is crystallized in the workplace and in the community is found in the formation of informal organizations, employee meetings to respond to employer abuse, and action on the shop floor in defiance of employer abuse. These social networks, for example among workers in the for-hire transportation industry, do not only emerge from the identity backgrounds of workers, but are shaped by their common struggles on the job.

In cases where workers are treated as a generic bloc, as with West Africans, they tend to switch identity from Senegalese, to French West Africans, to Africans. Despite the threat of job loss and deportation, on-the-job and community organizing leads to improved working conditions, respect, and dignity on the job. Organizing among transnational workers gains the attention of labor unions, which then see a chance to recruit new members and may provide resources to help immigrant workers mobilize at work and join the union.

The identities that already exist among workers through ethnicity, nationality, language, and religion are reinforced here in the States by the class identity immigrants are made to assume on the job. The ethnographic case studies of transnational immigrants that make up the heart of this book demonstrate that social identities are reinforced on a class basis in the restructured workplace. Employers' segmentation of transnational workers strengthens existing social networks and prevents the formation of new networks extending into the broader labor market. That is, immigrants cleave to traditional bonds based on ethnicity, nationality, language, and religion, and are not assimilated into the dominant society.

Religious Identity

A growing body of research demonstrates that immigrants retain and reinforce their religious faith upon arrival in the United States—even becoming more observant. For example, in a study of new immigrants, Ebaugh and Chafetz (2000) found that Buddhist, Greek Orthodox, and Zoroastrian faiths, transplanted through the founding of new institutions, have profoundly changed the character of Houston neighborhoods. An ethnographic study of religion in New York City's Chinatown by Guest (2003) shows that the dramatic growth in immigration from Fuzhou Province in China since the 1980s has reinforced Buddhist, Daoist, Protestant, and Catholic religious identities. Religion is an important means of gaining access to labor markets, solidifying labor enclaves, and establishing class bonds through friendships formed in churches and mosques.

[...] [R]eligion is an important part of identity and can strengthen class solidarity. Just as color and ethnicity are used to drive immigrants into certain labor niches, religion delineates boundaries between native-born and foreign workers. Immigrants—whether observant or not—frequently find it advantageous to refer to their religious faith to gain friends, find work, and form bonds on the job.

New immigrants from Mexico often go to churches to socialize, find job openings, and protest working conditions. Mexican churches in New York City neighborhoods are among the few forums for discussion about workplace conditions and the local labor market. At Our Lady of Guadeloupe, a Roman Catholic Church in Lower Manhattan, recent Mexican immigrants congregate for weekly services, religious, and national holidays. Workers use connections they make through fellow congregants to find leads to jobs in industries that often hire Mexicans. They join the church's Mexican immigrant organization, Tepeyac, for help during disputes with employers, and they frequently participate in demonstrations calling for a general amnesty for immigrants and for Mexican immigrant workers' rights. Brother Joel Magallan, pastor of the church, is a long-time advocate of those rights. In 2002, Our Lady of Guadeloupe sponsored the formation of the Mexican Workers Union (MWU) to help greengrocery workers organize and to advocate on behalf of fellow nationals in labor disputes with employers.

New immigrants from Islamic countries typically find jobs in the same industries as Muslims who preceded them. The personal transportation industry, comprised of taxicabs, limousines, and other for-hire vehicles, is a magnet for immigrants from the Muslim world, and most drivers are adherents of Islam. Interviews with for-hire vehicle drivers[3] demonstrate that Islamic faith overrides all other forms of identity, including language, nationality, and ethnicity. These ties lead to the formation of prayer groups held in workers' homes, workplaces, and the growing number of New York City mosques that become gatherings for discussion and debate about labor conditions.

Gender and the Division of Immigrant Labor

Patterns of gender stratification found in the general labor market are even more apparent among undocumented workers. Rarely do migrant workers of the same sex work in the same labor market. The gender differentiation is frequently reinforced by religion. Also, given the prohibition of male and female communication within civil society, even those women who work in the labor market tend to work in domestic work, garment factories, and other jobs in the lowest rungs of the economy segmented on the basis of gender. The transnational workers in this book's case studies are almost all male. The preponderance of men in the greengrocery, delivery, and for-hire driving industries stems from migration patterns and employers' reliance on gender stereotypes. The men in a family, rather than the women, typically make the first trips to the United States. Most female relatives commonly stay in their countries of origin to care for the families of transnational workers, although younger women frequently make the trek to New York City to work in the garment industry.

Some jobs in the nonunion economy, such as construction and driving, are stereotypically considered "men's work." Although food preparation is stereotypically "women's work," Latinos have had a history of working in the food service industry since the early twentieth century when they were recruited to work on American farms as contract laborers. However, women predominate in the apparel industry, make up the majority of domestic and childcare workers, and are increasingly found washing clothes in laundries. Like their male counterparts, female transnational workers usually arrive in the United States alone, without their families, precluding or greatly impeding permanent settlement and the establishment of immigrant communities.

Conclusion

The distinctiveness of migrant worker militancy in low-wage jobs above expectations and against the odds is critical to understanding native-born worker militancy as well. This unanticipated militancy is a product of the corporate restructuring that has created sub-minimum wage, dead-end, jobs below the poverty line. A major finding of this book is that immigrants tend to engage in collective action at least as much as native-born workers. However, at the same time this book finds that immigrants do not possess any inherently greater militancy or passivity than native workers. Cultures of militancy and passivity among all workers are structured by social relations producing ripe conditions for organizing. That is, immigrants do not have a cultural propensity to organize and native workers are not out-and-out hostile to organizing.

Three workplace conditions seem to produce greater militancy on the job among immigrant workers than native-born workers: first, collective social isolation that engenders stronger ties among immigrants than native-born workers in low-skill and low-wage jobs where organizing is frequently seen as the only way to improve conditions. Because immigrants work in jobs that tend to be more amenable to organizing, they are highly represented among newly unionized workers. The occurrence of strong social ties to the workplace drives immigrants to form their own embryonic organizations and to rely on unorthodox repertoires of struggle against their employers. The new social organizations formed by immigrants are ripe for union representation.

Second, employers play a major role in immigrant workers being more likely to organize than are native-born workers. Firms employing native-born workers tend to be larger and are often much harder to organize than the small businesses where immigrants in New York City work. The Merriam-Webster dictionary, published in June 2003, includes the new word *McJob*, defined as "a low-paying job that requires little skill and provides little opportunity for advancement." The reference reflects the relentless thirty-year economic restructuring that has created low-end jobs in the retail sector that pay low wages, provide few benefits, lack job security, and have poor working conditions. Corporate restructuring has downgraded both wages and working conditions among both native and immigrant workers. In another example, the retail giant Wal-Mart epitomizes the proliferation of postindustrial jobs in the retail industry that fail to pay enough to cover workers' basic needs.

Organizing against McDonalds or Wal-Mart is completely different from organizing against smaller employers who have fewer resources. Wal-Mart uses many of the same tactics against workers that immigrants contend with: failure to pay overtime, stealing time (intentionally paying workers for less hours than actually worked), no health care, part-time work, high turnover, and gender division of labor. The difference is that Wal-Mart has far more resources to oppose unionization than do the smaller employers who are frequently subcontractors to larger firms.

The redefinition of labor in the underground immigrant economy that this book examines is substantially different from low-wage nonunion work proliferating through the growth of chain stores and restaurants like Wal-Mart and McDonalds. Why do workers appear complacent in giant retail and restaurant chain stores while new immigrants frequently employed in smaller firms are so militant?

Under current labor law, both unorganized immigrant workers and native-born workers are hired and fired without due process at the behest of employers. As labor law has eroded, employers are emboldened to exploit workers to gain greater profits. There are no job protections, except those against discrimination—and these protections are weakly enforced. But, because native-born workers tend to be socially isolated and atomized in McJobs, they do not have the same opportunities immigrants have to resist through organizing and collective action. Employers may be aware that undocumented immigrants are legally vulnerable, but are unaware of the solidarity that is built up through collective social isolation.

Finally, the fact that native-born workers have an exit strategy and transnational workers do not is a significant and important difference. The notion of exit draws on Albert Hirschman's (1990) study, *Exit, Voice, and Loyalty: Responses to Decline in Firms, Organizations, and States*, which argues that the public and consumers have two different ways of demonstrating dissatisfaction with the quality of services. In this case, native-born workers have the option to exit from their jobs whereas immigrant workers are more prone to use voice to change the situation because they have far fewer options. By exercising voice, immigrant workers can push firms to improve their wages and working conditions. Workers employed at large firms like Wal-Mart and its ilk are unable to use voice, since they have little power and will be summarily fired for any form of dissent.

Labor–management conflict in the sprawling nonunion service sector is regulated by the state and business codes of conduct, which demarcate the boundaries of struggle. If you violate the terms of Wal-Mart's or McDonalds' employee manual by, say, arriving late, and then are summarily fired—due to social isolation on the job produced by constant employee turnover—no one is there to fend for you as is usually the case among undocumented workers employed in a small business.[4]

The expanding non-immigrant low-end service sector tends to produce unskilled part-time jobs that do not train workers in skills that keep them in the same labor market. Because jobs at the low end of the economy require little training, workers frequently move from one industry to the next. One day a native-born worker may work as a sales clerk for Target and the next day work for as a waiter at Olive Garden. Because they are not stuck in identity-defined niches, native-born immigrants can more easily exit a job they do not like, giving them less reason to organize and unionize.

Exit is, however, not the option of choice for most immigrant workers. Frequently, migrant workers engage in direct action against their employers to obtain higher wages and respect on the job. Employers firing new immigrant workers may risk a demonstration, picket line, or even a strike. Native-born workers employed by large and small employers protest through quitting and finding a new job elsewhere; they do not develop the same dense connections as do new immigrants driven into labor market niches who forge solidarity through working together.

Immigrant workers are pushed into low-wage labor market niches as day laborers, food handlers, delivery workers, and nannies; these niches are difficult if not impossible to escape. Consequently, with the exception of day laborers, immigrants tend to be employed for longer time spans in the same industry and with the same employer than are native-born workers. This longevity fosters greater solidarity for immigrants compared with native workers who may work in a litany of industries. [...] [I]mmigrant workers who are relegated to dead-end jobs in the lowest echelons of the labor market in food, delivery, and car service work show a greater eagerness to fight it out to improve their wages and conditions than do native workers who can move on to another dead-end job.

The perilous state of low-wage labor in New York City resembles the precarious conditions of the early twentieth century. In his account of immigrant organizing during the Progressive Era, Dubofsky notes that, from 1900 to 1910, the vast majority of low-wage workers in the city's industries were nonunionized Jewish and Italian immigrants. Throughout the following decade, labor unrest and strikes by these immigrant industrial workers remade the New York City labor movement. Union membership in the apparel industry increased from 30,000 garment workers in 1909 to 250,000 in 1913, primarily through the organization of female immigrants (Dubofsky 1969, 4).[5]

Early twentieth-century immigrant workers were more militant than the native-born because they had greater expectations for a better life in America. Dubofsky contends that, unlike native-born workers, they had not anticipated low wages and exceptionally arduous working conditions before they arrived in the United States. The occurrence of militancy and activism among immigrant workers, a key question this book seeks to answer, is partly addressed in this phenomenon of unmet expectations. Nearly ninety years later, low-wage immigrant workers labor under abusive conditions not unlike those of a century ago. Jarred by the harsh reality of working in New York City's unregulated sectors, recent immigrants regularly recount sorrowful stories of their unmet expectations in America.

Labor militancy among today's immigrants is no new, unique phenomenon. It is a response to the degradation of wages and working conditions over the past thirty years, after organized labor greatly improved working conditions from the 1940s to the 1970s. Those decades of labor power were a departure from the corporate domination, labor suppression, and class conflict that preceded and followed them. The breaking of the employer–employee compact, which had been established under the New Deal, by businesses in the 1970s, severely compromised the power of organized labor, leaving many workers with no recourse but renewed struggle within the workplace. Militancy among immigrants inside and outside of unions today is a response to business' thirty-year assault against American workers, largely without government penalties or substantial labor unrest. Economic restructuring and union concessions have given rise to a new workplace, where dissent is not filtered through union agents but is expressed by workers themselves.[6] That immigrant workers are at the vanguard of new organizing is startling, considering their paucity of resources and allies in organized labor. But the organizing is predictable, given workers' deep social ties built on the job and the absence of legal or employer regulations governing the workplace.

Endnotes

1. Guerin-Gonzalez and Strikwerda (1993) argue that "A vital and an often overlooked characteristic of labor migration is that in-migration of workers is actively encouraged and even initiated by employers in advanced industrial countries despite the presence of unemployed native-born workers who could be recruited for these jobs (16).

2. Hondagneu-Sotelo (2001) notes that women have assumed work in domestic services; adult male immigrants have largely replaced the native-born low-wage men in providing private transportation and making deliveries and adolescent boys in delivering newspapers and groceries, mowing lawns, and running errands.

3. One anonymous driver, interviewed after a gathering in defense of immigrant rights, spoke for many others at a meeting held in September 2003: "When we look for a job driving a car, we are asked two questions. The first is 'What country are you from?' This answers the second question, because usually people know your religion if they know where you are from. If people say they are from countries with large Muslim populations, they are then asked: 'Are you a Muslim?' Once they know that you are Muslim, they shake your hand and say 'Salaam Ale Ichim' (peace be unto you)."

4. In the case of Wal-Mart and a growing number of large retailers, the term "employee" is not even used. At Wal-Mart, employees are referred to as "associates." At Target, another big box store, employees are known as "team members." Thus, low-wage American workers do not see themselves as employees of businesses but in business for themselves, leading to a decline in class consciousness. The fact that workers in these establishments have limited job stability further erodes class solidarity.

5. Dubofsky (1969) makes clear that the abundance of low-wage labor did not deter immigrants from organizing to improve their conditions: "The metropolitan economy ... attracted a large proportion of less skilled immigrant workers who satisfied the needs of small trades with minutely subdivided operations. Lacking scarce skills and trade unions, the great majority of the city's workers suffered the anxieties wrought by low wages and economic insecurity. Realizing that conditions were far from ideal, that they were in fact often intolerable, the unorganized refused to accept poor conditions and unsatisfactory remuneration as either inevitable or permanent (13)."

6. The notion of a "working class New York" put forward by Joshua Freeman (2000) is rooted in the mid-twentieth century, when working-class conflict and power erupted throughout the United States. The absence of union strength today is reflected in greater business hostility toward labor, the erosion of labor standards, weaker labor laws, and a decline in government enforcement of worker safeguards. Still, Freeman asserts that New York remains a "working class" city due to its long legacy of mass labor militancy that created an abundance of unions.

References

Books, Chapters, Articles, Reports, and Press Releases

Bailey, Thomas, and Roger Waldinger. 1991. "The Changing Ethnic/Racial Division of Labor." In *Dual City: Restructuring New York*, ed. Mollenkopf, John and Manuel Castels. 73–78. New York: Russell Sage Foundation.

Basch, Linda, Nina Glick Schiller, and Cristina Szanton Blanc. 1993. *Nations Unbound: Transnational Projects, Postcolonial Predicaments and Deterritorialized Nation States*. Langhorne, PA: Gordon and Breach.

Briggs, Vernon M., Jr. 2001. *Immigration and American Unionism*. Ithaca: Cornell University Press.

Bronfenbrenner, Kate. 2000. "Uneasy Terrain: The Impact of Capital Mobility on Workers, Wages, and Union Organizing." Paper presented to U.S. Trade Deficit Review Commission, Washington, DC.

Buchanan, Patrick. 2001. *The Death of the West: How Mass Immigration, Depopulation and a Dying Faith Are Killing Our Culture and Country*. New York: St. Martin's Press.

Bureau of Labor Statistics. 2002. *Metropolitan Area at a Glance*. New York: U.S. Department of Labor, Northeast Regional Office.

Camarota, Steven A., and Nora McArdle. 2003. *Where Immigrants Live: An Examination of State Residency of the Foreign Born by Country of Origin in 1990 and 2000*. Washington, DC: Center for Immigration Studies, September.

Castles, Stephen. 2002. "The International Politics of Forced Migration." In *Fighting Identities: Race, Religion and Ethno-Nationalism*, ed. Leo Panitch and Colin Leys. 172–192. London: Merlin Press.

Dubofsky, Melvyn. 1969. *We Shall Be All: A History of the Industrial Workers of the World*. Chicago Quadrangle Books.

Ebaugh, Helen R.F., and Janet S. Chafetz, eds. 2000. *Religion and the New Immigrants: Continuities and Adaptations in Immigrant Congregations*. Lanham, MD: Rowman and Littlefield.

Foner, Nancy. 2001. *From Ellis Island to JFK: New York's Two Great Waves of Immigration*. New Haven: Yale University Press.

Foner, Nancy, Rubén G. Rumbaut, and Steven J. Gold, eds. 2000. *Immigrant Research for a New Century. Multidisciplinary Perspectives*. New York: Russell Sage Foundation.

Freeman, Joshua. 2000. *Working Class New York: Life and Labor since World War II*. New York: The New Press.

Freeman, Richard B., and Joel Rogers. 2002. "A Proposal to American Labor." *The Nation*, June 24, 18–24.

Guerin-Gonzalez, Camille, and Carl Strikwerda. 1993. *The Politics of Immigrant Workers: Labor Activism and Migration in the World Economy since 1830*. New York: Holmes & Meier.

Guest, Kenneth J. 2003. *God in Chinatown*. New York: New York University Press.

Harris, Nigel. 1995. *The New Untouchables: Immigration and the New World Worker*. London: I.B. Tauris Publishers.

Hirschman, Albert O. 1990. *Exit, Voice, and Loyalty: Responses to Decline in Firms, Organizations, and States*. Cambridge: Harvard University Press.

Hondagneu-Sotelo, Pierrette. 2001. *Doméstica: Immigrant Workers Cleaning and Caring in the Shadows of Affluence*. Berkeley: University of California Press.

Kieffer, David, and Immanuel Ness. 1999. "Organizing Immigrant Workers in New York City: The LIUNA Asbestos Removal Workers Campaign." *Labor Studies Journal* 24 (1): 12–26.

Levitan, Mark. 2000. *Building a Ladder to Jobs and Higher Wages: A Report by the Working Group on New York City's Low-Wages Labor Market*. New York: Community Services Society.

Levy, Frank, and Richard J. Murnane. 2004. *The New Division of Labor: How Computers Are Creating the Next Job Market*. Princeton: Princeton University Press.

Marcelli, E., M. Pastor, and P. Joassart. 1999. "Estimating the Effects of Informal Economic Activity: Evidence from Los Angeles." *Journal of Economic Issues* 33 (3): 579–607.

Merriam-Webster's *Eleventh New Collegiate Dictionary*. 2003. Springfield, MA: Merriam-Webster.

Minnite, Lorraine. 2004. "Legally Admitted Immigrants: Top 20 Source Countries to New York City Primary Metropolitan Statistical Areas, Fiscal Years 1992–2002." Tabulation. New York.

Portes, Alejandro, ed. 1995. *The Economic Sociology of Immigration*. New York: Russell Sage Foundation.

Portes, Alejandro, and Manuel Castels. 1991 "World Underneath: The Origins, Dynamics, and Effects of the Informal Economy." In *The Informal Economy: Studies in Advanced and Less Developed Countries*, ed. Alejandro Portes, Manuel Castels, and Lauren Benton. 11–37. Baltimore: Johns Hopkins University Press.

Sassen, Saskia. 1991. *The Global City: New York, London, Tokyo*. Princeton: Princeton University Press.

———. 1999. *Globalization and Its Discontents: Essays on the New Mobility of People and Money*. New York: New Press.

Smith, Michael Peter. 2001. *Transnational Urbanism: Locating Globalization*. Malden, MA: Blackwell.

Stafford, Walter. 1985. *Closed Labor Markets: Underrepresentation of Blacks, Hispanics and Women in New York City's Core Industries and Jobs*. New York: Community Service Society.

Stalker, Peter. 2001. *The No-Nonsense Guide to International Migration*. New York: Verso.

Tichenor, Daniel J. 2002. *Dividing Lines: The Politics of Immigration Control in America*. Princeton: Princeton University Press.

Waldinger, Roger. 1996. *Still the Promised City? African-Americans and New Immigrants in Postindustrial New York*. Cambridge: Harvard University Press.

Interviews

Anonymous Interviews with individuals, workers, union officials, and staff, November 1997–June 2004.

Define the following concepts/phrases:

economic restructuring	working class New Yorker
class-consciousness	pool of low-wage workers
over-exploitation	McJobs
informal sector	informalization
industrial geography	decline of union power

Answer the following questions:

1. Who were the immigrants that came at the beginning of the twentieth century?
2. What unions were organized for the new immigrants?
3. How did the Immigrant Act of 1924 reduce the immigration from outside northern Europe?
4. Discuss the changes in the migration law with the Hart-Celler Act of 1965.
5. How did the Immigration Reform and Control Act of 1986(IRCA) differ from the Illegal Immigration Reform and Immigrant Responsibility Act of 1996 (IIRAIRA)?
6. In the reading the author states that "There are two national immigration policies." Explain the differences between these policies.
7. How did downsizing, subcontracting, and outsourcing impact the working class and union power?
8. How did the service industry impact the "social geography of work in New York City"?

Guatemala's Ladino and Maya Migra Landscapes

The Tangible and Intangible Outcomes of Migration

Michelle J. Moran-Taylor

Introduction

As globalization and transnational processes intensify, these broader forces touch peoples' lives and localities in myriad ways. This article examines an increasingly vital policy and research concern—the impact of international migration on sending communities. It does this by looking at two ethnically, regionally, and historically distinct migrant communities of origin in Guatemala. International migration is the single most important social, cultural, and economic phenomenon affecting Guatemala. Over the last three decades, this human flow has grown dramatically, cutting across gender, generational, class, and ethnic boundaries. Today, nearly 15 percent of Guatemala's 12 million population migrates to the United States, and increasingly others as far afield as Canada. That figure will surely increase given the tattered economic conditions and hugely unequal distribution of income, land, and wealth in the country.

Departing from the overcrowded capital city of Guatemala, one leaves behind the mayhem and cacophony of buses, trucks, and cars. As one reaches the hinterland along the Atlantic Highway en route to the *Oriente* (East) or the Pan-American Highway in the opposite direction to the *Occidente* (West), striking changes appear in the physical landscape. Dozens of large billboards dot this terrain. Like those of Banrural and Western Union, billboards announce in bright gold letters the now better, quicker, and most certain way Guatemalans can get their money from the United States *"sin salir del pueblo"* (without leaving home). These ubiquitous features, in addition to rampant construction built with migrants' earnings sent home from their backbreaking jobs in the North[1], leave palpably visible traces in Guatemala's rural countryside. They mark the landscape as glaring reminders of the transnational connections Guatemalans maintain between their homeland and the United States and speak to the central role migrants play in sustaining the national economy.

Cash remittances currently comprise the largest source of foreign currency tunneled into Guatemala; for example, in 2007 Guatemalans living and working in the United States sent back home about $4.1 billion (Banco de Guatemala 2007). At a more localized level and according to my interviews, folks in migrant households receive on average each month $200 to $300. Because of the massive flows of cash remittances that enter migrant-sending countries like Guatemala, the relationship between international migration and development looms as a significant matter— an issue that emerges as a "hot" topic in many scholarly arenas. Hence the key question becomes: do economic remittances that migrants bring or send back home promote local development?[2] My argument here is that cash remittances help stimulate local development at the individual level rather than in projects that spawn vast effects at the community level. And, as a whole, consumption rather than investment takes precedence.

Although many studies address the economic consequences of migration and economic reasons for doing so, this article examines the concomitant economic and social effects of remittances in sending communities. Social remittances consider a variety of things that flow from migrants' places of arrival to the homeland, including ideas, behavior, and identities (Levitt 1999). As Levitt (2001:11) succinctly puts it, "They are the tools with which ordinary individuals create global culture at the local level." Several forces influence the transmission and impact of social remittances. Levitt (2001) outlines six criteria in her work: (1) "the nature of the remittance" (e.g., ideas about marketing, political leadership skills); (2) "the nature of the transnational system" (e.g., primarily its role in the character of migration and social networks); (3) "the messenger's characteristics" (e.g., class background); (4) "the target audience" (e.g., individual household member and the role that identity, civil status, and economic resources play); (5) "similarities and differences between sending and receiving countries" (e.g., existing normative, cognitive, and structural constraints that shape migrants' views and behavior); (6) "features of the transmission process" (e.g., arrives through multiple channels, original vs. building on earlier social remittances). In her study of Dominican transnational migrants, she paints social remittances as mostly beneficial, albeit she does acknowledge some negatives. While my study, too, considers the positive and negative outcomes that social remittances generate, I take the analysis one step further and highlight the ambivalence that they may also produce. In short, by presenting concrete examples from the ground up, the focus here is on emergent transformations due to both economic and social remittances on what I call "*migra* landscapes."[3]

Embracing a comparative ethnographic approach allows for several things: a more nuanced reality as well as key ethnic and geographic consequences of migration in Guatemala—both commonalities and differences. At the same time, it provides a better understanding of how increasing integration into a globalized economy alters life for people in the Guatemalan countryside. A cross-regional and cross-cultural emphasis also captures the uniqueness of the Guatemalan case to the study of transnational migration because it systematically examines how migration affects and unfolds within a national group—a group that is increasingly becoming an important Latino population in the United States. Equally significant, and following Eggan's (1954) "method of controlled comparison," such an approach permits us to visually juxtapose the major duality of Guatemalan society.

To capture a more holistic perspective of these migra landscapes, I explore the tangible and intangible ramifications of migration in Guatemala's Occidente and Oriente. Guatemala's Oriente is often justapoxed with the Occidente. Such schism develops and continues to govern Guatemalan society due to the dichotomous terms—Maya and Ladino[4]—in which the Central American country is typically cast: because of its distinctive ethnicities, because of its varied environments and differences forged during colonial times (e.g., tenure regimes, production objectives, and property relations), and because of particular political interests and historical accounts. Scholarly investigation, however, rarely compares both regions or pays attention to the Oriente.

Guatemala's eastern region is principally a Ladino-dominated area. Some indigenous people, however, do populate a few villages outside of the *municipios* (townships) in the departments of Zacapa, Chiquimula, Jalapa, and Jutiapa. Indigenous Maya residents in these eastern departments are not as visible as folks in the western highlands because they typically do not wear their *traje* (traditional clothing) and many have discontinued using Mayan languages. Several physical and social features distinguish these two regions. The Oriente is a hot and dry region long noted for its cattle ranches, large estates, poor quality land, and lack of irrigation.[5] In contrast, the Occidente, which is largely a Maya area, *minifundias* (small subsistence farms) prevail as well as cooler temperatures and greater rainfall.

A critical factor that currently sets apart these dichotomous regions concerns the role that NGOs (non-profit governmental organizations) play in the Occidente social landscape. Since ratification of the 1996 peace treaty, NGOs proliferated in the western highlands. A number of NGOs surfaced because foreign donors promised nearly a billion dollars of aid upon signing the internationally-brokered Peace Accord. Many NGOs sprung up because the state is now more open to organization, but also due to the heightened organization of Maya groups. Maya cultural activism in Guatemala has indigenous people coming together around a variety of causes (Fischer 2001; Fischer and McKenna 1996; Warren 1998). Altogether, I found that over a dozen NGOs of one kind or another operated within San Cristobal's boundaries. This particular social context, along with the complexities behind the formation and continuity of such organizations, contrasts remarkably with the Oriente. During the course of my fieldwork, in the township of Gualán and its surrounding villages, for example, I observed that NGOs and any other associations (e.g., CARE, WorldVision, Peace Corps, US Aid) remained conspicuously absent.

Guatemala's shift to a remittance-based economy (whereby humans are becoming the primary export commodity) constitutes a crucial phenomenon that needs to be examined; but in doing so, historical antecedents must be considered. Guatemala is a war-torn country. It is a country where its people endured nearly four decades of conflict between guerillas and the state leading to over 200,000 deaths or disappeared, leaving deep-seated wounds and long-festering resentment even within many migrant sending communities (Jonas 2000; North and Simmons 1999). This tumultuous period in Guatemalan history reinforced and deepened poverty for many people. But also, it paved the way for the neoliberal governments of the past decade to implement a range of policies (e.g., slashing of credit sources for small producers, privatization of former government-run services, violent suppression of attempts to create unions, to demand land reform, and most recently, the implementation of the Central American Free Trade Agreement—CAFTA) (Taylor, Moran-Taylor, and Rodman Ruiz 2006; Moran-Taylor n.d.). Such measures have systematically undercut the livelihoods of small-scale farmers throughout the country. In addition to these policies and the political violence experienced from the early 1960s to the late 1990s, other factors such as environmental conditions as well as cultural and/or individualistic (e.g., domestic violence) forces have propelled many Guatemalans to look North.

Overview of United States-Bound Guatemalan Migration

Although Guatemalan migrant flows to the United States continue to grow, little is known about this population movement. Studies that address Guatemalan migration tend to show migrants' adaptation to the United States and Canada as well as the new communities they create in their destination sites; such contributions include the work of Burns (1993), Hagan (1993), Repak (1995), Loucky and Moors (2000), Hamilton and Chinchilla (2001), and Fink (2003). Other research pays attention to the socio-psychological trauma among these migrants (Vlach 1992), the meaning of place and journey (Moran-Taylor and Richardson 1993), religion (Wellmeier 1998), and social networks (Hagan 1998; Menjívar 2002). While scholars primarily center on receiving communities in the United States, it is imperative to remember that international migration also expands and alters the rhythms of Guatemalan daily life.

In recent years, the Guatemalan northbound stream has experienced many of the trends associated with transnational migration (see Basch, Glick Schiller, and Szanton Blanc 1994; Glick Schiller, Basch, and Szanton Blanc 1992). Studies that take on a transnational migration perspective consider gender (Kohpahl 1998), migrant organizations (Hamilton and Chinchilla 1999), land attachments and exile (Montejo 1999), identity (Popkin 1999; Rodman 2006), ruptures (Nolin 2002), connections and communications (Moran-Taylor 2004), caretakers and children (Moran-Taylor n.d.), longings of return (Moran-Taylor and Menjívar 2005), as well as land and ethnic changes (Taylor, Moran-Taylor, and Rodman Ruiz 2006). Despite a developing literature on Guatemalan transnational migration, relatively little work explores the immediate and broader impact of migration in the homeland.

In Guatemala, pioneers of the journey North began to migrate in the 1960s. Subsequently, as the political violence intensified and economic opportunities eroded, greater numbers followed in the 1980s. In the 1990s, and more recently, emigration increased. A significant demographic feature characterizes emigration from Gualán and San Cristóbal to the United States. Whereas women and men in the eastern community of Gualán migrate in just about equal proportions, this tendency develops to a lesser extent among San Cristobaleños in the western highlands. In San Cristóbal, even though the northward movement initiated over three decades ago, the migrant flow remains largely male-centered. In addition to these gendered contrasts, there is also an intriguing regional dimension to the choice of United States destination: while individuals in Gualán chiefly gravitate to Los Angeles, California, those in San Cristóbal mainly target Houston, Texas. Such patterns develop because, as others observe (e.g., Alvarez 1987; Massey et al. 1987), migration is a social process involving kin and social networks between migrants' places of origin and destination. Further, the context of arrival and employment opportunities available at different United States localities fundamentally affect migrants' everyday experiences in the United States.

Methods

To conduct this cross-regional and cross-cultural study, I focused my research in the eastern Ladino-dominated municipio of Gualán (in the department of Zacapa) and in the western highlands, the Maya municipio of San Cristóbal (in the department of Totonicapán; see Map 1). These localities were selected because: (1) large streams of labor migration go to the United States; (2) strong transnational connections are sustained with United States receiving communities; (3) mature migration networks reflecting at least two generations of migrant experience exist; and (4) both sending communities have about 30,000 inhabitants. Factors that greatly distinguish these two study sites, in addition to ethnicity, history, and environment, include present-day conditions (e.g., the vast presence of NGOs shaping the social landscape). Crucially, and as I later argue, the nature of such conditions influence the kinds of community development outcomes that unfold in each region.

This article examines one aspect of a larger study that I carried out in Guatemala from 1999 through 2001, followed by brief visits in the summers of 2003 through 2006. The overall project incorporates survey and ethnographic research. Here I draw on the ethnographic material: participant observation, fieldnotes, personal journal, multiple informal interviews, and 54 in-depth, tape-recorded, semi-structured interviews lasting between two to three hours each. Using snowball sampling, I completed the interviews in a location that study participants selected. While employing such methods do not yield representative outcomes, by selecting individuals from diverse neighborhoods, this strategy ensures including individuals from a variety of socioeconomic backgrounds. I chose potential candidates based on the following criteria: that individuals have at least one year of residence in the United States and that they be at least 18 years old at the time of their departure from Guatemala. In both communities, I conducted the interviews in Spanish. While many townsfolk in San Cristóbal speak K'echi', usage of Spanish predominates too.

In all, I interviewed 30 females and 24 males (migrants and nonmigrants). The age of interviewees ranged from 18 to 82. The kinds of occupations that the study participants held widely varied from weavers, artisans, seamstresses, tailors, nurses, students, entrepreneurs, and the unemployed to NGO workers. My interviews followed a simple guide and always included questions about migration and employment histories; return migration; gender relations, roles, and identity; self-identity (e.g., attitudes and perceptions of ethnic identity); transnational flows (e.g., tangible and intangible and their frequency, density, and types); social relations; migration- related changes, and future migrants' goals.

Ladino Migra Landscapes: A View from the Oriente
The Tangible

Cash remittances are the bastion of Guatemala's economy. How these monies get spent varies. Like other migrants in the past and present (e.g, Levitt 2001; Wyman 1993), in Guatemala some migrant households invest their money in businesses; many others purchase homes or plots of land. Striking outcomes due to migra dollars that touch places like Gualán in eastern Guatemala include inflation of land prices. Lucas, for example, a man in his early forties, spent seven years in Los Angeles working in a tire shop, as many Gualantecos do.[6] Proudly, he showed me around his new taller (car mechanic shop) located on the town's outskirts and explained:

> This [Lucas firmly said pointing at his taller] I built with money from over there, the States. I purchased land when I first got back. I bought it for Q42,000 ($6,000) and now I wouldn't even sell it for Q100,000 ($13,000). I want to see if I can pay off my debts; I owe my brother some money. But also, I want to build my house here, if God helps me, right?

Lucas aims to launch a business that provides good, modern, and convenient service to his customers. He seeks to offer this service in a more "sophisticated" fashion rather than the average ones available in town. His plans include an air-conditioned panoramic waiting room with a small restaurant on its second floor, where customers can view their vehicles while being repaired. "At least *this*" Lucas emphatically said, "is one of the many ideas I have … from all the things I saw and experienced in the States." Like Lucas, many other returnees become purveyors of information (and goods) garnered in the United States and later transfer these back home. Importantly, Lucas's ideas and outlook on Gualán since his return illustrate, as does the research of Levitt (2001), how social remittances unfold in this particular context. In other words, they reveal the entrepreneurial visions Lucas transmits to his hometown. At the same time, his remarks point to the diverse ways in which migration can reorganize social life in the homeland.

What is also clear from Lucas's narrative—and his words echo many others—involves the far-reaching effects of migra dollars in fueling increases in both land and house prices in and around Gualán. No real estate listings are readily available for Gualán—land and houses typically sell by word of mouth. According to community members, house lot prices vary largely by neighborhood and their proximity to the town's center (see Table 5.2.1).

Among some Gualanteco migrant households, a strategy to deal with skyrocketing *finca* (farm) prices involves the purchase of land in cheaper and less desirable frontier areas. These returnees relocate or engage in the back-and-forth movement to the Petén—a department in Guatemala's northern rainforest lowlands (see Figure 5.2.1). There they purchase and raise livestock instead of setting up a business in town or taking up cattle ranching in the township's surroundings. Not surprisingly, as more cash remittances reach people's hands in Gualán, and as more migrants and returnees erect new homes and refurbish old ones, these structures extend the town's boundaries, dramatically reconfiguring settlement patterns and the physical terrain, particularly in newer neighborhoods.

Gualán these days teems with movement. Much of the town's urban hustle develops because of its fortuitous geographic location and history in the region as a site of commerce. While the town boosts with a host of small industries and businesses, migra dollars influence the cadence of Gualán's economy. The widespread housing boom generates new jobs and the establishment of small-scale businesses (e.g., hardware shops, cinder block factories). Little *tiendas* (shops), *paca* (second-hand Western-style clothing) shops, eateries, private courier services, and a slew of talleres (particularly car mechanic shops) proliferate because of migrants' earnings sent home. Increasingly, pick-up trucks, automobiles, and *micros* (small vans) make a greater presence in Gualán. Now, for a mere U.S. dollar, or often considerably less, micros haul people up and down Gualán's steep hills, around and about, to and from villages and towns. Cash remittances significantly boost the local transportation industry.

Altogether, though, migration mostly produces local development at the individual rather than community level. And while migration stimulates and supports some kind of local production in Gualán, this boost mainly materializes in the establishment of a few businesses. These endeavors, however, create very little employment with multiplier effects within the community. Returnees, for instance, those who set up car mechanic shops, usually hire only three to four men. Seldom do such ventures grow into bigger business enterprises.

At the individual level, migration affects Gualán in multiple forms. Some migrant households gain greater material desires and lean toward more consumption to display their heightened status. Social remittances that returnees bring or send back home help shape ideas of consumerism and the built environment too. Take the case of Nora and Sergio—both returnees. This

TABLE 5.2.1   House Lot Prices in the *Municipio* of Gualán, Zacapa

Area Price per m2 ($)	Price for lot size 10×20 m2 ($)	
Near Gualán's center	44	8,800
Barrio Puente de Zamora	31	6,200
Aldea Mayuelas	21	4,200
Barrio La Cienaga	12	2,500

Municipio refers to township, *barrio* to neighborhood, and *aldea* to village.

Gualanteco couple lives in the town's center and, by community standards, managed to climb the socioeconomic ladder. Nora and Sergio each own and run their specialty shops and even employ a security guard to keep an eye on their businesses. They moved residences from the outskirts to the town's center, hire nannies to care for their young children, send their eldest daughter to what locals consider a posh school in Guatemala City, fly their children to spend school holidays in the United States with relatives and learn English, and overall, participate in Gualán's "high society," Nora and Sergio belong, according to many locals, to the *nuevos ricos* (new rich) or those from the *alta* (high society) of Gualán.[7] But this new social status comes at a cost. To enjoy her newly gained social position in town, Nora, for instance, spent considerable time working as a live-in domestic in Chicago and Los Angeles. Meanwhile, others cared for her children back in Guatemala—a widespread practice that consistently emerges notably within Gualán, but increasingly throughout the country. This example underscores how individuals use migration to reposition themselves within a transnational class-structured space.

Furthermore, in her back-and-forth working ventures and while employed in this economic niche (i.e., as a domestic worker), Nora became quite familiar with the details and layouts of middle and upper-class American homes. In turn, Nora transferred these ideas to her community of origin and into her own house. Commenting on Nora's migratory experiences, Erminda, a niece and return migrant who spent her childhood in Los Angeles, told me with much admiration: "Yeah, she [Aunt] likes to own nice things—everything she owns is brand name and very pretty. Her house is precious, American style. As a babysitter she worked over there [in the United States]). *Sí, pero de gringuitos que tenían dinero, que estaban bien* (Yes, but for rich little gringos who were well off)."

Contradictory outcomes surface from such visible changes. While migration provides for higher standards of living, at the same time it generates a great deal of social inequality and alters traditional social hierarchies. For individuals for whom migration is not possible (due to their lack of economic resources), or perhaps not desirable, they look up to Gualantecos who have accomplished something. Among others in the community, migration engenders resentment and envy. What is also clear is that those able to make the journey North are individuals with some capital—not

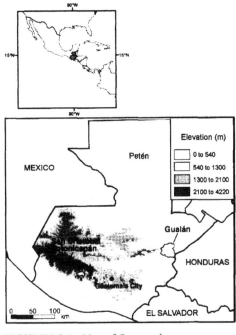

FIGURE 5.2.1   Map of Guatemala

the very poor. In general, prospective migrants who lack the economic means to make the north-ward trip, willing friends and family (particularly those already established in the United States) provide the needed funds to accomplish this goal.

The Intangible

Migration also causes striking transformations in Gualán that appear less tangible than those previously described. These changes include *el habladito* (speech alterations), peoples' attitudes, behavior, and local responses to such modifications. The ideas and behavior that migrants bring back, in other words, social remittances, clearly permeate different aspects of Gualán, especially el habladito.[8] Many returnees, of both sexes, come back speaking in *mexicano* tones, *mexicanadas* (Mexican slang), and/or Spanglish—Spanish and English—in their daily conversations. Izabél, a returnee in her early forties and a well-respected woman in Gualán, commented on the kinds of cultural changes that become readily noticeable in her town due to United States-bound migration:

> The Mexican things are the ones that flow back to Gualán—not the American cul-ture. What they [returnees and migrants] do is copy all the Mexican stuff—their way of living. In other words, everything that is untidy, dirty, because *puro* (real)

gringos don't live like that! In reality, though, ... what has come here is the Cholo [gang] culture—not the Mexican one.

Community members primarily perceive younger return migrants as mimicking "the Chicano and Cholo stuff." Older male and female returnees, they say, come back adopting more Mexican mannerisms. In Julia's view, a non-migrant teacher in her early forties, the mexicanadas migrants transfer back home relate to how they become *"mal hablados"* (poorly spoken and using foul language). When I chimed in that folks in Gualán, and in the Oriente as a whole, were "mal hablados" too, she then retorted: "Yes, here we use rough language, but they [Mexicans], their vocabulary is bad because they say, for example, *"la troca,"* (truck) and it's not that; *"el garbichero"* for *gabish* (garbage). The words, then, become misused ... the Mexicans change them."

The intangible effects of migration are not clear-cut. And contradictory portraits emerge of Gualanteco returnees. Locals quickly point out that return migrants (both male and female), for example, come back more stuck up, not humble, and/or acquire many vices while abroad. Marco, a Gualanteco returnee in his mid-thirties, assertively uttered, as he gave me a lift from a nearby village into town: "Those assholes, when they come back don't even acknowledge you when they pass by! When they return, they come with long hair, with earrings ... and can barely speak anymore." On the other hand, some Gualantecos sense that return migrants come back with improved demeanors. Summarizing some of the positive attitudes and behavior that returnees bring back a municipal worker told me: "People improve their *educación* (in this particular context it means attitudes and behavior). For example, they [returnees] come back more polite; if they have some rubbish to throw they search for a bin; if they smoke, they're more conscientious and respectful where this is done."

Localized expressions and constructions of race loom as particularly pertinent when addressing migration-related changes. Gualantecos, for instance, emphasize an improvement in returnees' social position and physical appearance. Community members repeatedly echo that return migrants *"vienen todos blanquitos"* (they all come back very white) and *"se blanquean"* (they whiten up) when they go over there [the United States]." Undoubtedly, such perceptions play a key role on discourses of *blanqueamiento* (whitening) of race in Guatemala—the idea that by mixing blood from a "whiter" to a "lower" race, the latter can be "improved" (see Nelson 1999; Smith 1995) and, in turn, result in class differentiations. But, in this context, in addition to phenotype, becoming white or whiter also entails changes in how an individual acts and dresses. And as people become whiter—real or imagined—as a result of a sexual liaison (Casaus Arzú 1992; Smith 1995) or migration (according to discourses Gualanteco migrants and non-migrants deploy), this phenotypical and behavioral transformation shapes local social constructions of identity. That is, it alludes to how race can be "improved" and altered—albeit ephemerally because of United States-bound migration.[9]

The question then becomes: if negative aspects are often highlighted, why do Gualantecos articulate such "improved" characterizations of returnees? Certainly, the money return migrants bring back or remit improves their standard of living and the daily rhythms that govern their lives back home. But also, when migrants originate from the villages and marry someone from the town (in the case of both Gualán and San Cristóbal), such a liason transcends as an upward move and an enhanced social standing—a practice evident at home too, but less acceptable and/ or repudiated in that context. Furthermore, many often regard *gringo* (American) culture in a positive light. The prospect of marrying a gringa, however, is seen in lesser terms. Returnees, for example, mention that "gringas are less *económicas*" (more consumer-oriented), "they're too liberal," (i.e., independent, autonomous, and/or "loose"), and "they're not familiar with their local culture." Gualantecos also mention that male returnees sometimes favor going back home to search for a bride in their community because female migrants become too spoiled in the United States. This happens, locals told me, as a result of two things: because of the money earned and because of the gringo ways that are quickly embraced (see also Grimes 1998).

Finally, Gualantecos speak about an improvement among returnees and migrants due to the kinds of employment secured in the United States. While abroad, Gualanteco migrants mainly hold low-paying jobs in the service and manufacturing sectors. For many individuals, this shift embodies a move away from arduous outdoor work or in the fields—jobs often construed as inferior and as an "Indian" task. Additionally, as migrant men and women labor indoors (e.g., factories, hotels, restaurants, private homes), they become less exposed to natural elements (that darken the skin). For some, this variation in employment may provide for a physical change in terms of slightly lightening (or whitening) a person's skin color. Hence, a localized view that "returnees come back *más blanquitos*" (a little more white). This discussion illuminates the perceived racism, "whitening," and other intangible transformations attending social remittances. Rather than just looking at the impact of social remittances as a balance that they may strike between beneficial and negative outcomes, this analysis reveals the ambivalence generated by social remittances. In sum, the picture painted here—a picture from below and from the Oriente—unveils some of the tangible and intangible aspects that deal with how transnational and return migration affects the Ladino-dominated sending community of Gualán, and importantly its people.[10] I now turn to explore how Maya migra landscapes reconfigure and reorganize people's lives in San Cristóbal, nestled in Guatemala's western highlands.

Maya Migra Landscapes: A View from the Occidente
The Tangible

San Cristóbal (see Map 1) parallels Gualán and many other Guatemalan communities in various ways. Much recent investment goes into house construction. Successful migrants in town and its periphery build lavish two and three-story concrete homes with cinder block and cement roofs. Such structures stand as status symbols and glaring reflections of migrants' accomplishments abroad. On the surface, this construction, however, does not reveal the perennial hardships migrants endure while working and living in the United States. And as brand-new houses spring up, so do a suite of new features. Many homes, for example, now include toilets instead of latrines, tiled and cement floors in lieu of dirt ones, and bigger doors and more windows that replace small openings. Structures housing "new" vehicles (typically second-hand cars purchased with migra dollars or *carros rodados* [vehicles brought back home during a southward trip] and often purchased at United States auctions) also become more evident in migrant homes. In short, elements previously absent in single-sized adobe dwellings and in much of Guatemala's countryside increasingly become more commonplace.

When San Cristobaleños return from the United States, instead of investing or carving out new businesses in their hometown, many gravitate to the thriving urban center of Quetzaltenango (Guatemala's second largest city) and its large market, where there exists a greater demand of goods. This is not to say that locals do not set up small enterprises in their community. Many do, particularly in the way of eateries and tailor shops. In Quetzaltenango's bustling center, however, San Cristobaleños prefer to launch businesses like bakeries or small shops to sell *cortes* (traditional cloth). Some return migrants even start up used-car dealerships (of carros rodados) in the peri-urban areas of that city. Moreover, in San Cristóbal, no banks currently operate to deal with the community's financial matters. Thus, locals often find themselves heading to Quetzaltenango.

San Cristóbal is a place long known for its textile production. Nearly half of the town's population consists of weavers (Municipalidad de San Cristóbal Totonicapán, Totonicapán 1998). Once back in the home community, return migrants take up the tradition of weaving (*cortes*)—a male-centered trade. In the process, and partly due to migra dollars that San Cristobaleños bring back home, some become more entrepreneurial and purchase additional *cajas* (weaving looms). Commonly, San Cristobaleño returnees (and others in the area who weave to eke out a living) hire others or employ family members to operate extra cajas within the household (Moran-Taylor and Richardson 1993).

Alternatively, return migrants in the tailoring business (e.g., producing gym pants for school uniforms) purchase additional industrial sewing machines to expand their resources in wholesale markets. These San Cristobaleños specifically target schools in the area of Quetzaltenango. The local development that such production activities bring to San Cristóbal, however, does not significantly alter the town's economic vitality, nor impact much of the town's physical landscape. Migra dollars have not facilitated productive investments, service opportunities, or infrastructure improvements (e.g., building roads, schools, water projects, cooperatives, sports and health facilities).

Migration brings about social and cultural change to San Cristobaleños in a multiplicity of other forms. Among some locals, household features may change because of family remittances. Migra dollars, for example, help some families make the switch from conventional wooden stoves or fires assembled on dirt floors (especially in outlying villages) to the convenience and more ecologically sound use of gas stoves. In spite the fact that many migrant households made the switch, I found that the vast majority of San Cristobaleños continue to purchase firewood. This outcome is hardly surprising given that 90 percent of rural Guatemalans use firewood to meet their basic needs such as cooking, boiling water, and heating (Naciones Unidas 1999).

With regards to technology (and mirroring Gualán), common items that become part and parcel of many migrant households include color televisions, stereos, VCRs, and camcorders. In dwellings with more expendable income, cellular telephones and washers increasingly become evident. While greater consumption patterns of electronic goods proliferate due to migration, in some homes the new items incorporated in family households do little to alter traditional life ways. Furthermore, instead of news or nuggets of information traveling via a letter, cassette, courier, or telephone call, owning a VCR, camcorder, and television allow migrants abroad and those who remain behind to stay connected more visibly. For San Cristobaleños who often support many traditional elements of their annual patron fiesta held in July, yet unable to make the journey back to Guatemala (because of their undocumented status or financial constraints), videos documenting the festivities back home offer an avenue in which migrants can participate, albeit vicariously, in events they miss and about which they reminisce. Video cameras and other electronic commodities owned by many migrant households permit San Cristobaleños to chronicle more easily and reproduce vignettes of the ordinary and extraordinary episodes of their lives and community (Moran-Taylor and Richardson 1993). With the advent of instant technology and use of computers, this change has enabled the flow, exchange, and sharing of significant events with greater speed between those who leave and those who stay. But the information-technology boom does not imply accessibility to computers, the internet (not to mention the know-how), and cellular telephones to all in San Cristóbal. For the most part, San Cristobaleños continue to keep in touch with loved ones by using *teléfonos comunitarios* (telephones rented out from peoples' homes, which typically include some makeshift cabin for greater privacy). While purchasing telephone cards and owning a cellular telephone have become more popular, the latter is still beyond the means of the vast majority, only gradually making their way to the countryside.

Migration results in more than visible consumer goods. Economic remittances configure other tangible aspects of people's daily lives like eating habits and health care—basic subsistence needs as well as improvements (Moran-Taylor and Richardson 1993). Many migrant households experience modifications in nutrition.[11] Instead of consuming only traditional staple foods of black beans and *tamalitos* (steamed com meal, shaped in oblong balls and wrapped in green com leaves, a traditional food in the western highlands), migrant households eat more meat, milk, and other non-standard items.

Another avenue in which migration yields some improvement concerns health-care practices.[12] This betterment is particularly true in the western highlands town of San Cristóbal.[13] Migrant households can now afford to purchase medicines or to pay for any other health-related expenses. Folks also mention that they prefer to receive medical treatment in privately-run local clinics rather than using community clinics available through the public healthcare system. In the past, women traditionally sought a midwife to assist with the delivery of their babies, but increasingly, San Cristobaleñas favor using a nurse at the local clinic or hospital. Thus, many women view this shift as a step up in health-care practices.

Life-cycle and community events constitute vital ways in which economic and social remittances transfer to migrants' places of origin too. Clearly, life-cycle events and traditions do not represent material things, but I include them in this section because of the tangible manner in which migra dollars can reinvigorate such features. Celebrations like the *quinceaños* (coming of age festivity) often turn into large and glamorous affairs. Migration affords those with greater disposable monies opportunities to throw grand parties with lavish meals. These events may even bring hundreds (sometimes 300 or more) of San Cristobaleños together and permit folks to display their material wealth and status within the community (Moran-Taylor and Richardson 1993). While migra dollars promote the enhancement and continuity of traditional life-cycle events (e.g., baptisms, first communions, quinceaños, weddings, and funerals), at the community level, financial transfers from migrants get funneled in various forms to the annual patron saint's fiesta. Participation in local festivities provides migrants a great deal of prestige and importance in their places of origin. Even though Guatemalan migrants in the United States get exposed to many American holidays and their associated traditions, these southbound flows do not filter back to their hometowns. Rather, in San Cristóbal (and Gualán) local festivities continue to draw much attention. And when comparing both towns in my study, in particular to how cash remittances are put into use for their annual fiestas (the single most important community celebration), San Cristobaleños experience a greater show of these monies.

Transnational migration studies stress the physical social process of migrants' movement back-and-forth, yet death can reinforce transnational ties too. In addition to fortifying transnational ties, the practice of organizing burials and funerals back home for deceased migrants demonstrates how Guatemalan migrants continue to maintain their orientations towards the homeland. During the course of my research, I observed that in both towns folks send the bodies of deceased loved ones back home to be buried. Ethnic differences emerge, however, in how San Cristobaleños regard their attachments to land.

Take the case of Don Vicente. He is a non-migrant San Cristobaleño in his fifties and the proud and busy owner of a funeral parlor. The funeral business comprises a ubiquitous trade in

San Cristóbal due to the artisan production of caskets (among many other woodcrafts) particular to the area. Donning a set of gold chains around his neck and a gold bracelet, Don Vicente, a short and dark-skinned fellow sporting a thin mustache, assertively depicted his funeral business in the following terms: "*funerarias sin fronteras*" (funerals without borders). While we sat in a small gloomy room abutting several stacked simple and elaborate wooden coffins in his business/home, he explained the specificities of his trade. Don Vicente primarily offers his service to San Cristobaleños in Houston and Los Angeles—prime United States destination places for people originating from this area. Showing me a wad of pastel-colored, squared receipts from his latest transactions, Don Vicente then pulls out his most recent transnational funeral arrangement (merely a few days old) and hands it over. The handwritten pale pink piece of paper reads: "Pepe Chuj, 25 years of age, perished on May 24, 2001 in Los Angeles, California. Place of birth: Pacanac [a village six kilometers from San Cristóbal]." Relatives of the deceased Maya migrant reside in Los Angeles. Like many others, this Maya family arranged to send the cadaver home for burial in their native land.

Once in Guatemala, loved ones left behind, migrant kin who journey back home (those without legal and financial limitations), and community members mourn the deceased day and night. Then slowly, somberly, and some sobbing stroll side-by-side—men form a single file flanking one edge of the narrow street; women, with their long, dark braided hair fully covered with thin black lace, along the other. As a few men, family members, and close friends gingerly carry the casket to the local cemetery in San Cristóbal's outskirts, the mourners quietly follow the procession through town. Curious onlookers peer from their little windows silently watching the drama; while others warily exchange whispers. Such responses to migrant deaths relate to how San Cristobaleños maintain strong attachments towards the land. According to Montejo (1999:188), Maya people abandoning their native land implies breaking away from the sacred ties "with the protective power that circumscribes the community, which is considered to be at the sacred center or navel of the universe." These ties to the land also become apparent when Guatemalan refugees in Mexico return to their homeland, places where their placenta often remains buried (Montejo 1999).

Bodies—dead or alive—going back to Guatemala become an integral part of the transnational connections that San Cristobaleños (like Gualantecos) continue to maintain and deploy with their places of origin. The costs involved in sending a cadaver can escalate to several thousands of U.S. dollars. To transport a body in a hermetically sealed coffin, airlines usually charge fees ranging from $2,000 to $2,500. But for his "transnational funeral package" Don Vicente's fees generally amount to about $3,000. Factored in this hefty sum include the costs of flying a cadaver back home, transporting the body from Guatemala City to San Cristóbal (a 185-kilometer stretch, usually taking between three to five hours to cover, depending on traffic, perennial queues, and road constructions), funeral services, and burial arrangements. Though Don Vicente handles his business affairs with the aid of a fax machine, soon he plans to make some technological changes. In order to provide better services to clients abroad, he hopes to install an Internet link and a computer at home. This way, Don Vicente told me, he could more quickly and efficiently connect with compatriots in the United States.

Indeed, this example truly captures at the ground level how small-town Guatemalan social life increasingly becomes transnationalized, as well as globalized. Above all, this profound transformation develops with more rapid and efficient transportation, the advent of varied kinds of telecommunications more readily available at peoples' fingertips, and the ways in which technology enhances transnational connections. Specifically, this case underscores several things: how technology may be mediated in and by a particular local situation; how folks produce global culture at the local level, and how certain kinds of transnational practices become more prevalent among some migrant families. This practice, however, may dwindle as more family members look North and choose to settle in their United States destinations; alternatively, as the second generation in the United States grows up and finds the attachments to their native land less sacred or their southward orientations less significant. Bringing this point to the fore is noteworthy because a central question that arises in the literature on transnational migration relates to whether or not transnationalism is merely a first generation phenomenon. The example of Don Vicente's "funerarias sin fronteras" casts light on the kinds of entrepreneurial responses that emerge at a localized level in the sending community due to international migration.

Sending bodies back home to be buried raises other interesting issues. How are, for instance, premature deaths handled due to violence? In the case of Los Angeles, *maras* (gangs), such as the "Mara Salvatrucha" and the "18th Street," initially formed in south central Los Angeles. Young migrant Guatemalan and Salvadoran males often join these gangs. But the maelstrom of gang rivalry can lead to premature and violent deaths. How, then, are the costs for such deaths born or shared? It is a question that community members in both townships in my study did not have to cope with yet. In much of Guatemala, however, the crime and violence experienced recently due to the deportation of gang members (and the gang culture flowing southward) has become an acute problem, as it has for many societies in El Salvador and Honduras.

The Intangible

How migration changes livelihoods and migra landscapes in San Cristóbal includes examining the effects that unfold in a less tangible manner, as well as those that are less visible to the naked eye. Here I attend, in particular, to language as well as the attitudes and behavior that migrants and returnees transfer back home. As in Gualán, mixed views surface on how locals perceive San Cristobaleño migrants and returnees. Some locals speak of an improvement as well as a decline in returnees' attitudes and demeanor in how they carry themselves. In Ana's words, a 38-year old, Maya non-migrant:

> Two outcomes emerge: If migrants go to civilize themselves or they don't. Like to leant about the niceties of gringo behavior, then they [returnees] come back imitating them. And, if not, they return worse ... or all arrogant—pretentious about the money they bring, dressing well, and eating only tinned foods.

When San Cristobaleños go to the United States and return to their community of origin, the migration experience impinges on language. In San Cristóbal, K'iche' is commonly spoken within the area and represents a key element of Maya ethnic identity. But this tradition appears to be dwindling among some individuals and families. More recently, some San Cristobaleños realize the great value of holding and passing on their native language to the next generation, especially given the current ethos and Maya activism in Guatemala. In spite of the recent ethnic cultural organizing and nationwide calls for teaching indigenous languages in public schools, many youngsters are losing the ability to speak their native language. Some people, namely non-indigenous Guatemalans, make disparaging remarks linked to these changes. They contend, for instance, that acquiring English-language skills may perhaps be more practical—especially in light of the prospects of United States-bound migration—rather than incorporating indigenous languages in the public schools' curriculum.

Though usage of the K'iche' language overwhelmingly decreased in past years in Guatemala, it appears even more evident among San Cristobaleño children in the United States. Also, the ability to speak K'iche and Spanish at home may become less desired as San Cristobaleño children in the United States gain greater fluency in English. In some United States localities with large Guatemalan populations (e.g., Los Angeles) it is not just less desirable to speak an indigenous language, but it drops out very quickly too. Despite such linguistic changes, San Cristobaleños—abroad and in the homeland—continue to strongly maintain connections to their roots in varied ways (e.g., use of traje, celebrating community festivities).

Whereas in rural areas the use of K'iche predominates, in San Cristóbal's *casco urbano* (town) both Spanish and K'iche' are widely spoken. Migration-related transformations associated with the use of Spanish concern speech alterations. When San Cristobaleños go back home, locals say that some individuals experience many changes in how they interject in their speech English words such as "oh" and "OK" or alternatively acquire other *cantaditos* (accents), like Mexican ones. These linguistic modifications community members associate with how some returnees become more pompous once back home. Additionally, as is the case with Gualantecos, stay-at-homers in San Cristóbal say that some returnees come back with many vices acquired from abroad; others come back with better habits. While mixed perceptions are expressed, what seems to take precedence among those who stay is a negative evaluation of returnees. In short, the tangible and intangible outcomes and effects of migration deeply reconfigure many aspects of life in San Cristóbal and in sending countries like Guatemala.

Discussion and Concluding Remarks

Migra landscapes emerge due to the massive flows of cash remittances (i.e., savings generated from employment in labor receiving countries such as the United States) that Guatemalan migrants send home. Cash remittances have become an essential area of contemporary study with entire local and even national economies increasingly dependent on migrants' earnings from abroad. Together, economic remittances and social remittances help create global culture at the local level (Levitt 2001), and in turn, help transform social and physical spaces into migra landscapes.

In terms of international development and migration, competing views emerge. One perspective highlights the negative effects for local development and emphasizes that migration aggravates unequal conditions in migrant-sending countries. Scholars supporting this argument claim that migra dollars lead to greater social inequality, generate an increased economic dependency among those who migrate, and increase consumption patterns without aiding local development (Dinerman 1978; Georges 1990; Gmelch 1980; Grasmuck and Pessar 1991; King 1986; Rhoades 1978; Rubenstein 1979). For other researchers, cash remittances and migration yield positive outcomes and help solve economic, social, and political problems for migrant-sending countries like Guatemala. Scholars argue that economic remittances invested in home communities promote local development (e.g., Durand, Parrado, and Massey 1996); and propel self-advancement of households, families, and villages (e.g., Cohen 2001, 2004). Another view that emerges in the literature is that cash remittances received by those who stay do not necessarily produce beneficial or negative outcomes. In his earlier work, Griffith (1985), for example, contends that remittances received primarily by Jamaican women are used to meet household expenses, and that they stimulate minor, short-term employment among migrant households' peasant farms—a practice that results in the reproduction of peasant livelihoods. Such an outcome emerges as a structural consequence of international labor migration among peasants, including the multiple demands on remittances with extended peasant families. Recently, when examining the impact of cash remittances on reproduction and development at home, Griffith (2006) further refines his argument and observes, for example, that these funds help maintain agricultural production, but also support the reproduction of labor. Although these studies illustrate how migrants' earnings sent back home may affect local development, conflicting viewpoints persist, exacerbated by the lack of systematic information on the frequency and amount of family remittances transferred (Grasmuck and Pessar 1991).

This article has explored some of the effects and outcomes of economic and social remittances in migrant sending regions. In the Guatemalan example, the economic weight that migrants bring to the country through cash remittances is remarkable and, thus, makes it an ideal case for assessing the impact of migration. It is vital to evaluate migration-related changes in sending regions to appreciate how transnational processes impinge on the lives and places of those who leave and those who stay. Throughout, I presented the various concrete forms in which economic and social remittances touch Guatemalan families (see Table 5.2.2). A critical part of this examination shows how these remittances affect social organization in migrants' places of origin.

For Levitt (2001), the story of Dominican transnational villagers is about trade-offs. I argue, however, that the story of Guatemalans goes beyond trade-offs. Migration does not impact only those who go North; migration reconfigures the livelihoods of thousands of Guatemalans across the socioeconomic spectrum in positive and negative forms. Crucially, the balances that social remittances strike between beneficial and negative consequences also generate ambivalence— an ambivalence that becomes less tangible. And in the Ladino example, it is an ambivalence that ultimately shapes notions of identity.

Beyond demonstrating the tangible, conspicuous, and often chronicled migration-induced changes in both communities, here I also examined a variety of other intangible transformations in people's lives. Importantly, the localization of the global experience in these towns carries for many a distinct Mexican cast, the intermediate filter and shaper before arriving in and departing from the North. Simply put, Mexico is something of a "cultural broker," to use Eric Wolf's (1956) well-known phrase, for global flow. Partly, this occurs as people are forced to move through Mexico in their overland ventures. Once in the United States, exposure to Mexican, as well as other Latino migrants, this contact colors the worldviews of Guatemalan migrants. They are the standard to which Guatemalans orient, at least with respect to real contact (compared to "white folk"). And while migration brings about contrasting effects and outcomes, parallel migration-related changes are also at work in both Guatemala's Oriente and Occidente.

The sharpest difference between the Oriente and Occidente Guatemalan towns in this study rests on how migration affects local development. Though in both places economic remittances promote some kind of local development, I argue that it occurs mostly at the individual level rather than in projects with multiplier effects at the community level. Not much channels into savings, economic production, and service development—primarily because many Guatemalans are struggling just to survive! When it comes to development at the community scale, in San Cristóbal the catalyst for change ensues from the recent flurry of NGOs in this highland region since the early 1990s—not migra dollars. This is a *big* difference with *big* consequences. Plainly, local development is not accomplished by the state. Rather, foreign NGOs largely promote and implement a wide number of projects throughout the western highlands. Although neoliberal policies deeply affected both the Oriente and Occidente regions, NGOs have played a distinctive

TABLE 5.2.2 Migration-Related Effects and Outcomes

Eastern town: Gualán	Western highlands town: San Cristóbal
Physical landscape and built environment alters, land inflation	Physical landscape and built environment alters, land inflation
Enhancement and continuity of life-cycle events and traditions	Enhancement and continuity of life-cycle events and traditions
Transnational practices e.g., burials are less pronounced*	Transnational practices e.g., burials are more pronounced
Alters constructions of race	Enhances ethnic identity
Entrepreneurial responses e.g., set up more businesses within the town's boundaries	Entrepreneurial responses e.g., set up more businesses outside the town's boundaries
Businesses established (e.g., auto workshops, second-hand clothing stores)	Businesses established (e.g., textile workshops and small stores)
Local development occurs mostly due to migrants' economic remittances	Local development occurs mostly due to international NGO's

*While sending loved ones back home to be buried is something both communities experience, for San Cristobaleños their inherent ties to the land make this example especially unique.

role in Guatemala's Maya heartland. When compared with Gualán, my research shows that cash remittances are not as key for local development in San Cristóbal. Rather, the monies that migrants abroad send home typically get sapped by multiple kin demands, get used to cover household expenditures, or get siphoned into consumption. In general, and as Cohen (2004) also observes, to a certain degree investments and savings do occur in Guatemala, but only after migrant households meet their needs.

In Guatemala's *Oriente Olvidado* (Forgotten East)[14] NGOs are virtually non-existent because this area and its people often attract little notice. This neglect goes beyond region, as the neglect of non-Maya people in general among academics and policy planners has merited far less attention. There is a reason for such oversight: the unevenness occurs because the region does not offer researchers the exoticism and romanticism of what they may deem "authentic." Throughout, then, this article offers a more balanced view of the impact of United States-bound migration and shows how rural life is changing in both Guatemala's Oriente and Occidente. In the end, whether economic remittances get launched into investments or sapped into consumption, one thing is clear. These monies constitute the sustenance of Guatemala's financial system, and for the foreseeable future, will continue to play a central role in the country's economy.

Endnotes

1. For migrants and those who stay behind, *el norte* (the North) simply means the United States or Canada.

2. For recent discussions on this debate, see for example, Durand, Parrado, and Massey (1996), Conway and Cohen (1998), and Cohen (2004).

3. In local parlance, Guatemalans refer to the United States Immigration and Naturalization Service as "la migra." When it comes to cash remittances that migrants send home from abroad, Durand, Parrado, and Massey (1996), call these monies "migra dollars."

4. Ladino refers to non-indigenous Guatemalans. This term, however, is fully loaded, and many Guatemalans would not self-identify in such terms. I capitalize both the labels of Ladino and Maya throughout this paper to assign both descriptors equal weight.

5. For a good historical discussion associated with power relations in this area, see McCreery (1994).

6. To maintain confidentiality, I use pseudonyms instead of the actual names of my informants.

7. While many locals in recent years catapulted to higher rungs of Gualán's society, from my conversations with community members, Gualantecos see a clear distinction between the new rich (either due to migra or *narco* [drug] money) and the old money class of elite cattle ranchers and coffee plantation owners.

8. Similarly, Gmelch (1992) in his study of Barbadian returnees from North American and Britain, observes that speech (and dress) notably alter.

9. For an insightful discussion of how historically the role that phenotype plays in constructions of race, particularly in Guatemala, see the work of Smith (1995). She points out that in Latin America throughout the post-colonial era the ruling class became more *mestizo* (mixed) and less white. She goes on to emphasize that color differences among the former group remain as an important dimension in how social ideologies unfold in Guatemala today.

10. I borrow the term "from below" from Guarnizo and Smith (1998). This concept captures how transnational processes and practices take place at the local level.

11. For research that explicitly deals with immigration, nutrition, and health-related outcomes among Maya children in the United States and Guatemala, see Smith et al. (2002).

12. While some migrant households may improve their health due to the influx of cash remittances, on the other hand, these monies may also allow folks greater flexibility to purchase over-the-counter drugs. Throughout Guatemala, for example, there exists a tendency to self-medicate, and in turn, overuse and abuse drugs (e.g., antibiotics).

13. The improvement in health locals report in San Cristóbal, in comparison to Gualán, may well derive from the fact that, as a whole, their department is worse off to begin with in terms of health.

14. Earlier in his historical and comparative work on colonial Guatemala, T. Little-Siebold (1993) dubbed this term.

References Cited

Alvarez, Robert

1987 Familia: Migration and Adaptation in Baja and Alta California, 1800–1975. Berkeley: University of California Press.

Banco de Guatemala

2007 Guatemala: Ingreso de Divisas por Remesas Familiares. URL<http://www.banguat.gob.gt/inc/ver.asp?id=/estaeco/remesas/remfam20012007.htm> (March 2, 2008).

Basch, Linda, Nina Glick Schiller, and Cristina Szanton Blanc

1994 Nations Unbound: Transnational Projects Postcolonial Predicaments and Deterritorialized Nation-States. Langhorne, Penn.: Gordon and Breach.

Burns, Allan F.

1993 Maya in Exile: Guatemalans in Florida. Philadelphia, Penn.: Temple University Press.

Casaus Arzú, Marta Elena

1992 Guatemala: Linaje y Racismo. San José, Costa Rica: FLACSO.

Cohen, Jeffrey

2001 Transnational Migration in Rural Oaxaca, Mexico: Dependency, Development, and the Household. American Anthropologist 103(4):954-967.

2004 The Culture of Migration in Southern Mexico. Austin: University of Texas Press.

Conway, Dennis, and Jeffrey Cohen

1998 Consequences of Migration and Remittances for Mexican Transnational Communities. Economic Geography 74(1):26-44.

Dinerman, Ina

1978 Patterns of Adaptation Among Households of U.S.-bound Migrants from Michoacán, Mexico. International Migration Review 12(4):485-501.

Durand, Jorge, Emilio A. Parrado, and Douglas Massey

1996 Migradollars and Development: A Reconsideration of the Mexican Case. International Migration Review 30(2):423-444.

Eggan, Fred

1954 Social Anthropology and the Method of Controlled Comparison. American Anthropologist 56(5):743-63.

Fink, Leon

2003 The Maya of Morganton: Work and Community in the Nuevo New South. Chapel Hill: University of North Carolina Press.

Fischer, Edward, and R. McKenna Brown, eds.

1996 Maya Cultural Activism in Guatemala. Austin: University of Texas Press.

Fisher, Edward

2001 Cultural Logics and Global Economies: Maya Identity in Thought and Practice. Austin: University of Texas Press.

Georges, Eugenia

1990 The Making of a Transnational Community: Migration, Development, and Cultural Change in the Dominican Republic. New York: Columbia University Press.

Glick Schiller, Nina, Linda Basch, and Cristina Szanton Blanc

1992 Transnationalism: A New Analytic Framework for Understanding Migration. *In* Towards a Transnational Perspective on Migration: Race, Class, Ethnicity, and Nationalism Reconsidered. Nina Glick Schiller, Linda Basch, and Cristina Szanton Blanc, eds. Pp. 1-24. New York: Annals of the New York Academy of Sciences.

Gmelch, George

1980 Return Migration. Annual Review of Anthropology 9:135-159.

1992 Double Passage: The Lives of Caribbean Immigrants Abroad and Back Home. Ann Arbor: University of Michigan Press.

Grasmuck, Sherri, and Patricia Pessar

1991 Between Two Islands: Dominican International Migration. Berkeley: University of California.

Griffith, David

1985 Women, Remittances, and Reproduction. American Ethnologist 12(4):676-690.

2006 American Guestworkers: Jamaicans and Mexicans in the U.S. Labor Market. University Park: Pennsylvania State University Press.

Grimes, Kimberly

1998 Crossing Borders, Changing Social Identities in Southern Mexico. Tucson: University of Arizona Press.

Guarnizo, Luis, and Michael P. Smith

1998 The Locations of Transnationalism. *In* Transnationalism from Below. Michael P. Smith and Luis Guarnizo, eds. Pp. 3–34. New Brunswick, N.J.: Transaction Publishers.

Hagan, Jaqueline

1993 Deciding to Be Legal: A Maya Community in Houston. Philadelphia, Penn.: Temple University Press.

1998 Social Networks, Gender, and Immigrant Incorporation: Resources and Constraints. American Sociological Review 63(1):55-67.

Hamilton, Nora, and Norma Stoltz Chinchilla

1999 Changing Networks and Alliances in a Transnational Context: Salvadoran and Guatemalan Immigrants in Southern California. Social Justice 26(3):4-26.

2001 Seeking Community in a Global City: Guatemalans and Salvadorans in Los Angeles. Philadelphia, Penn.: Temple University Press.

Jonas, Susanne

2000 Of Centaurs and Doves, Guatemala's Peace Process. Boulder, Colo.: Westview Press.

King, Russell

1986 Return Migration and Economic Problems. London, U.K.: Croom Helm.

Kohpahl, Gabriele

1998 Voices of Guatemalan Women in Los Angeles: Understanding Their Immigration (Latino Communities, Emerging Voices, Political, Social, Cultural, and Legal). New York: Garland Publishing.

Levitt, Peggy

1999 Social Remittances: A Local-Level, Migration-Driven Form of Cultural Diffusion. International Migration Review 32(124):926-949.

2001 The Transnational Villagers. Berkeley: University of California Press.

Little-Siebold, Todd

1993 Guatemala and the Dream of a Nation: National Policy and Regional Practice in the Liberal Era, 1871-1945. Ph.D. dissertation, Tulane University.

Loucky, James, and Marilyn Moors, eds.

2000 The Maya Diaspora: Guatemalan Roots, New American Lives. Philadelphia, Penn.: Temple University.

Massey, Douglas, Rafael Alarcon, Jorge Durand, and Humberto González

1987 Return to Aztlán: The Social Process on International Migration from Western Mexico. Berkeley: University of California Press.

McCreery, David

1994 Rural Guatemala, 1760-1940. Stanford, Calif.: Stanford University Press.

Menjívar, Cecilia

2002 The Ties that Heal: Guatemalan Immigrant Women's Networks and Medical Treatment. International Migration Review 36(2):437-466.

Montejo, Victor

1999 Tied to the Land: Maya Migration, Exile, and Transnationalism. *In* Identities on the Move, Transnational Process in North American and the Caribbean Basin. Liliana R. Goldin, ed. Pp. 185-202. Albany, N.Y.: Institute for Mesoamerican Studies, State University of New York at Albany.

Moran-Taylor, Michelle J.

2004 Crafting Connections: Maya Linkages between Guatemala's Altiplano and el Norte. Estudios Fronterizos 5(10):91-115.

n.d. When Mothers and Fathers Migrate North: Caretakers, Children, and Child Rearing in Guatemala. Latin American Perspectives. In press.

Moran-Taylor, Michelle J., and Cecilia Menjívar

2005 Unpacking Longings of Return: Guatemalans and Salvadorans in Phoenix, Arizona. International Migration 43(4):91-121.

Moran-Taylor, Michelle J., and Miles Richardson

1993 Place and Journey in the Lives of Guatemalan Migrants: Documenting the Undocumented. Southern Anthropologist 20(3): 12-22.

Municipalidad de San Cristóbal Totonicapán, Totonicapán.

1998 Censo Urbano. San Cristóbal Totonicapán, Totonicapán, Guatemala.

Naciones Unidas

1999 Guatemala: El Rostro Rural del Desarollo Humano. Guatemala City: Magna Terra Editores.

Nelson, Diane

1999 A Finger in the Wound: Body Politics in Quincentennial Guatemala. Berkeley: University of California Press.

Nolin, Catherine

2002 Transnational Ruptures and Sutures: Questions of Identity and Social Relations Among Guatemalans in Canada. GeoJournal 56(1):59-67.

North, Lisa, and Alan Simmons, eds.

1999 Journeys of Fear, Refugee Return, and National Transformation in Guatemala. Montreal, Canada: McGill-Queen's University Press.

Popkin, Eric

1999 Guatemalan Mayan Migration to Los Angeles: Constructing Transnational Linkages in the Context of the Settlement Process. Ethnic and Racial Studies 22(2):267-289.

Repak, Terry A.

1995 Waiting on Washington: Central American Workers in the Nation's Capital. Philadelphia, Pa.: Temple University Press.

Rhoades, Robert

1978 Intra-European Return Migration and Rural Development: Lessons from the Spanish Case. Human Organization 37:136-147.

Rodman, Debra

2006 Gender, Migration, and Transnational Identities: Maya and Ladino Relations in Eastern Guatemala. Ph.D. dissertation, University of Florida.

Rubenstein, Hymie

1979 The Return Ideology in West Indian Migration. Papers in Anthropology 20:21-38.

Smith, Carol

1995 Race-Class-Gender Ideology in Guatemala: Modem and Anti-Modern Forms. Society for Comparative Study of Society and History 37(4):723-749.

Smith, Patricia, Barry Bogin, M. Inés Varela-Silva, Bibiana Orden, and James Loucky

2002 Does Immigration Help or Harm Children's Health?: The Mayan Case. Social Science Quarterly 83(4):994-1002.

Taylor, Matthew, Michelle J. Moran-Taylor, and Debra Rodman Ruiz

2006 Land, Ethnic, and Gender Change: Transnational Migration and its Effects on Guatemalan Lives and Landscapes. Geoforum 37(1):41-61.

Vlach, Norita

1992 The Quetzal in Flight: Guatemalan Immigrant Families in the United States. San Jose, Calif.: Praeger Publishers.

Warren, Kay

1998 Indigenous Movements and their Critics, Pan-Maya Activism in Guatemala. Princeton, N.J.: Princeton University Press.

Wellmeier, Nancy

1998 Ritual, Identity, and the Mayan Diaspora. New York: Garland Publishing, Inc.

Wolf, Eric

1956 Aspects of Group Relations in a Complex Society: Mexico. American Anthropologist 58:1065-1078.

Wyman, Mark

1993 Round-Trip to America: The Immigrants Return to Europe, 1880-1930. Ithaca, N.Y.: Cornell University Press.

Define the following concepts/phrases:

transnational migration   migration

remittances   development

Answer the following questions:

1. How did author describe the geographical and historical background of Guatemala?
2. Discuss some of the reasons for Guatemalan migration to the United States.
3. How does the author describe social and economic remittances?
4. How do remittances impact some of the Guatemalan families?
5. What does the phrase "creating global culture at local level" mean?
6. Discuss the pro and cons of the two points of view regarding migration and economic development.

Latina Workers and Allies Mobilized to Close the Gender Pay Gap and Promote Fair Work Conditions

Monica Ramírez

NEARLY 100 ORGANIZATIONS ACROSS THE U.S. are latina-worker-growth_memetaking action today to raise awareness about the gender wage gap facing Latina workers. The most recent data reflects that Latina workers are being paid an average of 54 cents to the dollar paid to white male, non-Hispanic workers. This means that it takes Latinas 22 months to make the equivalent earnings that a white, non-Hispanic male worker is paid in just 12 months.

It is estimated that Latinas comprise nearly twice as many female workers than in 1994, increasing from 7.9 percent to 14.7 percent. Despite the fact that Latinas represent a growing percentage of the labor force, they are not necessarily more financially secure. In addition to equal pay violations, Latinas face wage theft, discriminatory job placement, failure to promote and train, job segregation and wide-spread sexual harassment. The situation is reported to be even more dismal for Latinas who are immigrants, indigenous Latinas, and Afro-Latinas.

The Latina gender wage gap has a detrimental impact on the Latina worker and her family. Thus, equal pay for Latinas is not "just" a Latina worker issue. It is a family, a children's, women's rights, labor and workers' rights issue that has consequences for our entire nation. When a Latina can not afford to put food on her table, a roof over head, save for her future or pay for her education or that of her children, this has a devastating impact for her and our country.

We cannot view pay discrimination in isolation. This injustice is part of a larger picture of inequality, where the many facets of our lives- our sex, race, documentation status, level of education, and relationship status, among other factors, are used against us in an attempt to keep us from maximizing our potential.

Latina workers and advocates, like me, have been organizing for change for years. While it is true that Latinas are being undervalued, cheated and sometimes discriminated against in multiple ways at work, we are also powerful. We are taking measures to hold wrong doers accountable and determine our own future.

There are amazing trailblazers who many of us have grown up admiring and who have inspired our own activism, like Dolores Huerta. She has dedicated her life's work to ensuring that Latina workers are not only counted as workers but also valued as human beings. In addition, other Latina labor leaders, like Aida Garcia, Dora Cervantes, Esther Lopez, Maricruz Manzanarez, Yanira Merino, Evelyn DeJesus, Maria Elena Durazo and many others, have been on the front lines organizing Latinas and other workers to stand up for fair wages and just conditions at work. There are workers, like an agricultural packing plant worker named Laura, and Araclis, a shop steward at a hotel in New Jersey, who have bravely spoken out against gender discrimination and have stood up to assert their rights.

In addition, there are thousands of women who are leading campaigns, like our sisters at Restaurant Opportunity Coalition (ROC) who are mobilized for "One Fair Wage" and our hermanas at the National Domestic Workers Alliance (NDWA) who have made significant advancements to increase protections for domestic workers at the state and federal levels.

Despite the odds, we are rising. We are rising up to speak out and stand up against unequal pay and all forms of oppression committed against our sisters, our brothers and ourselves. We are grateful to the multitudes of organizations and individuals who stand with us today and every day. The future of our nation depends on the ability for all of us to be paid what we are worth so that we can succeed and thrive.

Find more information about ways that you can stand with Latina workers at *www.latinaequalpay.org*.

■ Reading 5.3

Define the following concepts/phrases:

gender inequality

Restaurant Opportunity Coalition

gender wage gap

National Domestic Workers Alliance

activism

Answer the following questions:

1. According to the article, what kind of discrimination were women subjected to?
2. In 2016, what was the average salary to the dollar for Latinas in comparison to men?
3. What is the impact of gender wage gap for Latinas?
4. What is the root of lower wages among Latinas?
5. How are Latinas addressing the gender wage gap problem?
6. Who is Dolores Huerta?

Part VI

Ni Blancos Ni Negros: Latinos and the Politics of Race and Identity

Construction of Race and Ethnicity for and by Latinos

Edward Fergus, Pedro Noguera, and Margary Martin

S INCE THE 1990S, THE NATIONAL DISCOURSE on Latinos has focused on the growing presence of America's new largest minority group—who are they, where are they coming from, are they legal, and will they assimilate. Even though many scholars have documented the extraordinary diversity of the Latino population with respect to national origin, ethnic and phenotypic diversity, the face of Latinos on CNN, Fox News, and MSNBC is, more often than not, White or at best bronze (Candelario, 2007; Rivera, 2007).

According to the 2000 Census, over 35 million Latinos were living in the United States By mid-decade, this number rose to 42 million, and the 2007 American Community Survey estimates Latino groups at 45 million. The rapid and dramatic growth of the Latino population represented 51% of the change in racial/ethnic groups between 2000 and 2005 (Pew Hispanic, 2006). Given our shared border, the majority of the 42 million (64%) are Mexican, followed by Puerto Ricans (9.1%), Cubans (3.5%), Salvadorans (3.0%), and Dominicans (1.7%). In the 2000 Census, over 900,000 (2.7%) self-identified as Black Hispanic and 17.6 million (47.9%) as White Hispanic, and yet another 15 million (42.2%) identified as "some other race" (Logan, 2003). The Black Hispanic as an identification was most prominent among Dominicans (12.7%) followed by Puerto Ricans (8.2%), Cubans (4.7%), and finally Central Americans (4.1%) (Logan, 2003). On the other hand, White Hispanic identification is most prevalent among Cubans (85.4%) followed by South Americans (61.1%); Mexicans (49.3%); and then Puerto Ricans (49%). In 2007, these identification patterns changed; ACS estimates 677,000 (1.5%) self-identify as Black Hispanic and 24 million (54.3%) self-identify as White Hispanic and another 18 million (40%) self-identify as "other race." This difference in race and ethnic identification between 2000 and 2007 could either signal a particular migration pattern among Latino groups entering the United States or a shift in the identification patterns of Latino groups. Whatever the specific explanation for this shift, Latino groups still need to situate their identification as both a race and ethnicity.

Over the last three decades the US Census has situated Hispanics as a distinct ethnic group (Rodriguez, 2000). Since the enactment of Public Law 94-311, "Economic and Social Statistics for Americans of Spanish Origin." on June 16, 1976, Hispanic origin and race have been included jointly in the decennial census. Anyone familiar with the diversity among those who identify (and are identified as) Latinos will recognize the irony of this designation because Hispanics can come from any racial group. Still, the creation of the Hispanic category can be seen as somewhat of an accomplishment given that prior to 1980 Hispanics were identified as Hispanics, even though the rights and privileges accorded to Hispanics in terms of public education, housing, and even voting rights, were often not the same as those held by Whites (Ruiz, 2007).

In the 2000 Census, Latinos were required to answer both race and ethnicity questions: Question #7: Is Person 1 Spanish/Hispanic/Latino? And Question #8: What is Person 1's race? (See Figure 6.1.1)

These questions from the US Census continued maintained the distinction between race and ethnicity. That is, while race has historically been used in reference to essential biological group

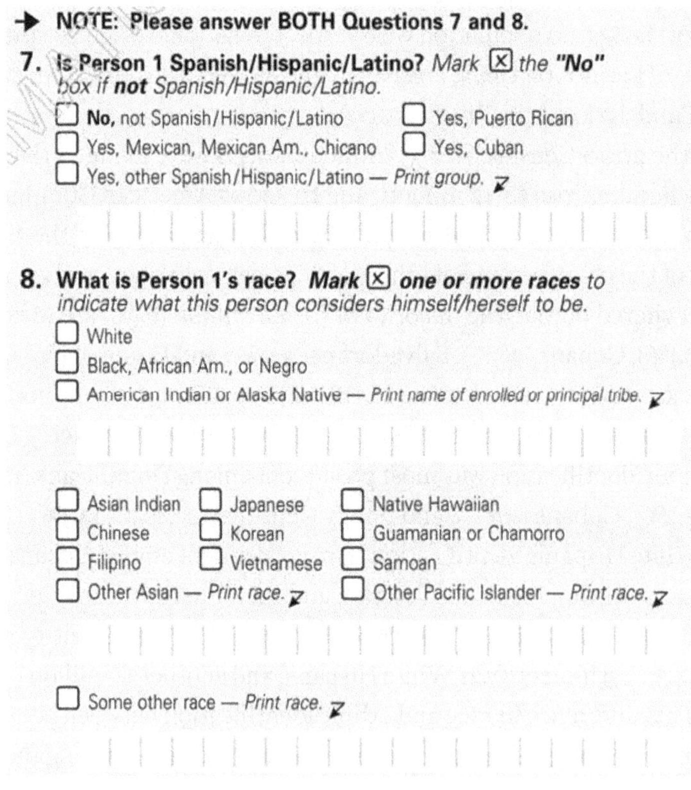

→ **NOTE: Please answer BOTH Questions 7 and 8.**

7. Is Person 1 Spanish/Hispanic/Latino? *Mark ☒ the* ***"No"*** *box if* ***not*** *Spanish/Hispanic/Latino.*

☐ **No,** not Spanish/Hispanic/Latino ☐ Yes, Puerto Rican
☐ Yes, Mexican, Mexican Am., Chicano ☐ Yes, Cuban
☐ Yes, other Spanish/Hispanic/Latino — *Print group.*

8. What is Person 1's race? ***Mark*** ☒ ***one or more races*** *to indicate what this person considers himself/herself to be.*

☐ White
☐ Black, African Am., or Negro
☐ American Indian or Alaska Native — *Print name of enrolled or principal tribe.*

☐ Asian Indian ☐ Japanese ☐ Native Hawaiian
☐ Chinese ☐ Korean ☐ Guamanian or Chamorro
☐ Filipino ☐ Vietnamese ☐ Samoan
☐ Other Asian — *Print race.* ☐ Other Pacific Islander — *Print race.*

☐ Some other race — *Print race.*

FIGURE 6.1.1 United States Census Form 2000.

differences, ethnicity has primarily been used to draw distinctions between groups based upon religion, culture, language, and even nationality. Given the confusion surrounding these categories, it is not surprising that the operation of these policy definitions utilized by the federal government do not serve as a basis for everyday race-making (Lewis, 2003) for those who identify as Latino.

For many Latinos, the meaning making of what is race and ethnicity is a complex process. For many, it can involve an ongoing tension between the subjective (who I think I am) and objective (who others think I am) dimensions about race that may not be easily resolved (Fergus, 2004). For others, especially recent immigrants, there is the additional confusion that arises from the fact that the categories operative in Latin America are not operative in the U.S. context. For example, whereas phenotype figures prominently in the racial categories utilized in most Latin American countries, the United States has historically treated racial categories as immutable, rooted in biology, and tied to the Black–White binary (Almaguer, 1994). And yet for other Latinos, the use and non-use of racial categories is tied to perceived social meanings of self-identifying as White, Black, or Asian. And these social meanings have significance in everyday mobility. For example, the educational attainment of those who identify as Black Hispanic is higher than White Hispanic (a mean 11.7 years vs. 10.5 years), however Black Hispanics have a lower median income, higher unemployment, and higher poverty rates than White Hispanics (Logan, 2003). Such discrepancies in the relationship between income and educational attainment are highly significant because for most groups in American society there is a high degree of correspondence between these patterns. Similar differences between Black and White Latinos have also been noted in studies on skin color and labor market participation (Espino & Franz, 2002), and political activities and attitudes (Hochschild, et. al., 2006). Such complexities and ambiguities necessitate the exploration of the following question: how should Latinos fit into the U.S. social landscape with respect to the well established race and ethnicity constructs? More importantly, should Latinos utilize current race constructs that are based on a Black–White paradigm to explain the "otherizing" of Latinos, or is a tri-fold racial hierarchy as articulated by Bonilla-Silva (2004) necessary? Or should Latinos solely be constructed as an ethnicity with differing racial categories? Also, given the subjective nature of these racial designations one question that emerges is just how "White" and/or "Black" are Latinos? That is, even though they may lay claim to Whiteness or Blackness to what degree are they accepted and treated as White or Black in the communities where they reside?

The purpose of this chapter is to provide a historical outline of the predominant theories on race and ethnicity and what they have meant for those who identify as Latino. We also examine the ways in which the concept of race does and does not consider the interaction of markers such as language, skin color, and culture found among Latino national groups. Drawing upon Cornell and Hartmann's (1998) construct of race as external and ascribed, and ethnicity as an internally constructed concept, we extrapolate on the applicability of race and ethnicity and its utility to the experiences of Latinos. Our particular focus is in the theoretical expansion of the discourse on race and ethnicity, and its potential in interpreting disparate social mobility and educational outcomes within Latino groups, such as the high drop-out rate among Mexicans, Puerto Ricans, and Dominicans and the low drop out rate among White Cubans.

Theoretical Conversations of Race/Ethnicity
The Meaning of Race as Social Construct

Numerous social scientists have pointed out that U.S. notions of race and ethnicity have been premised on a Black–White dichotomy or continuum. This dual framework of race and ethnic construction subjugates all groups to define themselves within this dichotomy or continuum (Bashi & McDaniel, 1997; Bonilla-Silva, 2004). As Andrew Hacker (1992) suggests, "[i]n many respects, others groups find themselves sitting as spectators, while the two prominent players try to work out how or whether they can co-exist with one another" (p. 38). The dominant paradigm of race, which positions Whites as the superior group and Blacks as the inferior (the ultimate "other"), has shaped the ways in which Americans have thought about race and racial disparities. Throughout much of the 19th century, race was used as the primary basis for determining rights and status in American society, and those regarded as non-Whites—Asians, Native Americans, Latinos, and even some Eastern Europeans—were generally denied privileges held by Whites (Fredrickson, 2002). For example, prior to a Supreme Court ruling early in the 20th century that Armenians were in fact Whites (this was a reversal of an earlier ruling), they experienced many of the same forms of discrimination that non-Whites were subjected to—segregated housing and education, limited rights in the courts, etc. (Takaki, 1987). After World War II and especially after the passage of civil rights legislation and changes in immigration policy in the mid-1960s, the system of racial hierarchy became complex even as the Black–White paradigm remained intact. Increasingly, groups were assigned status by virtue of their proximity to either Blacks or Whites. The relative success of Asians in education and employment led to an "upgrading" of Asians such that they were increasingly regarded as "honorary Whites" (Lee, 1994). Meanwhile, Latinos were more often than not lumped together with Blacks and Native Americans as disadvantaged minorities.

Regardless of the time period, Latinos have posed a quandary for those who sought to situate them within the American racial hierarchy. This is because diversity related to region, nationality, socioeconomic status and, most importantly, phenotype, has played an important role in determining how Latinos have been treated. Several scholarly analyses of the discrimination experienced by Latinos in the United States have consciously or unconsciously ignored this diversity as they have applied the dominant Black–White racial paradigm to an examination of the Latino experience. For example, although Carnoy's *Faded Dreams* (1998) provides a well-documented historical analysis of the ways in which changes in federal policies related to civil rights have affected opportunities for African Americans, his treatment of Latinos is at best superficial. Rather than taking the time to carefully interrogate the variegated experience of Latinos, Carnoy simply throws in "and Latinos," as though the Latino experience could be assumed to be equivalent to that of Blacks (Carnoy, 1998). A similar approach has been taken in several other important scholarly treatments of race in recent years (Massey, 1998; Omi & Winant, 1989). While such an approach may have been useful in cases where Latinos have been subject to blatant forms of discrimination on the basis of race, this paradigm has not been as useful for understanding the nuanced social histories of Latinos when other factors, namely, immigration status, nationality or phenotype, may have been more important in understanding the experience of particular groups. For example, long before the ban on inclusion was lifted for Blacks, there are several examples where Latinos played professional baseball, served in the military, attended White segregated schools, and held public office in states that practiced blatant racial discrimination (Almaguer, 1994). Such examples should not be taken as proof that Latinos were treated as Whites because they co-exist with other examples of blatant discrimination directed specifically at Latinos (e.g., racial segregation in schools). However, the historic contradictions and inconsistencies in the treatment of Latinos should force us to rethink the narrow restrictions created by the Black–White paradigm of race.

Biology Confuses Us

Throughout most of the 20th century, the social construction and social discourse on race treated group differences as though they were rooted in innate biological distinctions (Lipsitz, 1998). Within this framework, racial differences were regarded as conferring certain biologically determined advantages on Whites—superior intellect, and disadvantages on Blacks—a proclivity for criminal and licentious behavior. With Blacks serving as the negative reference point, membership in the White racial category was used as the basis for extending important rights and privileges to some, and denying these to others (Omi & Winant, 1989). By essentializing race in this way, and supporting these racist notions with numerous pseudo-scientific studies that argued physical differences existed (i.e., neurological, IQ, cranial, etc.; Jensen, 1979; Morton, 1849), "Whiteness" and "Blackness" could be used as the basis for constructing a racial hierarchy. Latinos, like Asians, people of mixed racial heritage, middle easterners, and others, were in turn placed along the Black–White racial hierarchy, never as equal to Whites, but above Blacks. While such a position of limited privilege contained its own hardships and indignities, Latinos could find solace in the fact that at least they were better off than Blacks.

This biological-based race definition began formally with the development of the Eugenics Education Society in 1907 (later Eugenics Society). As a term, "eugenics" involves the scientific marking of hereditary traits. "Scientists" associated with eugenics were preoccupied with finding ways to promote genetic traits associated with superior intellect and physical ability, and discouraging and even eliminating those associated with inferiority. One part of the agenda of the Eugenics Education Society was to utilize the information of hereditary traits in the explanation of "poverty and pauperism" (Kenny, 2004). Prominent researchers, Charles Galton Darwin, Leonard Darwin, Robert Baker, and others argued the inequalities experienced by Blacks, Latinos, and Native Americans were due to genetic deficiencies that were reflected in cultural attributes. Long after the Society lost its influence and credibility (due in part to its similarity with Nazism), this line of research assisted in the development of terms such as "culture of poverty" and "cultural deficiency." The publication of *The Bell Curve* (1996) by Hernstein and Murray and recent comments by Nobel Laureate Charles Watson, serve as a potent reminder that the idea of innate racial superiority of Whites over Blacks is still very much alive in this country.

With few exceptions, for much of the 20th century sociologists moved away from the notion of race as a biological concept (i.e., skin color, hair texture, and other features). With the emergence of the Chicago School of sociology social scientists began treating race as a social construct (e.g., DuBois, 1899; Drake & Cayton, 1945; Myrdal, 1944) that had to be understood as a by-product of the particular historical experience of the United States. In what is widely regarded as one of the most important theoretical treatments on race in the last twenty years, Omi and Winant (1994) argue that even though early efforts to use race as a demarcation of social status and privilege attempted to use physical variations among humans as the basis for their system of classification, they were forced to recognize that such distinctions were arbitrary and fraught with ambiguity. Given America's long history of race mixing, there is a high degree of variability with respect to phenotype within group. Therefore, it is the social meanings that humans place upon physical markers such as hair texture and skin color that matter far more than any "objective" or "scientific" distinctions. Winant defines race as "a concept that signifies and symbolizes sociopolitical conflicts and interests in reference to different human bodies" (2000, p. 172), and he adds that there is a contextualization that assigns meaning to biological or physical features. That is, even though the darkness of Black skin color has been used to justify discrimination against them, some Blacks are light enough to "pass" and as light as individuals classified as White. For this reason, several scholars have treated the American concept of race as a social construct that can only be understood within the context of America's sordid history of race relations (Cornell & Hartmann, 1998).

Other research on race as a social construct and the perpetuation of racial inequities also illuminated the presence of racial hierarchies with an awareness that they operate differently in relation to multiple groups (Bashi & McDaniel, 1997). The construct of racial hierarchy is loosely defined as the stratification of racial categorization with Whites at the top and Blacks at the bottom (Song, 2004). The stratification of Whites on top comes from social and economic-based privileges in the form of institutionalized racism that has allowed for wealth accumulation and other forms of social mobility (Bobo, Keugel, & Smith, 1997; Hacker, 1992). The stratification of Blacks at the bottom is determined by a socio-history of negative social and economic policies based on the privileging of Whites and subjugating of Blacks. Much of this racial hierarchy construct is situated on a history of discrimination and systematic exclusion, which few groups have experienced similar to Native Americans and Black Americans. Although there is much agreement in the presence of a racial hierarchy, there is less agreement as to what groups are experiencing it the worst and more importantly whether it is a static hierarchy. Proponents of the Black–White binary model of racial hierarchy (e.g., Feagin, 2000; Hacker, 1992) posit this framework is the basis of oppression for other non-White groups. Feagin argues that the oppression other groups experience (i.e., Arabs, Latinos, Asians) experience is based on an anti-Black framework; "white elites and the white public have long evaluated, reacted to, and dominated later non-European entrants coming into the nation from within a previously established and highly imbedded system of antiblack racism" (pp. 204–205). This argument is exemplified in the experiences of non-U.S. native Blacks also experiencing racial discrimination, even though they assert a Black immigrant identity (Kasinitz, 1992; Waters, 1994). In addition, proponents of the Black–White model also look to the dominant narrative of assimilation (i.e., gaining English language proficiency, attainment of U.S. citizenship, etc.) as having occurred among Black Americans but not resulting in the social mobility found among European immigrants.

On the other side of this conversation are the proponents of the racial hierarchy who consider the racialization experiences of other groups beyond Blacks and Whites as expanding our notions of the racial hierarchy (Almaguer, 1994; Bashi & McDaniel, 1997; Bonilla-Silva, 2004). This line of research posits a need for expanding racial hierarchy beyond Black–White and to consider other factors beyond skin color, such as religion (Arab-Americans), citizenship (Latinos), culture (Indians), and language. Several researchers note the experiences of race riots (Yoon, 1997), and the racial tensions between Black Americans and Asians, and Mexicans (Murguia & Foreman, 2003) as representing some of the inapplicability of the Black–White model. More specifically, the Black–White model of racial hierarchy centers racial discrimination and oppression as solely skin-color bound, however the discrimination research on new immigrants, particularly Asians and Latinos exemplify oppression as multimodal.

The construction of race and its racial hierarchy matters significantly for Latinos because the daily operation of these hierarchies primarily relies on skin color. The skin color variation among Latinos highlighted earlier and the differential outcomes along these variations makes the application of racial hierarchy a very pertinent construct in defining who is allowed to be Latino and what are the social mobility consequences. Numerous studies of Latinos and these variations illuminate the slippery operation of this racial hierarchy because it presents that some Latinos are not able to exist as Latino but rather solely Black or White. For instance, in a study of Puerto Ricans in New York City, Rodriguez and Cordero-Guzman (1992) noted that among 240 randomly selected Puerto Ricans, 40% of the sample saw themselves differently from the way in which they perceived that Americans (Whites) viewed them. Additionally, the participant's ethnic/racial identification was strongly influenced by their perceptions of how Americans identify them. For example, participants that believed North Americans viewed them as White were more inclined to identify themselves as White. Such findings were also apparent in a study of Mexican Americans in which the 546 respondents used various ethnic identities depending on context in order to minimize their social distance from those with whom they interacted (Saenz & Aguirre, 1991). In another study of high school Mexican and Puerto Rican students of varying skin color (i.e., White-looking, Hispanic/Mexican-looking, and Black/Biracial-looking), there was a continuing vacillating of race and ethnicity identification (Fergus, 2004). More specifically, the darker skin Latinos primarily situated a Black identity within their interactions with African Americans, while the lighter skin Latinos went back and forth between a White and/or an ethnic identity. Such differences also moderated their perceptions of opportunity and engagement in school. Other studies of skin color variation among Chicanos in the southwestern United States also noted differences in educational attainment between dark and light skin Chicanos (Murguia & Telles, 1996), as well as Dominicans and Cubans (Aguirre & Bonilla-Silva, 2002). In these studies, we are able to understand that multiple Latino groups are cognizant of how skin color signifies a racial and ethnic identification, as well as in aggregate analyses of social, economic, and educational outcomes a racial hierarchy is present along the color line. And, in the everyday race-making of Latinos, this racial hierarchy based on skin color has substantive consequences for life chances. However, the question that remains of race and racial hierarchy is what are the markers that allow for Latinos to make movement up and down this hierarchy? And since language and other cultural attributes are described as pertinent in the self-identification of Latinos, what do those markers mean in the operation of Latinos within the racial hierarchy? Some of the literature on ethnicity and its construction focuses on the self-ascription of ethnic labels due to structural forces faced by specific groups, some of which includes conversations on race but it has been limited in regards to Latinos. The following discussion is to unpack what this self-ascription notion of ethnicity has constructed about Latinos, particularly in understanding various social outcomes.

Latino as an Ethnic Label

The ethnicity or ethnic label research on Latinos has explored what undergirds the selection of specific ethnic tags, and, as a result of this research, we understand ethnicity as a complex construct among Latino groups. During the 20th century, the research on ethnicity[1] attended to the ways in which ethnicity was formed, maintained, and, in some instances, diminished by language, culture, immigrant status, identity labels, occupational status, and other factors (e.g., Barth, 1969; Gordon, 1975; Greeley, 1971; Handlin, 1951; Lieberson, 1980; Novak, 1973; Park, 1914). The propensity in early ethnicity research, which focused on extrapolating the assimilation process of European immigrants, described ethnicity or ethnic labels as fading overtime and resulting in a homogenous "American identity." This research, known as assimilation and pluralism (e.g., Glazer & Moynihan, 1963; Handlin, 1951), examined ethnicity as a diminishing factor among immigrant groups and situated the absorption of an American identity as an inevitable product. Park (1914, p. 615) defined assimilation as "a process of inter-penetration and fusion in which persons and groups acquire the memories, sentiments, and attitudes of other persons and groups, and by sharing their experience and history, are incorporated with them in a common cultural life." Such an explanation of did not explain the persistence of non-American ethnic labels found among Latino groups, especially the emergence of a Chicano and Puerto Rican identity during the 1960s civil rights movements. Various researchers began refuting the inevitability of an American ethnic label and offered a differing rendering in which attention was given to the presence of ethnicity as a matter of "interest" and "context" in which the individual has a choice of identifying or not (Espiritu, 1992).

Early discussions of ethnicity as "communities of interests" involved Glazer and Moynihan's (1963) research on Blacks, Puerto Ricans, Jews, Italians, and Irish in New York City. Glazer and Moynihan assert this group of ethnic immigrants' retention of their ethnic identification is because of common interests and in major cities religion and race are the two areas of interests that defined ethnic groups. Unlike Germans who come from differing religious backgrounds, Jews, Italians, and Irish maintained their respective religious institutions (i.e., Judaism and Catholicism) that exist for the specific purpose of serving ethnic interests. However, Glazer and Moynihan consider ethnic identification amongst Italians and Irish as declining from one generation to another and a new Catholic identification as emerging. Subsequently, even though they note racial discrimination and culture as significant factors in the ethnic identification among Blacks, Chicanos, and Puerto Ricans, Glazer and Moynihan are unable to articulate how interests are structured by race and racial identifications. Despite this theoretical shortcoming, this instrumentalist perspective introduced the notion that Latinos developed an ethnicity that was tied to contextual interests.

Barth (1969) introduced a major shift in this instrumentalist discourse on ethnic labels by suggesting that ethnicity is about boundaries—who is in and who is out. Barth's focus was primarily on the self-ascription and the ascription of others that create an ethnic or cultural boundary. Those boundaries of ethnicity involve structural and agency conditions. On the structural side, Yancey, Erickson, and Julian (1976) suggest that "the development and persistence of ethnicity is dependent upon structural conditions characterizing American cities and position of groups in American social structure" (p. 391). Yancey et al. suggest that ethnic identity is not a discrete variable but rather a continuous identification; "ethnicity may have relatively little to do with Europe, Asia or Africa, but much more to do with the exigencies of survival and the structure of opportunity in this country" (p. 400). In addition, they site changes in ecological and structural conditions, such as labor market opportunity and housing environment, as assisting in the maintenance and development of ethnic associations and affiliation. Unfortunately, Yancey et al. do not develop the persistence of ethnic identity among contemporary ethnic groups (e.g., Puerto Ricans, Mexicans, Africans, Black Americans, Asians, and West Indians) but they note a difference in ecological and structural conditions from European immigrants. These differences are identified in some of the status attainment research which outlined Blacks and Latinos experiencing ecological factors in distinct ways that moderate and mediate their social mobility (Portes & Wilson, 1976). Therefore, such researchers have conveyed ethnic identification can be both a function of how they enter the economic structure, such as laborers or professionals, and the structural conditions they endure (e.g., residential segregation and employment discrimination); for instance the entrée of Cubans during the 1960s versus the Marielitos in the 1980s.

Although, discourse on ethnicity has continued to develop this notion of situational or structural construction of ethnic identification, there has been little attention to how these structural conditions facilitate ethnic cohesion, particularly given its importance in the development of a Latino and Hispanic identification also known as panethnicity. Espiritu (1992) operationalizes panethnicity as a politico-cultural collectivity made up of peoples of several, hitherto distinct, tribal or national origins. Among Latinos, the construction of a collective panethnicity emerged in the 1970s with the use of "Hispanic" to ascribe various groups with an overarching label for political mobility. The resulting effect of an official use of Hispanic was the treating of Latinos as if they represent a real cultural and historical group (Portes & MacLeod, 1996). The use of a Hispanic label not only lumped together subgroup boundaries between Puerto Ricans, Dominicans, Panamanians, and other Latin American countries but also "encourage[d] individuals to broaden their identity to conform to the more inclusive ethnic designation" (Espiritu, 1992, p. 6). In some regions of the United States, use of the word Hispanic did not erase cultural distinctions among ethnic groups but rather was used to designate a particular political and economic orientation. Massey (1993) contends that the term "Hispanic" does not have any real existence beyond its original use as a statistical device:

> There is not a "Hispanic" population in the sense that there is a Black population. Hispanics share no common historical memory and do not compromise a single, coherent, community ... Saying that someone is Hispanic or Latino reveals little or nothing about likely attitudes, behaviors, beliefs, race, religion, class, or legal situation in the United States. The only thing reasonably certain is that either the person in question or some progenitor once lived in an originally colonized by Spain. (pp. 453–454)

These labels imposed by nation-states upon immigrant groups from Latin America do not illustrate the heterogeneity of these immigrant groups:

> Procrustean, one size fits-all pan-ethnic labels such as Asian, Hispanic, Black are imposed willy-nilly by the society at large to lump ethnic groups together who may hail variously from Vietnam or Korea, India or China, Guatemala or Cuba, Haiti or Jamaica, and who differ widely in national and class origins, phenotypes, languages, cultures, generations, migration histories, and modes of incorporation in the United States. Their children, especially adolescents in the process of constructing and crystallizing a social identity, are challenged to incorporate what is "out there" into what is "in here," often in dissonant social contexts. (Rumbaut, 1994, p. 749)

Although these labels have been constructed by nation-states, their usage has allotted Latinos political and economic leverage. For instance, Padilla (1985) notes that in Chicago during the early 1970s, Mexicans and Puerto Ricans adopted a collective Latino or Hispanic identity for a common struggle. The two groups united as a "Hispanic" collective in order to acquire Hispanic representation by voting for a Hispanic political candidate making Latino/Hispanic a situational ethnic identity that is

> fabricated and becomes most appropriate or salient for social action during those particular situations or moments when two or more Spanish-speaking ethnic groups are affected by structural forces [e.g., discrimination in housing, education, and employment] and mobilize themselves as one to overcome this impact. (p. 4)

Also pertinent to understand within this conversation of ethnic cohesion is the decision-making processes by which individuals elect to use particular ethnic labels. Nagel (1994) asserts "ethnic identity ... is the result of a dialectical process involving internal and external opinions and processes, as well as the individual's self-identification and outsider's ethnic designations—i.e., what you think your ethnicity is, versus what they think your ethnicity is" (p. 154). Self-identification involves a "layering" effect that sustains various meaning for the individual and group. For example, Padilla (1985) and Pedraza (1992) note that amongst Latinos that self-identifying as Mexican, Cuban, Puerto Rican, Dominican, Latino, or Hispanic serves various purposes and functions with the different groups. As Nagel (1994) illustrates,

> an individual of Cuban ancestry may be a Latino vis-a-vis non-Spanish-speaking ethnic groups, a Cuban-American vis-a-vis other Spanish-speaking groups, a Marielito vis-a-vis other Cubans, and white vis-a-vis African Americans. The chosen

ethnic identity is determined by the individual's perception of its meaning to different audiences, its salience in different social contexts, and its utility in different settings. (p. 155)

The shift in boundary making conversation opens the door to the question of how these boundary making activities occur and who dictates the perimeters. This is where the self-ascription process of ethnicity meets the external ascription process of race, how does race and ethnicity interact when it comes to those that self-ascribe as Latino? A myriad of research demonstrates that this interaction functions differently among various Latino populations and has implications for mobility (e.g., Fergus, 2004; Gomez, 2000; Murguia & Telles, 1996; Rodriguez, 1992, 2000). And in some ways this research has also suggested the possibility of self-ascribed ethnicity as dominant in intra-group situations and race as dominant in inter-group situations. In other words, "while an individual can choose from among a set of ethnic identities, that set is generally limited to socially and politically defined ethnic categories with varying degrees of stigma or advantage attached to them" (Nagel, 1994, p. 156). For instance, ethnic identity functions differently among White Americans and Americans of African ancestry; "white Americans have considerable latitude in choosing ethnic identities...Americans of African ancestry, on the other hand, are confronted with essentially one ethnic option Black" (Nagel, 1994, p. 156). This difference in latitude is noted in a study of Mexican and Puerto Rican high school students of different skin color, in which the lighter-skin students were allowed to be White and Latino, but the darker-skin students were limited to solely a Latino identity (Fergus, 2004). Such differences in the latitude of ethnic options demonstrates the boundary of individual ethnic options and the significant role outside agents play in restricting available ethnic identities. Even though, dark-skin Latinos may distinguish themselves in intra-racial settings, such distinctions are unimportant in inter-racial settings because of the power of race as a socially defining mechanism of U.S. society. However, race is interpreted in such contexts as biological, i.e., there is something physical that makes someone Black or Latino. Therefore, in discussing the self-ascription of individuals and groups, it is critical to note that there are limits to individual choice and external ascription plays an important role in restricting available ethnic labels. And much of this external ascription is the moment in which race as a biological construct takes center stage as demonstrated in the popular identification of individuals like Tiger Woods as Black, George Lopez as Mexican, Zoe Saldana as Black, Cameron Diaz as White, and Jimmy Smits as Latino.

Discussion

The presence of Latinos in the United States, unlike any other group, in some ways challenges and in other ways disrupts the manner in which race and ethnicity has been constructed. Both constructs are developed from the social experiences of Blacks and Whites; however the emergence of Latinos who can be easily situated in both categories and along the continuum, raises questions as to the breadth and depth of these categories. As we've outlined, neither category has sufficiently accounted for the dynamism of Latino groups, which, in turn, has limited our theoretical and empirical conversations of what is occurring with the Latinos in the United States.

The consideration of Latinos into the racial hierarchy discourse has been at best a sideline approach or afterthought (Bonilla-Silva, 2004). Even though, the social construct conversation continues to situate the meaning of race as continuously shifting, it is premised on the Black–White experience of race as a social construct. This is also apparent in some of the racial hierarchy literature on other racialization markers (Bashi, 1998; Bonilla-Silva, 2004); the meaning of power and privilege of self-identification in relation to external identification is premised on skin color power and privilege of Blacks and Whites. Such bifurcation continues to locate the notion of race as a social construct of skin color and facial/hair features of Blacks and Whites. Theories of race as a social construct need to involve more integration that argues the positionality of power and privilege as also bound to experiences of language, immigrant/non-immigrant, and skin color variation labels (i.e., White, Black, Brown, *mestizo*, *indio*, *guero*, negro, Moreno, etc.).

The shift s in ethnicity conversation from assimilation to pluralism to primordialism attend to the significance of language, immigrant status, and other markers as relevant in the self-ascription of ethnic identification. However, this research has not systematically considered individual and group consequences of this dialectical process of ethnic identity in relation to labor market opportunity, educational opportunity and resilience, and perceptions of individual opportunity. Particularly when juxtaposing to notions of power and privilege in positionality, which racial hierarchy conversations illuminate as directing social and economic mobility. For instance, do dark-skin Latinos experience labor market employment opportunities and participation in similar ways as light-skin Latinos? How would these dark-skin Latinos fair if they exhibited a Spanish accent? Or Spanish surname? The conversation of Latinos as solely a self-ascription prevents us from understanding the realities and tensions that exist when Asians from Venezuela speak Spanish and identify as Chino-Latinos.

As we continue to explore the empirical realities of Latinos in the United States, it will necessitate a theoretical expansion of race and its racial hierarchies as it pertains to other markers beyond skin color. Such expansion can allow for understanding the realities of how Spanish language (e.g., "Yo quiero Taco Bell," "Living la vida loca") and accents, undocumented immigrant status, and the Latinization of food (e.g., "Mexican" cheese) serve to position the role of Latino group culture as subordinate to dominant White culture. And such positionality illustrates the power of Whiteness in otherizing Latinos as a cultural phenomenon. Also, by limiting the conversation of Latinidad to an ethnic label dialogue, our research has only centered its theoretical and empirical exploration as to what it means for Latinos to call themselves Hispanic, Mexican, Puerto Rican, Dominican, etc. As we establish the new frontiers of research regarding Latinos, positionality, power, and self-ascription need to be critical elements of theoretical and empirical exploration when looking at language, skin color, immigrant status, and culture of Latino groups in the United States.

Endnote

1. Throughout this review we will use ethnicity and ethnic identity interchangeably.

References

Aguirre, B. E., & Bonilla-Silva, E. (2002). Does race matter among Cuban immigrants? An analysis of the racial characteristics of recent Cuban Immigrants. *Journal of Latin American Studies*, 34(2), 311–324.

Almaguer, T. (1994). *Racial fault lines.* Berkeley: University of California Press.

Barth, F. (1969). *Ethnic groups and boundaries: The social organization of culture difference.* Boston: Little, Brown.

Bashi, V. (1998). Racial categories matter because racial hierarchies matter: A commentary. *Ethnic and Racial Studies*, 21, 959–968.

Bashi, V., & McDaniel, A. (1997). A theory of immigration and racial stratification. *Journal of Black Studies*, 27, 668–682.

Bobo, L., Kluegel, J. R., & Smith, R. A. (1997). Laissez faire racism: The crystallization of a 'kinder, gentler' anti-black ideology. In S. A. Tuch & J. Martin (Eds.), *Racial attitudes in the 1990s: Continuity and change* (pp. 15–44). Greenwood, CT: Praeger.

Bonilla-Silva, E. (2004, November). From bi-racial to tri-racial: Towards a new system of racial stratification in the USA. *Ethnic and Racial Studies*, 17, 931–950.

Candelario, G. (2007). Color matters: Latina/o racial identities and life chances. In J. Flores & R. Rosaldo (Eds.), *A companion to Latina/o studies* (pp. 337–350). New York: Blackwell.

Carnoy, M. (1998). *Faded dreams: The politics and economics of race in America.* New York: Cambridge University Press.

Cornell, S., & Hartmann, D. (1998). *Ethnicity and race: Identities in a changing world.* Thousand Oaks, CA: Pine Forge Press.

Drake, S., & Cayton, H. (1945). *Black metropolis.* Chicago: The University of Chicago Press.

DuBois, W. (1899). *The Philadelphia negro: A social study.* Philadelphia: The University Pennsylvania Press.

Espino, R., & Franz, M. (2002). Latino phenotypic discrimination revisited: The impact of skin color on occupational status. *Social Science Quarterly*, 83, 612–623.

Espiritu, Y. (1992). *Asian American panethnicity: Bridging institutions and identities.* Philadelphia: Temple University Press.

Feagin, M. (2000). *Racist America.* New York: Routledge.

Fergus, E. (2004). *Skin color and identity formation: Perceptions of opportunity and academic orientation among Puerto Rican and Mexican youth.* New York: Routledge.

Fredrickson, G. M. (2002). *Racism: A short history.* Princeton, NJ: Princeton University Press.

Glazer, N., & Moynihan, D. P. (1963). *Beyond the melting pot: The Negroes, Puerto Ricans, Jews, Italians and Irish of New York City.* Cambridge, MA: MIT Press.

Gomez, C. (2000). The continual significance of skin color: An exploratory study of Latinos in the Northeast. *Hispanic Journal of Behavioral Sciences, 22,* 94–103.

Gordon, M. (1975). Toward a general theory of racial and ethnic group relations. In N. Glazer & D. P. Moynihan (Eds.), *Ethnicity: Theory and experience* (pp. 84–110). Cambridge, MA: Harvard University Press.

Greeley, A. M. (1971). *Why can't they be like us? America's white ethnic groups.* New York: E.P. Dutton.

Hacker, A. (1992). *Two nations: Black and white, separate, hostile, unequal.* New York: Scribner.

Handlin, O. (1951). *The uprooted.* Boston: Little Bay Books.

Hernstein, R., & Murray, A. (1996). *The bell curve: Intelligence and class structure in American life.* New York: Free Press.

Jensen, A. R. (1979). *Bias in mental testing.* New York: Free Press.

Kasinitz, P. (1992). *Caribbean New York.* Ithaca: Cornell University Press.

Kenny, M. (2004). Racial science on social context. *Isis, 95,* 394–419

Lee, S. J. (1994). Behind the model-minority stereotype: Voices of high- and low-achieving Asian American students. *Anthropology and Education Quarterly, 25,* 413–429.

Lewis, A. (2003). *Race in the schoolyard.* New Brunswick, NJ: Rutgers University Press.

Lieberson, S. (1980). *A piece of the pie: Blacks and white immigrants since 1880.* Berkeley: University of California Press.

Lipsitz, G. (1998). *The possessive investment in whiteness.* Philadelphia: Temple University Press.

Logan, J. (2003). *How race counts for Hispanic Americans.* Unpublished manuscript. University at Albany, NY: Mumford Center.

Massey, D. (1993). Latinos, poverty, and the underclass: A new agenda for research. *Hispanic Journal of Behavioral Sciences, 15,* 449–475.

Massey, D. (1998). *Worlds in motion: International migration at the end of the millenium.* Oxford, UK: Oxford University Press.

Morton, G. (1849). *An illustrated system of human anatomy.* Philadelphia: Grigg, Elliott and Co.

Murguia, E., & Foreman, T. (2003). Shades of whiteness: The Mexican American experience in relation to Anglos and Blacks. In A. W. Doane & E. Bonilla/Silva (Eds.), *White out: The continuing significance of racism* (pp. 63–79). London: Routledge.

Murguia, E., & Telles, E. (1996). Phenotype and schooling among Mexican Americans. *Sociology of Education, 69,* 276–289.

Myrdal, G. (1944). *An American dilemma.* New York: Harper Press.

Nagel, J. (1994). Constructing ethnicity: Creating and recreating ethnic identity and culture. *Social Problems, 41*, 152–176.

Novak, M. (1973). *The rise of the unmeltable ethnics: Politics and culture in the seventies.* New York: Macmillian.

Omi, M., & Winant, H. (1989). *Racial formation in the United States: From the 1960s to the 1990s.* New York: Routledge.

Padilla, F. (1985). *Latino ethnic consciousness.* Notre Dame, IN: University of Notre Dame Press.

Park, R. E. (1914). Racial assimilation in secondary groups. *American Journal of Sociology, 19*, 606–623.

Pedraza, S. (1992). *Ethnic identity: Developing a Hispanic-American identity.* Paper presented at the 5th Congreso Internacional sobre las Culturas Hispanas de los Estados Unidos, Madrid, Spain.

Pew Hispanic Center. (2006). *Pew Hispanic Center tabulations of 2005 American community survey.* Washington, DC: Pew Hispanic Center.

Portes, A. (1996). *The new second generation.* New York: Russell Sage Foundation.

Portes, A., & Bach, R. L. (1985). *Latin journey: Cuban and Mexican immigrants in the United States.* Berkeley: University of California Press.

Portes, A., & MacLeod, D. (1996). What Shall I Call Myself? Hispanic identity formation in the second generation. *Ethnic and Racial Studies, 19*(3), 523–547.

Portes, A., & Wilson, K. L. (1976). Black-white differences in educational attainment. *American Sociological Review, 41*, 414–431.

Rivera, R. (2007). Between blackness and Latinidad in the hip hop zone. In J. Flores & R. Rosaldo (Eds.), *A companion to Latina/o studies* (pp. 351–362). New York: Blackwell.

Rodriguez, C. (1992). Race, culture, and Latino "Otherness" in the 1980 census. *Social Science Quarterly, 73*, 930–937.

Rodriguez, C. (2000). *Changing race: Latinos, the census, and the history of ethnicity in the United States.* New York: New York University Press.

Rodriguez, C., & Cordero-Guzman, H. (1992). Placing race in context. *Ethnic and Racial Studies, 15*, 523–542.

Ruiz, V. (2007). Coloring class: Racial constructions in twentieth-century Chicana/o historiography. In J. Flores & R. Rosaldo (Eds.), *A companion to Latina/o studies* (pp. 169–179). New York: Blackwell.

Rumbaut, R. G. (1994, Winter). The crucible within: Ethnic identity, self-esteem, and segmented assimilation among children of immigrants. *International Migration Review, 28*(4), 748–794.

Saenz, R., & B. Aguirre. (1991). The dynamics of Mexican ethnic identity. *Ethnic Groups, 9*, 17–32.

Song, M. (2004). Who's at the bottom? Examining claims about racial hierarchy. *Ethnic and Racial Studies, 27*, 859–877.

Takaki, R. (1987). *From different shores: Perspectives on race and ethnicity in America.* New York: Oxford University Press.

Waters, M. (1994, Winter). Ethnic and racial identities of second-generation black immigrants in New York City. *International Migration Review, 28*(4), 795–821.

Yancey, W., Erickson, E., & Julian, R. (1976). Emergent ethnicity: A review and reformulation. *American Sociological Review*, 41(3), 391–403.

Yoon, In-Jin. (1997). *On my own*. Chicago: The University of Chicago Press.

Reading 6.1

Define the following concepts/phrases:

Public Law 94-311

black and white binary

race and ethnicity

race as a social construct

Eugenic Education Society

Answer the following:

1. Provide the economic and social statistics for Americans of Spanish origin (Latinos).
2. In what consists the three approaches to analyze race relations in the United States?
3. Write an essay addressing how Latinos challenge the prevailing white-black paradigm of race relations.

■ Reading 6.2

Statement in Support of Black Lives

Mujeres Unidas y Activas

MUJERES UNIDAS IS A GROUP OF Latina immigrant women with the dual mission of personal transformation and building community power. Among our core values are compassion, learning, and solidarity. We call upon those core values to guide us in our work and to drive how we want to be in relationship to other communities seeking justice. We recognize the importance of standing with our Black brothers and sisters in this crucial moment as well as long term in our shared fight for liberation.

As immigrants to this country we understand that our acts solidarity must go beyond simply proclaiming Black Lives Matter. We must take a hard look at ourselves and motivate ourselves to learn about the history of the place we have come to live. We must study and deeply understand not only the history and legacy of racism but also specifically anti-Black racism and the ways in which we as immigrants both benefit from and are harmed by it. We must recognize the ways in which we are impacted by systematic racism as immigrants, but also the ways it uniquely attacks Black people and communities.

Our understanding must also extend back to our home countries—to the history and legacy of slavery and racism there and the ways in which we deny, erase and disparage blackness and our own Black heritage in our families, communities and societies. We must understand how anti-blackness is embedded into our language and our social structures and how detrimental that is to all of us.

It is our responsibility to share what we have learned with our friends and our families, with our children and our neighbors, to have conversations that may be difficult but are necessary if we are truly committed to creating a just world.

With humility and love we recognize that we have a big learning curve as we lift up Black struggle. We understand that our silence is complicit and that complicity is deadly. There is an urgent need for us to join our voice to the millions of other voices screaming for justice. We commit to centering Black Latinx voices, experience, and leadership.

To our Black brothers and sisters, we see you. We love you. Your lives matter.

With love,
Mujeres Unidas Activas

Reading 6.2

Define the following concepts/phrases:

Mujeres Unidas   legacy of racism
Black Lives Matter

Answer the following questions:

1. How has the solidarity of Latinas with Black Lives Matter manifested?
2. What are the core values of the Mujeres Unidas?
3. How can the racialization and systematic discrimination of black Americans become a teaching lesson for Latinas?

Part VII

Culture and Identity in the Latino Community

Historical Perspectives on Latinos and the Latin Music Industry

Deborah Pacini Hernandez

I F LATINOS' RACIAL AND CULTURAL HYBRIDITY has always been problematic within the United States, it has been particularly vexing for music industry personnel seeking the illusory comforts of neat and impermeable marketing categories. In the United States, a domestic "Latin" music industry specializing in Spanish-language music of Latin American origins has always existed alongside (but secondary in influence to) an English-only mainstream popular music industry that has viewed U.S. Latinos and their musics as Latin American (i.e., foreign). Although the commonly used term "Latin music industry" suggests a monolithic entity, this industry has always included multiple layers and players—some with strong connections to Latin America, some without—whose domains of activity have often overlapped and intersected with each other as well as with the mainstream music industry. Moreover, many of the most influential players in the Latin music industry—even in the case of small domestic independent labels—have *not* themselves been Latino. Some of these non-Latinos whose professional lives revolved around Latin/o musics have been personally engaged with Latino communities, although for others, Latin music has simply been another product that could turn a profit if marketed effectively. All Latin music industry personnel, however, regardless of their own ethnic and racial backgrounds, have had to ply their trade within a complicated network of multiple ethnically, racially, and culturally defined communities and markets whose boundaries have always been porous and unstable.

Keith Negus's elegantly simple but profound axiom that "industry produces culture and culture produces industry" is particularly useful for examining how the Latin music industry and its personnel have influenced the development of Latin/o music in the United States. Negus observes that "industry produces culture" (i.e., the music industry is not simply a machine that records and sells products—in this case, sound recordings), but he suggests that the corollary, "culture produces industry," is equally significant because the culturally constructed predispositions and values of the individuals who carry out the work of the music industry strongly influence (in both positive and negative ways) the range of sounds and images emerging from that industry.[2] This is true whether the industry personnel in question are Latino or not: Recording company personnel's cultural biases inevitably affect the structure of the music industry itself. As Negus notes, "Recording companies distribute their staff, artists, genres, and resources into divisions defined according to social-cultural identity labels, such as black music division, Latin division, domestic division, international department. Such practices can be viewed as a direct intervention into and contribution towards the way in which social life is fragmented and through which different cultural experiences are separated and treated unequally."[3] This chapter explores the early, segmented history of the Latin music industry in order to illuminate the shifting relationships between commercial music production and socially constructed notions of ethnicity, race, and nationality; Chapter 7 extends this narrative into the 1980s and beyond, when immigration and globalization further destabilized the relationships between the industry producing Latin music and the identities of the populations presumed to be consuming it.

Marketing Ethnic Sounds: The Early Years

The phonograph was invented toward the end of the nineteenth century, but the technological, economic, and legal structures necessary for the infant recording business to thrive did not coalesce until the first decades of the twentieth. The Columbia and Victor companies, for example, initially held a monopoly on recording thanks to their patents, but subsequent legal challenges and technological changes opened the doors for smaller companies to enter the business of recording and selling music. In the 1920s, over 150 small companies had sprouted up,[4] and record players, originally a novelty unaffordable to most people, had come down drastically in price, by 1927 selling over a million units per year.[5] Developments in radio broadcasting and reception technology similarly made the dissemination of recorded music accessible to people throughout the nation, even those with very limited resources.

Chronologically paralleling these developments in the recording and broadcast industries was a burgeoning population of immigrants who added a profusion of styles and languages into the pool of sounds that could be recorded and sold. Record companies quickly understood the potential value of this particular segment of the market, as the following letter sent by Columbia to its dealers in 1909 indicates: "Remember that in all large cities and in most towns there are sections where people of one nationality or another congregate in 'colonies.' Most of these people keep up the habits and prefer to speak the language of the old country … . To these people records in their own language have an irresistible attraction, and they will buy them readily."[6] Another piece of correspondence from 1914 reveals the industry's understanding of how it could take advantage of the adjustment process immigrants were undergoing:

> With [thousands] of miles between them and the land of their birth, in a country with strange speech and customs, the 35,000,000 foreigners making their home here are keenly on the alert for anything and everything which will keep alive the memories of their fatherland—build them a mental bridge back to their native land. They are literally starving for amusements. With no theatres, except in one or two of the largest cities, few books in their native tongue, it is easy to realize why the talking machine appeals to them so potently, so irresistibly. Their own home music, played or sung by artists whose names are household words in their home-land—these they must have. They are patriotic, these foreigners, and [it is] their own intense desire that their children, brought or born in this *new* country shall share their love of the old.[7]

The first recordings of immigrant musics made in New York were created by Okeh Records, founded by a German immigrant, Otto Heineman, in 1918.[8] An unexpected 1920 hit recording by African American vaudeville singer Mamie Smith proved that black musicians singing black vernacular music would sell well within the black community (and even beyond). Recognizing the economic potential of vernacular music, Okeh sent out roving recording units throughout the United States in search of undiscovered talent under the direction of Ralph Peer. Peer is justifiably famous as a central figure in the development of U.S. popular music, because, as an executive of Okeh and then Victor, he was responsible for the earliest field recordings of the black, ethnic, and regional musics that coalesced into the blues, gospel, jazz, and "country" styles now considered quintessentially "American." In the process of transforming traditional folk music into a commercially viable art form, he also coined the race-based marketing terms "race music" and "hillbilly" music.[9] While the musicians he worked with represent a veritable who's who of early U.S. popular music, it is less well known (or commented upon by U.S. popular music scholars) that his corpus of early American musical recordings also included the first recordings of Mexican-origin music in the United States, among them performances by Mexican-born singer and first Mexican American recording star Lydia Mendoza. These musicians were paid very modest one-time fees, although most struggling musicians, like Mendoza, welcomed the opportunity to record in order to increase their audience base.

From its very beginning, the music business reflected and reified the prevailing bipolar racial imaginaries and hierarchies characteristic of the U.S. social structure. English-speaking artists were classified by race rather than by genre, and the resources devoted to producing and marketing each category varied accordingly: White musicians and styles received far more resources than the "race music" made by blacks. Region and class also played a part in drawing the boundaries of these categories, resulting in the designation "hillbilly" for the musical styles preferred by rural whites, while music by and for the urban middle classes remained unmarked and was simply referred to as "popular." Non-English-language musics, in contrast, were categorized collectively as "ethnic," with subcategories defined by country of origin or language. It is important to note that while the music industry insisted on coding musics according to race, class, and region for marketing purposes, audiences listening to radio and buying records often ignored these divisions and consumed whatever appealed to them. For example, some African American listeners and dancers enjoyed "white" Tin Pan Alley music as well as "Latin-tinged" Tin Pan Alley and film music, and likewise some white listeners ventured beyond the boundaries of Tin Pan Alley. "Ethnic" Latino/a listeners similarly had eclectic tastes in English-language popular musical genres (both those coded black and white)—and [...] the interest of Latino musicians and audiences in "non-Latino" genres has remained constant to this day.

The early years of the twentieth century, when immigration to the United States was reaching record levels, were extraordinarily fertile times for ethnic music. Columbia and Victor actively sought to record music abroad so they could sell it to particular ethnic and national groups in the United States as well as back to the countries of origin. Music company personnel traveling in Latin America in search of musics to record were typically unfamiliar with local customs, so they depended on middle-class businessmen to identify musicians suitable for recording. (These businessmen were often furniture store owners who sold record players, which were then contained in large furniture-like cabinets.) Given the bourgeois backgrounds of such cultural mediators, the musics recommended to visiting talent scouts tended to be those considered "nice" enough to be listened to by the middle- and upper-class families who were purchasing record players, which at the time were relatively expensive. As a result, the first recordings made in Latin America were of musics with prominent European-derived aesthetics, such as the Puerto Rican *danza* or the Colombian *bambuco*; the vernacular musics associated with the more populous but poorer, lower status, and racially subordinated sectors of Latin American society, such as the *bomba* music favored by Afro–Puerto Ricans or Dominican *palo* music, were not considered material appropriate for recording.[10] Later, after realizing the difficulties of recording in Latin America—for example, in the Caribbean, the tropical heat would sometimes melt the acetate masters—record companies concluded that it was more efficient to bring or attract Latin American musicians to their studios in New York to record, transforming that city into a mecca for ambitious and talented musicians from throughout the hemisphere and, subsequently, into a creative crucible for Latin/o American musical developments throughout the twentieth century.[11]

In the early decades of the U.S. recording industry, fledgling record companies were open to experimentation, willing to record and press even small runs of music for limited audiences. They realized, for example, that most immigrants, being of working-class origins, preferred vernacular styles, such as accordion-based musics, to the more "refined" musics being recorded in Latin America for bourgeois audiences. As had happened in Latin America, U.S. record companies seeking local ethnic talent depended on middle-class businessmen (again, often furniture store owners) who could identify the musicians and styles that would appeal to a particular ethnic or national community. While predisposed to recommend "nice" ethnic music, such as the *canciones mejicanas* sung by Lydia Mendoza, these ethnic businessmen were generally more amenable to the idea of recording vernacular music than their Latin American counterparts. Thus, if the first recordings made in Puerto Rico were Eurocentric danzas, in New York they were more likely to be the *jíbaro* music and *plenas* loved by working-class Puerto Rican migrants.[12] In the Southwest, Bluebird (a subsidiary of RCA) and Decca were tapping the market for working class–oriented Mexican music as early as the mid-1930s, recording popular Texas Mexican accordion musicians, such as Narciso Martínez and Santiago Jiménez.[13] By the end of the 1930s, even the poorest migrant worker could hear recordings of vernacular Mexican American music playing on jukeboxes in bars and restaurants located in the *colonias* (ethnic neighborhoods) that had sprung up in and around towns and cities throughout Texas and the Southwest between 1890 and the 1920s.[14] Even during the Depression, the market for vernacular music remained strong, particularly when the price of records dropped by half.

Record companies began recording Mexican American musicians in Los Angeles during these same years and under very similar circumstances. Okeh, Bluebird, Decca, Victor, and Columbia scoured Los Angeles's Mexican barrios (neighborhoods), seeking ethnic talent with the help of Mexican American intermediaries, recording local musicians in makeshift studios (often set up in hotel rooms), and paying the performers a pittance for each recording.[15] Los Angeles's first Mexican recording star was the Mexican-born Pedro J. González, who recorded with his group, Los Madrugadores. Considered to be performers of "high-quality" Mexican music, González and Los Madrugadores benefited from daily exposure on González's pioneering Spanish-language radio program, which was hugely popular among working-class Mexican Angelenos in the 1930s.[16]

Although recording ethnic music was a fairly profitable business in local terms, vernacular music associated with communities considered to be nonwhite did not make it into the U.S. musical mainstream, where the real money was. More cosmopolitan music from urban middle- and upper-class Latin America, in contrast, had a better chance of being accepted by non-Latino audiences and thus was of much greater interest to the major record companies. Owning the publishing rights to Latin American music popular within U.S. Spanish-speaking ethnic communities that could also appeal to mainstream audiences (especially when translated into English by white performers) could be, in fact, quite lucrative; every time a song was performed in the United States, the owner of the rights received a fee, whether it was performed live or on a recording by the original artist or covered by other artists. (Indeed, the voracious appetite for acquiring such rights placed the U.S.-based music industry in the company of businesses such as Standard Oil and United Fruit, who in these same years were similarly scouring Latin America for other resources, such as oil, rubber, and bananas, that could be sold at a premium within the United States.)

One of the most successful U.S. music publishers obtaining rights to Latin American music was E. B. Marks, who developed the industry's largest catalogue of Latin American music, some of which, translated into English and given new arrangements, became mainstream Tin Pan Alley hits.[17] Another successful music publisher who exerted an enormous influence on the circulation of Latin/o American popular music in the United States was Ralph Peer, who, on his first visit to Mexico City in 1928, had an epiphany when he "discovered" Mexican composer Agustín Lara; then, while overnighting in San Antonio on his way back to New York, Peer heard a version of "El Manisero" ("The Peanut Vendor"), a song written by Jewish Cuban composer Moises Simons and sung by Rita Montaner, which had become wildly popular in Havana.[18] Recognizing the potential for Latin America to be "a popular music resource for U.S. listeners,"[19] Peer opened offices in Havana and Mexico City to facilitate the acquisition of his eventually sizable catalogue of Latin American music. In subsequent years, Peer extended his reach throughout Latin America, from Puerto Rico to Argentina, signing major Latin American musicians, such as Lara and Dámaso Pérez Prado. Peer's catalogue of songs eventually contained some of the most well-known Latin American standards, including such chestnuts as "Bésame Mucho," "Granada," and "Perfidia."

Given the profitability of publishing rights, non-Latino music publishers such as Peer and Marks had as many vested interests in widely promoting their musical property as the labels who originally recorded it, and it was in no small part thanks to their efforts that Latin American styles permeated the mainstream popular music landscape in the first half of the twentieth century.[20] When consumed by mainstream audiences in the United States, however, Latin styles were typically performed by musicians who were neither Latin American nor Latino. In the 1910s and 1920s, for example, the Argentine tango was popularized by the theatrical presentations of professional dancers Irene and Vernon Castle, not by local Latino musicians (Argentine or otherwise) residing in New York's thriving Spanish-speaking community.[21] Mexican music was also popular in the mainstream arena in the early decades of the twentieth century, but the music produced by Mexican Americans in the Southwest did not circulate widely beyond the boundaries of these communities. Thus, until the mambo-inspired Latin music boom of the late 1940s and early 1950s, mainstream interest in Latin and Latin-tinged music did not necessarily translate into receptivity to musics performed by U.S. Latinos.

In summary, several characteristics of the Latin/o music industry were established early on. First, if the recording of Spanish-language music initially depended on the recommendations of middle-class ethnic or Latin American nationals who understood local tastes, the mainstream-oriented recording industry that produced, promoted, and profited from them was run primarily by people who were not connected in any organic way to the communities whose musics they were marketing. Second, from the very beginning, the Latin music industry consisted of two "streams" of music that converged in the United States: recordings made in Latin America and "ethnic" recordings made in the United States. Third, music industry personnel have always had to negotiate the sensibilities of separate but overlapping audiences—well-established Latino communities, newer immigrants from Latin America, Latin American nationals, and mainstream English-speaking listeners attracted to exotic ethnic sounds—whose musical practices and preferences, as I discuss below, have been shaped by different imaginaries of race and racial difference.

Latinos Market Themselves: The Latino Music Industry in the Early Years

As the U.S. music industry expanded, U.S. Latinos were not unaware that they, too, could profit by fulfilling the desires of their coethnics for culturally relevant music—and without being distracted, as was often the case with the major record companies, by trying to produce "Latin" music that would be acceptable to nationwide mainstream audiences. The record business, however, was highly dependent on infrastructural support—access to radio airwaves and related necessities, such as adequate performance venues, distribution outlets, press coverage—most of which was owned or controlled by non-Latinos. With few exceptions, then, Latino-owned/Latino-operated recording ventures did not take root and thrive until sufficiently substantial and economically diversified Latino communities emerged with the capacity to support a parallel infrastructure of radio, theaters, newspapers, and record stores catering to Spanish-speaking consumers.

Not surprisingly, the first Latino forays into the commercial music business took place in New York, the capital of the U.S. recording industry as well as the nation's premier immigrant-receiving city. As small businesses in New York's Puerto Rican community proliferated and a middle class emerged in the 1920s, some astute entrepreneurs, realizing they were in a position to take advantage of their community's rich musical scene began investing some of their capital in the music business. For example, Julio Roqué, a successful dentist, established the city's first Spanish-language radio program, *Revista Roqué*, in 1924, which featured a variety of Latin American music, including that of his own orchestra.[22] Another pioneering entrepreneur—even more remarkable because she was a woman—was Victoria Hernández, the sister of prominent Puerto Rican musician and composer Rafael Hernández. Like her brother, Victoria Hernández, who arrived in New York in 1919, was a classically trained musician, although she never developed ambitions for a career in music performance. After saving money from her jobs in a textile factory and giving piano lessons, in 1927 she was able to open up Almacenes Hernández, the first locally owned music store in the Puerto Rican section of Harlem that came to be known as El Barrio.[23] Recognizing music's centrality to the Spanish-speaking community's social and cultural fabric, other ethnic entrepreneurs followed suit: As Virginia Sánchez Korrol has noted, record stores "spread quickly throughout the *colonia hispana* and came to symbolize the Latin settlements as the candy store had characterized other ethnic immigrant neighborhoods. Emanating from these establishments were the rhythms of *el Son, la Guaracha,* Puerto Rican *plenas* and *aguinaldos,* combined with the romantic *boleros* and *danzas.*"[24]

In her groundbreaking study of Puerto Rican musicians in New York, Ruth Glasser observes that in addition to selling records, these record stores served as meeting places for musicians, where they could listen to new releases and receive tips about opportunities for gigs. Moreover, when record companies, such as Victor and Columbia, sought local ethnic talent, record store owners were among their best sources of referrals. Taking advantage of her connections, Victoria Hernández became her brother Rafael's manager, booking dates and negotiating contracts and recording sessions with Victor, not only for Rafael but for other barrio musicians as well. Around the same time, she also established the country's first Latino-owned record label, Hispano, which recorded the local Puerto Rican groups Las Estrellas Boricuas and Los Diablos de la Plena. Victoria's pioneering recording label collapsed after she lost her capital in the 1929 bank crash, but, since ethnic recordings remained profitable throughout the Depression, her record store survived, and she continued to serve as an intermediary between local musicians and the major record companies.[25]

The second Puerto Rican entrepreneur to venture into the ethnic recording business in New York also did so after gaining experience as a record store owner. Gabriel Oller, born in Puerto Rico to an educated family (his father was a teacher), was brought to New York by his parents in 1917. Deciding he wanted a career in the entertainment industry, he earned a degree in electronics before opening up his record store in El Barrio, a respectful distance away from Victoria Hernandez's store. In 1934, he founded the Dynasonic label and began recording local musicians—trios and quartets—playing Puerto Rican styles; he was particularly successful selling traditional *aguinaldos* around Christmas time. Oller's Dynasonic label was small—he never pressed more than two hundred copies of any recording—but, unlike Victoria Hernández's label, it survived the Depression, releasing records by such well-known musicians as Noro Morales as well as local neighborhood trios and quartets. He later established two other record labels, Coda and SMC (Spanish Music Center), that were active in the 1940s and 1950s.[26] Hernandez's Hispano and Oller's Dynasonic labels were both relatively short lived, and neither had much distribution beyond New York, but they are significant because they were the first Latino-owned/Latino-operated record labels in the United States, predating by some years comparable ventures that emerged in Texas and the Southwest in the 1940s.

During World War II, shortages of the shellac used to manufacture records prompted the major record companies to drop or reduce their ethnic and foreign catalogues in favor of their more lucrative mainstream offerings. After the war ended, the majors renewed their interest in musics produced in Mexico and other Latin American countries, but they did not resume the recording of U.S.-based ethnic musics. Mexican American entrepreneurs took advantage of the void left by the departure of the majors and the simultaneously expanding Mexican-origin population in the Southwest. Beginning in the mid-1940s, a slew of Mexican American–owned companies sprang up in Texas, the most important of which were Ideal (1946) and Falcon (1948), but which also included Rio (1948), Corona (1947), and other smaller companies, such as Alamo, Gaviota, and Del Valle. In Los Angeles, ethnically owned companies, such as Azteca, Aguila, Tri-Color, and Taxco, similarly began springing up in the late 1940s to satisfy the demand for locally produced music.[27] Another small Los Angeles-based company specializing in ethnic music that was not Mexican American–owned but that played a significant role in promoting Mexican Angeleno music in the postwar period was Imperial Records, founded by Lew Chudd in the late 1940s. Chudd's Imperial began as a folk music-oriented label with strong interests in Mexican music and later became one of the most important Mexican Angeleno music labels in Los Angeles, recording top local groups such as Los Madrugadores and Lalo Guerrero; Imperial also recorded in Texas.[28]

Non-Latinos in the Postwar Latin Music Industry

In contrast to the Southwest, where the major record companies' interest in vernacular music diminished during the war, New York's more cosmopolitan and lucrative Latin music business not only survived but thrived throughout the 1940s. Latin music's popularity had exploded in the years prior to the outbreak of World War II and was given an additional boost when Hollywood was enlisted by the Franklin Roosevelt administration to combat German influence in Latin America by producing films with friendly images of Latin Americans. Latin American-themed musicals were among Hollywood's most popular products, and they supplied mainstream U.S. audiences with a range of (mostly) Mexican, Cuban, Brazilian, and Argentine styles (and a few stars, such as Carmen Miranda, as well). Latin music was given another boost during the 1941 struggle between the publishing company ASCAP and radio stations regarding broadcast royalties. During the dispute, ASCAP refused to allow radio stations to play any ASCAP-owned music on the air, but the extensive catalogue of Latin American music held by Peer's company, Peer International (associated with ASCAP's rival BMI), helped fill the void, for a short time giving Latin music unprecedented access to the mainstream radio airwaves from coast to coast.[29] Even during the war, when the major recording companies dropped Latin music artists from their rosters, New York's extensive entertainment infrastructure provided alternative venues for live Latin music and dancing.

In the late 1940s and early 1950s, the mambo craze set in motion in Mexico by the Cuban bandleader Dámaso Pérez Prado arrived in New York and spilled beyond the boundaries of New York's primarily Puerto Rican and Cuban Spanish-speaking communities. Bands specializing in mambos and other urban-oriented Spanish Caribbean dance musics began performing in ballrooms throughout the city to enthusiastic audiences of diverse ethnic and racial origins—African

Americans, Italians, Poles, but especially Jews. Indeed, Jewish engagement with mambo was so extensive that Jewish fans known as "mamboniks" became the subject of numerous pop tunes with such names as "It's a Scream How Levine Does the Mambo." In his seminal article on Jewish and Latino cultural and musical interactions in New York, Josh Kun notes that Jews, Cubans, and Puerto Ricans had been interacting since the early twentieth century, when Puerto Ricans and Cubans first began moving into East Harlem (later El Barrio), then predominantly Jewish.[30] As Jews began moving out of El Barrio in the 1930s and 1940s, many of the performance venues originally constructed by and for the Jewish community were "recycled" into venues catering to the surrounding Puerto Rican community (although often the buildings remained in Jewish hands).[31] Throughout the late 1940s and 1950s, Jewish-owned performance venues, from the legendary Palladium Ballroom located in midtown Manhattan to the Jewish resort hotels in the Catskills, provided steady work and crucial spaces for Spanish Caribbean Latinos to develop their music beyond the boundaries of the Spanish Caribbean community itself.[32]

When the major record companies began dropping Latin music artists from their rosters in the 1940s during the war, some Jewish entrepreneurs seized the opportunity to enter the record business. The most active of the Jewish-owned Latin record company owners were Sidney Siegel, who in 1944 founded Seeco (and later its subsidiary, Tropical Records), and George Goldner, who founded the even more influential Tico Records in 1948. Seeco's Siegel was personally familiar with the Puerto Rican community and its musical tastes, since prior to establishing his label he owned a variety store in El Barrio called Casa Siegel, which sold records, among other household products, to his mostly Puerto Rican clients.[33] Seeco specialized in a wide variety of Mexican, Caribbean, and Latin American musicians recorded in their countries of origin—even if it meant that its recordings were not as polished as Tico's, which were recorded in New York. Goldner, whose wife was Puerto Rican, was more directly engaged in New York Latin music, participating actively in Tico's studios and imprinting a particular sound that defined New York Latin dance music. As the pseudonymous author of an online history of Tico Records notes, "His Tico tracks were bold, sassy, and tailored strictly to the tastes of big city consumers. He and Alan Weintraub often bathed them in a rippling echo, making them sound as if they were being placed in a subway station. Tico Records was about fancy, dressed-up Latin dance music, and the keyword was sophistication."[34]

Seeco's roster was more diverse and far-flung than Tico's, including many of Latin America's most important musicians, from Cuba's legendary Trio Matamoros to Mexico's famous Trio Los Panchos.[35] Nonetheless, throughout its approximately two decades of activity, Siegel's Seeco recorded virtually all of New York's top Latin musicians, from Machito (born Francisco Grillo) and Celia Cruz to Arsenio Rodríguez. When major label interest in Latin music rebounded in the 1950s in the wake of the success of mambo and then cha-cha, Seeco was listed by *Variety* as the second most successful label in Latin music after RCA.[36] Goldner's Tico label, however, managed to lure away musicians made famous by Seeco and eventually compiled the most extensive roster of New York's Latin music stars. Together, Tico and Seeco dominated the New York–based Latin music business throughout the 1940s and 1950s. (As they had done in Latin America, the majors signed U.S.-based Latino musicians only after they had proven successful in the Latin music market—for example, RCA signed Tito Puente away from Tico in 1955.)

As independent labels, neither Tico nor Seeco owned their own pressing or distribution companies, but they did have more access than their Latino counterparts to economic and social capital that allowed them to promote their music beyond the confines of New York's Latino community. Crucial to Goldner's success was his access to English-speaking radio audiences via his personal and business relationships with personnel working on English-language radio shows (e.g., disc jockeys Symphony Sid, Art "Pancho" Levy, Bob "Pedro" Harris), encouraging (or paying) them to play the Latin music he was producing. One example of such synergies was a fifteen-minute radio show hosted by disc jockey host Dick "Ricardo" Sugar, who was hired by Goldner to play Tico's recordings (it was legal to do so then); one of Tico's artists, Puerto Rican bandleader Tito Puente, was catapulted into citywide stardom via this practice.[37] These DJs' willingness to play Latin music produced by local Latin/o American musicians on their radio shows (as opposed to the Tin Pan Alley and Hollywood versions of it) also drew non-Latino dancers to the Palladium; Wednesday nights in particular became known for their appeal to the "gringo crowd," which often included celebrities.[38] Goldner also organized and financed a nationwide tour for his musicians, "Mambo USA"—although it turned out to be a financial disaster in provincial cities and regions of the United States, where mambo's popularity did not, as in New York City, serve as a bridge for crossing racial and ethnic boundaries.

Local Latino entrepreneurs found it difficult to compete with the majors and the better-funded and better-connected independent companies, Tico and Seeco. Nevertheless, what they lacked in connections to the non-Latino world was at least partly compensated for by their solid grounding in New York's Puerto Rican/Latino community. One such entrepreneur was Al Santiago, born in New York into a family of musicians and raised surrounded by musicians active in the Latin music scene; indeed, he himself was a musician until he decided he did not have the talent to make a career in performance. In 1955, Santiago opened up Casalegre, a record store, and, thanks to his adept use of local Spanish-language media to advertise his records, he became so successful that he decided to parlay his knowledge of Latin music into a record company. Since he lacked cash, he founded Alegre Records around 1956 with a partner, Ben Perlman, who owned a store next to Casalegre.[39] With most of the major Latin music stars under contract with the far-better-financed Tico or Seeco, Santiago signed young but up-and-coming Latino artists who the more established labels were not interested in. Santiago's willingness to provide recording opportunities to young musicians paid off with Johnny Pacheco, who scored a major hit with his first *pachanga* recording; Santiago is also credited with being the first to sign future salsa stars Eddie Palmieri and Willie Colón. In the early 1960s, Santiago recorded seminal live music jams by the Alegre All-Stars (imitating a similar Cuban All-Stars format that had been organized and recorded by the Panart label in Havana), a model that would later be successfully replicated by the next Latin music industry powerhouse, Fania Records.

Latin music had been a reasonably profitable business during the height of the mambo craze, but sales of a typical record were generally modest, around five thousand units; a big hit might sell one hundred thousand. A hit in the national pop market, in contrast, could sell millions of records.[40] In 1953, as mainstream interest in Latin music began waning as young people of all races and ethnicities turned their attention toward the dynamic new sounds of R & B and rock 'n' roll, Goldner established two new labels, Rama and Gee, in order to promote doo-wop. Goldner scored several major national hits (including the Crows' "Gee"), whose profits dwarfed what he was earning from Latin music, and in 1957, he sold Tico to Morris Levy, the owner of the Birdland nightclub (and a reputed Mob boss). Goldner remained active in Latin music, however, continuing to produce for Tico. In 1965, he founded a new label, Cotique, to capitalize on boogaloo, a hybrid of Spanish Caribbean aesthetics and African American R & B rhythms that at the time looked like it might gain traction on the national stage.[41] By the end of the 1960s, however, the boogaloo had disappeared from view, displaced by the more roots-oriented salsa that resonated better with the spirit of the cultural nationalism and identity politics that would mark the 1970s.

In summary, during the height of the cross-cultural Latin music boom of the 1940s and 1950s, Latino-owned labels, such as Santiago's Alegre and Oller's SMC and Coda, played important historical and cultural roles in New York's Latin music industry, but economically they remained minor players. Santiago sold his label to Morris Levy in the early 1960s, but, with the further decline of interest in Latin music on the national stage during that decade [...], even Tico and Seeco foundered as the Spanish Caribbean Latin music upon which these labels had thrived disappeared from the national stage.

Moving in and Branching Out: Latinos in the Latin Music Business in the Rock 'n' Roll Era

On the West Coast, the lure of rock 'n' roll had a similar effect on non-Latino entrepreneurs. Chudd's Imperial Records, which had been one of the most active and successful labels producing Mexican American artists, abandoned them in the 1950s in order to pursue work with more lucrative rhythm and blues and pop artists (e.g., Fats Domino and Ricky Nelson).[42] With the majors and then Imperial out of the picture, Mexican American labels specializing in music performed by Mexican Americans, whether in California, Texas, or other parts of the Southwest, largely had the domestic field to themselves. They did, however, have to compete with an extraordinarily robust—and geographically proximate—Mexican music industry. To a degree not matched in the domain of Spanish Caribbean music, Mexican music produced in Mexico was actively and effectively supported by Mexico's film industry, which released a steady stream of musicals featuring Mexican music's biggest recording stars (and turned lesser-known musicians into stars). Indeed, Mexico provided most of the Spanish-language films viewed by Spanish-speaking moviegoers throughout the United States, providing invaluable visibility to Mexican styles and stars. In New York, Spanish-speaking Latinos enjoyed the Mexican music promoted in such films as well as touring Mexican artists for whom New York was an indispensable stop, but Mexican music did not seriously compete with the dynamic Spanish Caribbean dance music being performed and recorded locally. In Los Angeles, in contrast, where Hollywood's film and music industries were closely connected to their counterparts in Mexico City, local Mexican American musicians had to compete directly with Mexican musicians. This is not to suggest that interest in local Mexican Angeleno musicians did not exist; Billy Cardenas, for example, who became the most influential producer of Los Angeles Chicano rock in the 1970s, got his start scouting out local mariachi bands to record for Bill Lazarus's Crown Studios.[43] But in a city where top Mexican acts toured regularly and had records produced and distributed by such major record companies as RCA, Mexican American musicians performing Mexican music were at a clear disadvantage.[44] ([...] this structurally unequal relationship between Mexican and Mexican American record producers remains in place to this day.)

Mexican Angeleno musicians with interests in rock 'n' roll, on the other hand, benefited from Los Angeles's centrality to mainstream U.S. popular music production in the 1950s (and beyond). Most rock 'n' roll-oriented record companies, however, were owned by non-Mexicans. The Del-Fi label that Ritchie Valens helped put on the map, for example, was owned by Bob Keane. Interestingly, Keane had spent part of his childhood in Mexico, where his father worked as a contractor, so he was receptive to Mexican Americans and their Mexican-tinged rock 'n' roll. Known for its successful doo-wop groups, Del-Fi was one of the labels sought by Mexican American rock 'n' roll and R & B artists, such as Chan Romero and the Carlos Brothers.[45] One notable and major exception to the dominance of non-Mexican rock 'n' roll producers was the partnership between Eddie Davis and the Mexican American Billy Cardenas, who in the 1960s and 1970s managed and produced for various record labels virtually every major Chicano rock artist (e.g., Cannibal and the Headhunters, Thee Midniters, the Premiers, the Blendells [...]). As David Reyes and Tom Waldman point out, the complementary interests and cultural resources of each partner worked to their advantage: Cardenas, who was responsible for scouting new talent, grew up in the Mexican American community but loved rock 'n' roll; Davis, in contrast, a former altar boy who had grown up fascinated with Mexican music, "used his record company connections to procure studio time and distribution deals."[46]

Texas and other more provincial parts of the Southwest, in contrast, had no equivalent to either Los Angeles's powerful film and music industries, to New York's international Latin music industry, or to both cities' ethnically diverse demographics, which had advantages as well as disadvantages for Mexican American entrepreneurs and musicians. As Manuel Peña has argued, Mexican American–owned companies may have been small and undercapitalized, but their grounding in the local community, and their consistent and unwavering support for regional musics such as conjunto, allowed them to thrive without the interference of larger companies.[47] In New York, in contrast, the hegemony of the commercially profitable big-band style of Latin music actually limited industry access to smaller ensembles specializing in more folk-oriented vernacular musics.

On the other hand, young Texas Mexicans in the 1960s, such as Sunny Ozuna and Little Joe Hernandez, who were seeking careers in rock 'n' roll rather than with vernacular styles, encountered more difficulty finding recording opportunities than their counterparts in Los Angeles, where Mexican American rock 'n' roll was more central to the local musical scene. Most Texas Mexican–owned music labels were not interested in English-language pop music, and, conversely, non–Mexican American labels were not interested in Mexican American acts.[48] One notable but fleeting exception was the independent Louisiana-born Cajun record producer Huey Meaux, who in the early 1960s signed Sunny Ozuna and his group the Sunglows and was able to move their song "Talk to Me" into the mainstream national arena, including a performance on *American Bandstand*. When the group failed to produce another hit song, however, Meaux convinced Ozuna to turn to the Mexican ethnic market instead, despite the fact that Ozuna "hate[d] Spanish music."[49] [...] Ozuna and others like him resisted being confined to the Mexican American market until the Chicano movement of the late 1960s, when Mexican-origin music was validated as an expression of ethnic pride and self-determination, even among assimilated youths.

In 1967, the small Dallas-based Zarape Records coined the term "*Onda Chicana*" to link Little Joe and the Latinnaires' rock 'n' roll–inflected music to the Chicano movement, providing their hybrid musical style with a symbolically appealing moniker.[50] Ambivalence toward Mexican American rock 'n' roll remained, however, and Mexican American producers came to the conclusion that they would do better commercially with music more strongly grounded in long-popular local styles, such as polka-ranchera. Even Sunny Ozuna and Little Joe eventually embraced performance styles foregrounding more audibly Mexican aesthetics, and they established their own labels, Buena Suerte and Key-Loc, respectively, to produce it.[51] Performers of vernacular Mexican American music, whose music did not threaten to disrupt perceived ethnic boundaries, benefited from the continuing vitality of pioneering Texas-based labels such as Ideal and Falcon that had been established in the 1940s, as well as dozens of newer ones that sprouted up in the 1960s and 1970s. Some of these labels were started by musicians who could not get a record deal with an established label; Freddie Martinez, for example, founded the later hugely successful Discos Freddie in 1969 for just this reason.[52]

As for the East Coast music industry in the 1960s and beyond, if rock 'n' roll displaced New York Latin music as the dance music of choice for trend-conscious urban cosmopolitans—and disrupted the Latin music industry that had once catered to them—Spanish Caribbean music remained vital within New York's Puerto Rican community. The music did, however, move toward a more explicitly roots-oriented style that came to be known as salsa. [...] [S]alsa was a grassroots phenomenon arising out of the urban decay and official neglect experienced by Latino New Yorkers in the 1970s, and it was nourished by the ideology of self-determination promoted by the Puerto Rican civil rights movement. Yet if salsa itself was a spontaneous grassroots musical phenomenon, its hegemonic image as the quintessential sound of Latin music (and *latinidad* itself) acquired in the 1970s was the product of the savvy business practices of salsa's premier record label, Fania.

Founded in 1964 by the Dominican-born Johnny Pacheco and Jerry Masucci, Fania was originally intended to replicate Alegre Records' earlier success in promoting Pacheco's pachangas.[53] Pacheco's first recordings with the fledgling Fania label were literally peddled out of the trunk of a car, but, given Pacheco's name recognition in Latino New York, the releases did reasonably well based on word of mouth. What really stimulated Fania's success, however, was the confluence of several unfolding developments: the marginalization of music from Cuba as a result of the postrevolutionary U.S. embargo of Cuba; the desires of New York's most well-known Latin musicians to leave the ailing Tico, Alegre, and Seeco labels; and the dramatic expansion of the Puerto Rican community in New York in the wake of labor surpluses created on the island by the industrialization programs collectively referred to as Operation Bootstrap.[54] New York Puerto Rican and Cuban musicians calculated that a new label co-owned by Pacheco promised a better future, especially in the context of the city's rapidly growing Puerto Rican community; within a few years, Fania had signed virtually every significant Latin musician in New York, from such well-established artists as Celia Cruz and Ray Barretto to newer up-and-coming artists such as Ruben Blades and Willie Colón. Even Tito Puente, discouraged from a disappointing experience with RCA, signed on with Fania. Indeed, Fania's roster of Latin music stars was so extensive, and it produced so many hit salsa records, it has been called "the Latin Motown."

Unlike Tico and Seeco, Fania did not (initially) attempt to appeal to non-Latino mainstream audiences; nor, like Seeco, did Fania sign talent from Mexico or other Latin American countries whose musics had long enjoyed small but consistent audiences in the United States. Instead, to use a contemporary political term, it sought to appeal to its musicians' base, New York's Puerto Rican and other Latino communities. By the early 1970s, having transformed salsa into the quintessential sound of Latin music in New York, Fania began making skillful use of Spanish-language media to market the Fania "brand" of New York–based Afro-Cuban and Puerto Rican dance music to Latinos and Latin Americans beyond New York. Fania's 1972 film *Our Latin Thing*, documenting a seminal collective performance by its biggest stars at the Cheetah nightclub, proved to be extraordinarily effective in spreading dynamic images of Fania's Latino musicians of diverse national backgrounds (and their enthusiastically dancing fans) to urban Latinos/as in other parts of the United States as well as throughout Latin America, bolstering salsa's image as a counterweight to the power of U.S. rock. Throughout the 1970s, Fania was the undisputed powerhouse producer of hip, sophisticated Spanish Caribbean Latin dance music that was virtually synonymous with the concept of Latin music itself. In 1975, Fania extended its dominance of New York Latin music even further by purchasing Tico and Alegre from Levy as well as Goldner's Cotique label, giving Fania access to the rich back catalogue of music produced by the stars it had under contract. It has been said that Fania deliberately "scuttled the label [Tico] to eliminate competition with … Fania";[55] whether or not this is true, the significant fact is that Fania faced little competition from either Latino-owned or non-Latin labels during its formative decades.

By the end of the 1970s, Fania was becoming a victim of its own successes among urban U.S. Latinos and Latin Americans. As salsa became more profitable, Fania's stars were lured away by contracts with major record companies such as Elektra, A&M, and Columbia. Others left for smaller labels, because they believed they were not receiving royalty payments commensurate with Fania's international sales. In 1979, Fania ceased producing records, although it continued to release music from its back catalogue.[56] Contributing to Fania's decline, the hegemony of salsa itself as the quintessential Latin dance music came under challenge in the 1980s with the rise in popularity of Dominican merengue—even among salsa's core Puerto Rican constituency […]. By the early 1990s, Latino-owned record companies were sprouting up in New York to market Spanish Caribbean musics other than salsa, such as the Dominican-owned J&N, which specialized in merengue and bachata.[57]

Fania's centrality to New York's Latin music industry was further sidelined by the rise of Ralph Mercado, a concert promoter and artists' manager whose Latin music empire would dwarf Fania within a decade. Mercado, born of Dominican and Puerto Rican parents, began his career in the 1960s as a concert promoter, organizing dances in New York's Puerto Rican community. (He also promoted non-Latino artists, including James Brown.) In 1972, he established the RMM Management Company and began signing local artists, mostly salsa musicians, some of whom, such as Tito Puente, were Fania's top stars. As Puente noted, "Everyone took advantage of Latin musicians back then … . As a promoter Raffi [Mercado] was different. He respected us … and he's a man with ethics. Everyone who was anybody went with Raffi."[58] Since he was not directly competing with Fania in record production and distribution at the time, Mercado and Masucci collaborated frequently and effectively in promoting the New York salsa sound to their mutual benefit. Mercado, for example, was responsible for booking the Fania All-Stars into the Cheetah nightclub in 1971 and arranging for the filming of what became *Our Latin Thing*. Mercado also promoted major salsa concerts in New York, including the annual Madison Square Garden concert featuring the artists who recorded with Fania. Mercado's role in promoting Latin music in the post-Fania period is discussed in Chapter 7; for now, it is important to credit his groundbreaking work in promoting Fania's musicians in the early days of salsa, when New York's Latin music business, after years of dominance by non-Latinos, was reverting into Latino hands.

The mainstream music industry's disinterest in the vibrant sounds of cultural empowerment and resistance produced by New York Latino musicians in the 1960s and 1970s may have provided opportunities for Latino entrepreneurs, but their location within (primarily) New York Spanish Caribbean communities also prevented these musicians and styles from achieving the place they deserve in the history of U.S. popular music, despite their profound influence on a generation of U.S. Latinos and Latin Americans. As a *New York Times* columnist observed in 2006, when Emusica, the company that purchased Fania's catalogue in 2005, began reissuing high-quality recordings, "Today Motown looms gigantic in American cultural memory, a cornerstone of the 60's nostalgia industry, the subject of innumerable books and documentaries, its hits still ubiquitous on the airwaves decades after they made the charts. Fania, on the other hand, is recalled mostly by collectors and Latinos of a certain age. And where Motown's records have been endlessly reissued and anthologized, Fania's catalog languished for years, its master tapes moldering in a warehouse in Hudson, N.Y."[59]

In subsequent decades, the segmented, layered nature of the Latin music business would once again change shape in the wake of major waves of immigrants from all over Latin America, who began transforming the cultural demographics of the major U.S. Latino record-producing centers—New York, Los Angeles, and Texas—and contributing to the emergence of a new center: Miami. The mainstream music industry, which had largely ignored the musics being produced within U.S. Latino communities since the 1950s, reconsidered their position in the late 1980s when the economic potential of so many Spanish-speaking newcomers became impossible to ignore. As the majors reentered the Latin music business, smaller independent, Latino-owned labels that once had the field to themselves found themselves competing with the powerful, deep-pocketed majors—although this time, music industry personnel, even in the majors, were far more likely to include Latinos than in the past. The growing U.S. Spanish-speaking, Latin American–oriented market segment, however, created new dilemmas for a music industry gearing up to market ethnically marked "Latin" music across ethnic and geographic lines, within the United States as well as to Latin America. While growing numbers of foreign-born Latinos reinforced the Latin American image of Latin music, most Latinos continued to be U.S.-born, bicultural, bilingual, and culturally distinct from the newcomers.[60] [...].

Endnotes

1. "Mainstream" is an imprecise but often-used shorthand term for those musics receiving more financial resources, media exposure, and critical attention than those "marginal" musics located along the periphery of the nation's popular music landscape. Although to many people the term "mainstream" might invoke cultural expressions associated

with the Eurocentric "core culture" of the United States, since the emergence of rock 'n' roll in the 1950s, African American musicians and styles have figured prominently in the U.S. musical mainstream, complicating clear-cut associations of "mainstream" with the musical practices of Euro-descendants. Latin American and Latino musics have also influenced various mainstream styles, although they have not received recognition commensurate with their contributions. Nevertheless, while mainstream popular music may be quite diverse in terms of origins, content, and styles, its language has always been English-only: Other than a few novelty songs that have occasionally appeared on hit-parade lists, music in any language other than English has yet to achieve sustained visibility in the mainstream arena.

2. Keith Negus, *Music Genres and Corporate Cultures* (London: Routledge, 1999), 14–30.

3. Keith Negus, "La cultura, la industria y la matriz de la salsa: El negocio de la música en los Estados Unidos y la producción de la música Latina" [Culture, Industry and the Salsa Matrix: The Music Business in the United States and the Production of Latin Music], *Revista de Ciencias Sociales* 4 (1998): 27–52.

4. Pekka Gronow, "Ethnic Recordings: An Introduction," in *Ethnic Recordings in America: A Neglected Heritage* (Washington, DC: American Folklife Center, 1982), 6.

5. Ibid., 3.

6. Ibid.

7. Richard K. Spottswood, "Commercial Ethnic Recordings in the United States," in *Ethnic Recordings in America: A Neglected Heritage* (Washington, DC: American Folklife Center, 1982), 55.

8. Alan Sutton, "The Origins of Okeh," available at http://www.mainspringpress.com/okeh.html (accessed November 17, 2007).

9. Ibid.

10. Chris Strachwitz and Cristóbal Díaz Ayala, liner notes to *Lamento Borincano: Early Puerto Rican Music: 1916–1939* (Arhoolie 7037–38). See also Ruth Glasser, *My Music Is My Flag: Puerto Rican Musicians and Their New York Communities, 1917–1940* (Berkeley: University of California Press, 1995), 133–135.

11. Within a few decades, most Latin American nations established their own domestic music industries, which allowed Latin American musicians to develop their careers without traveling abroad, at which point U.S.-based companies simply bought the rights to proven hits or signed successful musicians.

12. Strachwitz and Díaz Ayala, liner notes to *Lamento Borincano*, 7.

13. Manuel Peña, "The Emergence of Conjunto Music, 1935–1955," in *Puro Con-junto: An Album in Words and Pictures,* ed. Juan Tejeda and Avelardo Valdez (Austin: Center for Mexican American Studies and Guadalupe Cultural Arts Center, 2001), 16–17.

14. Jukeboxes played an important role in disseminating music to poor and working-class listeners unable to purchase record players in Latin America as well; I document the role of jukeboxes in the Dominican Republic in *Bachata: A Social History of a Dominican Popular Music* (Philadelphia: Temple University Press, 1995), 54–55.

15. See George Sánchez, *Becoming Mexican American: Ethnicity, Culture and Identity in Chicano Los Angeles, 1900–1945* (New York: Oxford University Press, 1993), 182–183. One indication of the freewheeling nature of the ethnic music business at this early stage was that one of the earliest recordings made in Los Angeles, the song "El Lavaplatos," was recorded in 1930 by no fewer than three groups on three different labels. The song was recorded by its composer Jesús Osorio and Manuel Camacho for Victor, by Los Hermanos Bañuelos for Brunswick/Vocalion, and by Chávez y Lugo for Columbia; see Steven Loza, *Barrio Rhythms: Mexican American Music in Los Angeles* (Urbana: University of Illinois Press, 1993), 22.

16. For more on Pedro González and Los Madrugadores, see Loza, *Barrio Rhythms*, 33–34; and Chris Strachwitz and Zac Salem, "Pedro J. González y los Madrugadores," liner notes to *Pedro J. González y los Madrugadores, 1931–1937* (Arhoolie Folklyric CD 7035, 2000). See also *Break of Dawn*, Isaac Artenstein's fine 1988 biopic based on González's musical career and political activism in Los Angeles, and Paul Espinosa's 1983 documentary, *Ballad of an Unsung Hero*.

17. Steve Traiman, "What a Difference a Song Makes (100th Anniversary Edward B. Marks Music Company)," *Billboard* 106, no. 41 (October 8, 1994): 8.

18. In 1925, Peer left Okeh and signed on to work with the Victor Recording Company, which later agreed to allow his publishing company, Southern Music, which he founded in 1928, to retain the publishing rights to the music recorded by the musicians he had signed to Victor. Peer, it should be noted, did not own the rights to "El Manisero," which became the first authentically Latin music song to become a top hit nationally after it was recorded in New York in 1931 by Cuban bandleader Don Azpiazú's orchestra with singer Antonio Machín. The rights to "El Manisero" had been acquired by the other major non-Latino holder of publishing rights to Latin American music, E. B. Marks, who released a version of the song, with English lyrics written by Louis Rittenberg, as "The Peanut Vendor." The song received additional mainstream exposure when it was included in the 1931 Hollywood musical *Cuban Love Song*, sung by Lawrence Tibbet. See Ned Sublette, *Cuba and Its Music: From the First Drums to the Mambo* (Chicago: Chicago Review Press, 2004), 399. Another English-language version was written by Azpiazú's sister-in-law, Marion Sunshine, and Wolfe Gilbert; see Gustavo Pérez Firmat, "Latunes: An Introduction," *Latin American Research Review* 43, no. 2 (2008): 185.

19. Richard M. Sudhalter, "Ralph S. Peer: A Life of Infinite Variety and Many Achievements," available at http://www.peermusic.com/aboutus/rsp01.cfm (accessed July 2007).

20. For an extensive discussion of how Latin American music influenced the U.S. mainstream popular music landscape in the 1930s, 1940s, and 1950s, see Pérez Firmat, "Latunes," 180–203.

21. John Storm Roberts, *The Latin Tinge: The Impact of Latin American Music on the United States* (1979; repr. New York: Oxford University Press, 1999), 45.

22. Glasser, *My Music Is My Flag*, 111.

23. Christopher Washburne, *Sounding Salsa: Performing Latin Music in New York City* (Philadelphia: Temple University Press, 2008), 12. See also Glasser, *My Music Is My Flag*, 107–109.

24. Virginia E. Sánchez Korrol, *From Colonia to Community: The History of Puerto Ricans in New York City* (1983; repr. Berkeley: University of California Press, 1994), 80–81.

25. Glasser, *My Music Is My Flag*, 107–109, 143–144.

26. Max Salazar, interview with Gabriel Oller, in *Mambo Kingdom: Latin Music in New York* (New York: Schirmer Trade Books, 2002), 19–23.

27. Chris Strachwitz with James Nicolopulos, *Lydia Mendoza: A Family Autobiography* (Houston: Arte Público Press, 1993), 356–358; Loza, *Barrio Rhythms*, 78.

28. Strachwitz with Nicolopulos, *Lydia Mendoza*, 357. Another Los Angeles–based company specializing in Mexican music that also recorded in Texas was Globe Records, but Strachwitz reports that otherwise little is known about it, including the ethnicity of its original owners.

29. In spite of the linguistic similarities between their names, there appears to be no relationship between Ralph Peer's Peer Music and the Mexican company Peerless, one of the most important Mexican-based music labels. The likeliest explanation for the similarity is that the owners of the Mexican company were trying to replicate the branding success of the well-known U.S.-based company. Peer Music, it should be noted, has continued to be a powerhouse in Latin music publishing, holding the rights to hit songs by such major Latin/o artists as Mark Anthony, Julio Iglesias, Paulina Rubio, and Thalia (not to mention hits by English-language superstars, such as Frank Sinatra, Johnny Cash, and the Beatles). See "Company History," available at http://www.peermusic.com/aboutus/companyhistory.cfm (accessed July 2007).

30. Josh Kun, "Bagels, Bongos, and Yiddishe Mambos, or the Other History of Jews in America," *Shofar* 23, no. 4 (Summer 2005), 50–68. See also "The Mamboniks," a Web site archiving information on the history of Jews in the Latin music businesses, available at http://mamboniks.blogspot.com (accessed January 2009).

31. See Roberta L. Singer and Elena Martínez, "A South Bronx Music Tale," *Centro Journal* 16, no. 1 (Spring 2004): 177–201.

32. For more on Jewish interest in Latin music, see Ralph J. Rivera's fine documentary, *Through the Eyes of Larry Harlow: El Judío Maravilloso* (Tropical Visions Entertainment Group, 1998).

33. Kun, "Bagels, Bongos."

34. Stuffed Animal (pseudonym), "Mambo USA, Morris Levy and Rhythm 'n' Blues," 4 (pt. 2 of "Mambo Gee Gee: The Story of George Goldner and Tico Records"), available at http://www.spectropop.com/tico/index.htm (accessed February 2009).

35. See Don Charles, "The Seeco Records Story," in "Seeco Album Discography," by Don Charles, David Edwards, and Mike Callahan, available at http://www.bsnpubs.com/latin/seeco.html (accessed February 2009).

36. "Sidney Siegel and Seeco Records," posted by The Snob, January 11, 2007, available at http://mamboniks.blogspot.com/2007/11/sidney-siegel-and-seeco-records.html (accessed February 2009).

37. Steven Loza, *Tito Puente and the Making of Latin Music* (Urbana: University of Illinois Press, 1999), 9.

38. Vernon Boggs, *Salsiology: Afro-Cuban Music and the Evolution of Salsa in New York City* (New York: Excelsior Music Publishing, 1992), 214. See also Washburne, *Sounding Salsa*, 41.

39. Ibid., 203–227; see also John Child, "Profile: Al Santiago," February 23, 1999, available at http://www.descarga.com/cgi-bin/db/archives/Profile36 (accessed January 5, 2009).

40. Boggs, *Salsiology*, 212.

41. Stuffed Animal, "Mambo Gee Gee." For more on boogaloo, see Juan Flores, "'Cha Cha with a Backbeat': Songs and Stories of Latin Boogaloo," in *From Bomba to Hip-Hop: Puerto Rican Culture and Latino Identity* (New York: Columbia University Press, 2000), 79–112.

42. In an interview with Steven Loza, former Imperial artist Lalo Guerrero expressed resentment at Chudd for this change in direction: "They cancelled all of us Chicanos out. They threw the Chicanos out because they were making too much money off the blacks." Loza, *Barrio Rhythms*, 77.

43. David Reyes and Tom Waldman, *Land of a Thousand Dances: Chicano Rock 'n' Roll from Southern California* (Albuquerque: University of New Mexico Press, 1998), 58.

44. There were some exceptions, however, such as the Texas-born Chelo Silva, who, in the 1940s, recorded with the powerful Mexican company Peerless (no relationship to Ralph Peer) and later with Columbia. Manuel Peña, *Música Tejana: The Cultural Economy of Artistic Transformation* (College Station: Texas A&M University Press, 1999), 65.

45. Reyes and Waldman, *Land of a Thousand Dances*, 37–38.

46. Ibid., 56. See also Mark Guerrero, "Billy Cardenas: East L.A. Manager and Record Producer of the 60s," available at http://markguerrero.net/misc_48.php (accessed February 2009).

47. Peña, *Música Tejana*, 97.

48. A poignant scene in the film *Selena* dramatizes the dilemma for aspiring Texas Mexican rock 'n' rollers. As a youth, Selena's father, who played in a rock 'n' roll band, was hired to play in a club, but when the owners saw that the band members were Mexican, they canceled the contract. When they attempted to play rock 'n' roll in a Mexican venue, the patrons booed and threw bottles at them.

49. In 1965, Meaux scored another hit with a Texas Mexican group, but not until he had hidden its identity with a faux-British name: the Sir Douglas Quintet. See Joe Nick Patosky, "Huey P. Meaux: The Crazy Cajun" (excerpt from "Sex, Drugs, and Rock and Roll," *Texas Monthly* 24, no. 5 [May 1996]: 116), available at http://www.laventure. net/tourist/sdq_meaux.htm (accessed February 2009).

50. Peña, *Música Tejana*, 162.

51. Ibid., 163–175.

52. Jennifer LeClaire, "Latin Music Mecca Freddie's Stars Continue to Shine a Spotlight on Tejano Music," available at http://www.hispaniconline.com/trends/2004/sep/briefcase/trendsetters.html (accessed November 21, 2007).

53. The Italian American Masucci, a lawyer and personal friend of Pacheco's, had no prior interest in or knowledge of Latin music, but he agreed to handle the business end of the company. Izzy Sanabria, "The World's Greatest Force in Latin Music," liner notes to *Fania: 1964–1994* (Musicrama/Koch B000008UGE, 1994).

54. For a full description and analysis of Fania's emergence, see Washburne, *Sounding Salsa*, 15–23. For more on Operation Bootstrap, see, for example, Edna Acosta-Belén and Carlos E. Santiago, *Puerto Ricans in the United States: A Contemporary Portrait* (Boulder, CO: Lynne Reiner Publishers, 2006); and César J. Ayala and Rafael Bernabé, *Puerto Rico in the American Century: A History since 1898* (Chapel Hill: University of North Carolina Press, 2007).

55. Stuffed Animal, "The Last Gasp, Fania, and the Death of George Goldner," 5 (pt. 5 of Stuffed Animal, "Mambo Gee Gee"), available at http://www.spectropop.com/tico/TICOpart5. htm (accessed April 28, 2009).

56. John Lannert, "Salsa Pioneer Jerry Masucci, 63, Dies, Fania Records Co-Founder Made Latin Style a Hit," *Billboard*, January 10, 1998.

57. J&N Records, for example, was established in New York and later expanded, with offices in the Dominican Republic; Karen Records, in contrast, originally established in the Dominican Republic, later opened up offices in Miami.

58. Quoted in Alisa Valdes, "The Berry Gordy of Tropical Latin Music," *Boston Globe*, June 21, 1998.

59. Judy Rosen, "The Return of Fania, the Record Company That Made Salsa Hot," *New York Times*, June 4, 2006.

60. See Robert Suro and Jeffrey Passel, "The Rise of the Second Generation: Changing Patterns in Hispanic Population Growth," a study published by the Pew His-panic Center, October 14, 2004, available at http://pewhispanic.org/files/reports/22.pdf (accessed August 12, 2007).

■ Reading 7.1

Define the following concepts/phrases:

musical hybridity

transnationalism

globalization

cultural citizenship

race music

miscegenation

Latin American hybridity

Latin music boom 1940–1950

Answer the following questions:

1. What are the main characteristics of the Latino Music Industry at the beginning of the twentieth century?
2. Describe the Mexican American pioneers in the Southwest music industry.
3. Why was salsa Music a success in the New York Latino market?
4. Explain the Fania success in the East Coast music industry?
5. Analyze the author's phrase … "salsa as the quintessential sound of Latino Music and Latinidad."
6. How did Latinos in the two major metropolises, New York and Los Angeles, respond to rock 'n' roll during the '60s and '70s?
7. Discuss the linkages between the Mexican music industry and the Chicano movement.
8. How did Miami become an essential center of the Latino music industry during the 1980s?

I Am Joaquín

An Epic Poem

Rodolfo "Corky" González

I am Joaquín
Lost in a world of confusion,
Caught up in a whirl of a
    gringo society,
Confused by the rules,
Scorned by attitudes,
Suppressed by manipulations,
And destroyed by modern society.
My fathers
  have lost the economic battle
and won
  the struggle of cultural survival.
And now!
  I must choose
Between the paradox of Victory of the spirit, despite physical hunger
     Or
  to exist in the grasp
of American social neurosis,
sterilization of the soul
  and a full stomach.
Yes,
I have come a long way to nowhere,

Rodolfo Gonzales, "I Am Joaquin," *Message to Aztlan: Selected Writings of Rodolfo "Corky" Gonzales*, pp. 16-29. Copyright © 2001 by Arte Público Press. Reprinted with permission.

Unwillingly dragged by that
  monstrous, technical
  industrial giant called
          Progress
and Anglo success ...
  I look at myself.
    I watch my brothers.
      I shed tears of sorrow.
        I sow seeds of hate.
  I withdraw to the safety within the
circle of life ...
          MY OWN PEOPLE
I am Cuauhtémoc,
Proud and Noble
    Leader of men,
King of an empire,
civilized beyond the dreams
of the Gachupín Cortez.
Who is also the blood,
  the image of myself.
I am the Maya Prince.
I am Nezahualcóyotl,
Great leader of the Chichimecas.
I am the sword and flame of Cortez
                    the despot.
                And
I am the Eagle and Serpent of
            the Aztec civilization.
I owned the land as far as the eye
could see under the crown of Spain,
and I toiled on my earth
and gave my Indian sweat and blood
    for the Spanish master,
Who ruled with tyranny over man and
beast and all that he could trample
                  But...
    THE GROUND WAS MINE ...

I was both tyrant and slave.
As Christian church took its place
in God's good name,
to take and use my Virgin Strength and
                              Trusting faith,
The priests
    both good and bad
                    took
But
  gave a lasting truth that
      Spaniard,
          Indio,
            Mestizo
Were all God's children
And
  from these words grew men
      who prayed and fought
                        for
their own worth as human beings,
      for
        that
          GOLDEN MOMENT
            of
          FREEDOM.
I was part in blood and spirit
  of that
      courageous village priest
                          Hidalgo
in the year eighteen hundred and ten
who rang the bell of independence
and gave out that lasting cry:
  "El Grito de Dolores, Que mueran
  los Guachupines y que viva
  la Virgen de Guadalupe..."
I sentenced him
        who was me.
I excommunicated him my blood.

I drove him from the pulpit to lead
  a bloody revolution for him and me...
    I killed him.
His head,
  which is mine and all of those
  who have come this way,
I placed on that fortress wall
  to wait for independence.
Morelos!
    Matamoros!
        Guerrero!
All Compañeros in the act,
STOOD AGAINST THAT WALL OF
                INFAMY
  to feel the hot gouge of lead
    which my hand made.
I died with them ...
  I lived with them
    I lived to see our country free.
Free
  from Spanish rule in
  eighteen-hundred-twenty-one.
    Mexico was free ? ?
The crown was gone
      but
all his parasites remained
        and ruled
        and taught
  with gun and flame and mystic power.
I worked,
I sweated,
I bled,
I prayed
  and
waited silently for life to again
                    commence.
  I fought and died

for
  Don Benito Juárez
Guardian of the Constitution.
I was him
    on dusty roads
        on barren land
as he protected his archives
    as Moses did his sacraments.
He held his Mexico
        in his hand
            on
        the most desolate
        and remote ground
        which was his country,
And this Giant
        Little Zapotec
gave
    not one palm's breath
of his country to
    Kings or Monarchs or Presidents
of foreign powers.
I am Joaquín.
I rode with Pancho Villa,
    crude and warm.
A tornado at full strength,
nourished and inspired
    by the passion and the fire
    of all his earthy people.
I am Emiliano Zapata.
    "This Land
        This Earth
            is
            OURS"
The Villages
    The Mountains
        The Streams
            belong to the Zapatistas.

Our Life
Or yours
is the only trade for soft brown earth and maize.
All of which is our reward,
  A creed that formed a constitution
    for all who dare live free!
"this land is ours ...
      Father, I give it back to you.
          Mexico must be free ..."
I ride with Revolutionists
              against myself.
I am Rural
    Coarse and brutal,
I am the mountain Indian,
      superior over all.
The thundering hoofbeats are my horses.
The chattering of machine guns
is death to all of me:
  Yaqui
    Tarahumara
      Chamula
        Zapotec
          Mestizo
            Español
I have been the Bloody Revolution,
The Victor,
The Vanquished,
I have killed
  and been killed.
      I am despots Díaz
      and Huerta
and the apostle of democracy
      Francisco Madero
I am
the black shawled
faithful women
who die with me

or live
depending on the time and place.
I am
 faithful,
  humble,
   Juan Diego
   the Virgin de Guadalupe
Tonantzin, Aztec Goddess too.
I rode the mountains of San Joaquín.
I rode as far East and North
  as the Rocky Mountains
     and
all men feared the guns of
      Joaquín Murrieta.
I killed those men who dared
 to steal my mine,
   who raped and Killed
              my love
              my Wife
Then
I Killed to stay alive.
I was Alfego Baca,
 living my nine lives fully.
I was the Espinosa brothers
 of the Valle de San Luis
All
were added to the number of heads
that
 in the name of civilization
were placed on the wall of independence
Heads of brave men
who died for cause and principle.
Good or Bad.
    Hidalgo! Zapata!
    Murrieta! Espinosa!
are but a few.
They

dared to face
The force of tyranny
        of men
         who rule
          By farce and hypocrisy
I stand here looking back,
and now I see
        the present
and still
  I am the campesino
  I am the fat political coyote
            I,
of the same name,
          Joaquín.
In a country that has wiped out
all my history,
stifled all my pride.
In a country that has placed a
different weight of indignity upon
         my
         age
         old
         burdened back.
       Inferiority
is the new load ...
  The Indian has endured and still
emerged the winner,
  The Mestizo must yet overcome,
  And the Gauchupín we'll just ignore
I look at myself
 and see part of me
who rejects my father and my mother
and dissolves into the melting pot
 to disappear in shame.
  I sometimes
    sell my brother out
and reclaim him

for my own, when society gives me
   token leadership
         in society's own name.
I am Joaquín,
who bleeds in many ways.
The altars of Moctezuma
            I stained a bloody red.
 My back of Indian slavery
      was stripped crimson
  from the whips of masters
  who would lose their blood so pure
  when Revolution made them pay
Standing against the walls of
 Retribution.
        Blood ...
      Has flowed from
      me
on every battlefield
      between
Campesino. Hacendado
  Slave and Master
      and
   Revolution.
I jumped from the tower of Chapultepec
  into the sea of fame;
My country's flag
   my burial shroud;
With Los Niños,
     whose pride and courage
could not surrender
      with indignity
      their country's flag
To strangers ... in their land.
Now
 I bleed in some smelly cell
 from club,
 or gun,

or tyranny,
I bleed as the vicious gloves of hunger
  cut my face and eyes,
as I fight my way from stinking Barrios
 to the glamour of the Ring
  and lights of fame
  or mutilated sorrow.
My blood runs pure on the ice caked
hills of the Alaskan Isles,
on the corpse strewn beach of Normandy,
the foreign land of Korea
                    and now
                    Vietnam.
Here I stand
        before the court of Justice
                Guilty
for all the glory of my Raza
            to be sentenced to despair.
Here I stand
        Poor in money
 Arrogant with pride
            Bold with Machismo
            Rich in courage
                    and
        Wealthy in spirit and faith.
My knees are caked with mud.
My hands calloused from the hoe.
I have made the Anglo rich
        yet
 Equality is but a word,
  the Treaty of Hidalgo has been broken
  and is but another treacherous promise.
My land is lost
            and stolen,
My culture has been raped,
            I lengthen
  the line at the welfare door

and fill the jails with crime.
    These then
are the rewards
       this society has
For sons of Chiefs
        and Kings
        and bloody Revolutionists.
Who
gave a foreign people
    all their skills and ingenuity
to pave the way with Brains and Blood
for
those hordes of Gold starved
Strangers
Who
changed our language
and plagiarized our deeds
           as feats of valor
           of their own.
They frowned upon our way of life
  and took what they could use.
       Our Art
       Our Literature
       Our Music, they ignored
so they left the real things of value
and grabbed at their own destruction
       by their Greed and Avarice
They overlooked that cleansing fountain of
      nature and brotherhood
Which is Joaquín.
  The art of our great señores
      Diego Rivera
      Siqueiros
      Orozco is but
another act of revolution for
the Salvation of mankind.
  Mariachi music, the

heart and soul
of the people of the earth,
the life of child,
and the happiness of love.
The Corridos tell the tales
of life and death,
    of tradition,
Legends old and new,
of Joy
 of passion and sorrow
of the people ... who I am.
I am in the eyes of woman,
        sheltered beneath
her shawl of black,
        deep and sorrowful
        eyes,
That bear the pain of sons long buried
        or dying,
        Dead
on the battlefield or on the barbed wire
        of social strife.
Her rosary she prays and fingers
endlessly
    like the family
working down a row of beets
    to turn around
    and work
    and work
    There is no end.
Her eyes a mirror of all the warmth
    and all the love for me.
And I am her
And she is me.
    We face life together in sorrow,
    anger, joy, faith and wishful
    thoughts.
I shed tears of anguish

as I see my children disappear
behind a shroud of mediocrity
never to look back to remember me.
I am Joaquín.
      I must fight
      And win this struggle
      for my sons, and they
      must know from me
      Who I am.
Part of the blood that runs deep in me
Could not be vanquished by the Moors.
I defeated them after five hundred years,
and I endured.
      The part of blood that is mine
      has labored endlessly five-hundred
      years under the heel of lustful
          Europeans
          I am still here!
I have endured in the rugged mountains
  of our country.
I have survived the toils and slavery
  of the fields.
          I have existed
in the barrios of the city,
in the suburbs of bigotry,
in the mines of social snobbery,
in the prisons of dejection,
in the muck of exploitation
and
in the fierce heat of racial hatred.
And now the trumpet sounds,
The music of the people stirs the
      Revolution,
Like a sleeping giant it slowly
rears its head
to the sound of
      Tramping feet

Clamoring voices
Mariachi strains
Fiery tequila explosions
The smell of chile verde and
Soft brown eyes of expectation for a
better life.
And in all the fertile farm lands,
the barren plains,
the mountain villages,
smoke smeared cities
We start to MOVE.
La Raza!
Mejicano!
Español!
Latino!
Hispano!
Chicano!
or whatever I call myself,
I look the same
I feel the same
I Cry
and
Sing the same
I am the masses of my people and
I refuse to be absorbed.
I am Joaquín
The odds are great
but my spirit is strong
My faith unbreakable
My blood is pure
I am Aztec Prince and Christian Christ
I SHALL ENDURE!
I WILL ENDURE!

Answer the following questions:

1. Look on the internet for information about Juan "Corky" González (biography and activism).
2. According to the poem, who is Joaquín?
3. How does the literary style of the poetry reflect the Chicano/Latino literary trend?
4. How is Joaquín's geographical reality and being Chicano manifested? Provide two examples from the poem.
5. Discuss how the stanza below (page 255) articulates issues about dual identity, immigrants' struggle, and assimilation.

I am Joaquin
Lost in a world of confusion,
Caught up in a whirl of a
    gringo society,
Confused by the rules,
Scorned by attitudes,
Suppressed by manipulations,
And destroyed by modern society.
My fathers
have lost the economic battle
and won
the struggle of cultural survival.
And now!
I must choose
Between the paradox of
Victory of the spirit,
despite physical hunger
Or
 to exist in the grasp
of American social neurosis,
sterilization of the soul
 and a full stomach.
Yes,

I have come a long way to nowhere,
Unwillingly dragged by that
monstrous, technical
Industrial giant called
     Progress
and Anglo success...
I look at myself.
I watch my brothers.
I shed tears of sorrow.
I sow seeds of hate.
I withdraw to the safety within the
circle of life...

AmeRícan

Tato Laviera

we gave birth to a new generation,
AmeRícan, broader than lost gold
never touched, hidden inside the
puerto rican mountains.

we gave birth to a new generation
AmeRícan, it includes everything
imaginable you-name-it-we-got-it
society.

we gave birth to a new generation,
AmeRícan salutes all folklores,
european, indian, black, Spanish
and anything else compatible:

AmeRícan,   singing to composer pedro flores' palm
               trees up high in the universal sky!

AmeRícan,   sweet soft spanish danzas gypsies
               moving lyrics la española cascabelling
               presence always singing at our side!

AmeRícan,   beating jíbaro modern troubadours
                 crying guitars romantic continental
                 bolero love songs!

AmeRícan,   across forth and across back
                 back across and forth back
                 forth across and back and forth
                 our trips are walking bridges!
                 it all dissolved into itself, an attempt
                 was truly made, the attempt was truly
                 absorbed, digested, we spit out
                 the poison, we spit out in malice,
                 we stand, affirmative in action,
                 to reproduce a broader answer to the
                 marginality that gobbled us up abruptly!

AmeRícan,   walking plena-rhythms in new york,
                 strutting beautifully alert, alive
                 many turning eyes wondering,
                 admiring!

AmeRícan,   defining myself my own way any way many
                 many ways Am e Rícan, with the big R and the
                 accent on the í!

AmeRícan,   like the soul gliding talk of gospel
                 boogie music!

AmeRícan,   speaking new words in spanglish tenements,
                 fast tongue moving street corner "que
                 corta" talk being invented at the insistence
                 of a smile!

AmeRícan,   abounding inside so many ethnic english
                 people, and out of humanity, we blend
                 and mix all that is good!

AmeRícan,	integrating in new york and defining our own destino, our own way of life,
AmeRícan,	defining the new america, humane america, admired america, loved america, harmonious america, the world in peace, our energies collectively invested to find other civili- zations, to touch God, further and further, to dwell in the spirit of divinity!
AmeRícan,	yes, for now, for i love this, my second land, and i dream to take the accent from the altercation, and be proud to call myself american, in the u.s. sense of the word, AmeRícan, America!

■ Reading 7.3

Answer the following questions:

1. Look on the internet for information about Tato Laviera (biography, activism, and literary work).
2. According to the poem, who is "AmeRícan"?
3. How does the literary style of the poem reflect the Nuyorican/Latino literary trend?
4. How is his geographical reality (being Puerto Rican and living in America) manifested in his poem, "AmeRícan"? Provide an example from the poem.
5. In the stanza below from the poem "AmeRícan," Tato Laviera (page 273) deconstructs the word "AmeRícan" as an attempt to dig into his dual identity. Discuss how the writer employs language to describe his double cultural experience.

AmeRícan,	*defining myself my own way anyway many many ways AmeRícan, with the big R and the accent on the í!*

CPSIA information can be obtained
at www.ICGtesting.com
Printed in the USA
BVHW050255110221
599813BV00002B/21